THE CHALLENGES OF JUSTICE IN DIVERSE SOCIETIES

Cultural Diversity and Law

Series Editor:
Prakash Shah, School of Law, Queen Mary, University of London, UK

Around the world, most states are faced with difficult issues arising out of cultural diversity in their territories. Within the legal field, such issues span across matters of private law through to public and constitutional law. At international level too there is now considerable jurisprudence regarding ethnic, religious and cultural diversity. In addition, there are several layers of legal control – from communal and religious regulation to state and international regulation. This multiplicity of norm setting has been variously termed legal pluralism, inter-legality or inter-normativity and provides a fascinating lens for academic analysis that links up to cultural diversity in new and interesting ways. The umbrella of cultural diversity encompasses various population groups throughout the world ranging from national, ethnic, religious or indigenous groupings. This series particularly welcomes work that is of comparative interest, concerning various state jurisdictions as well as different population groups.

Also in the series

Law and Religion in the 21st Century
Relations between States and Religious Communities
Edited by Silvio Ferrari and Rinaldo Cristofori
ISBN 978-1-4094-1143-7

Muslim Marriage in Western Courts
Lost in Transplantation
Pascale Fournier
ISBN 978-1-4094-0441-5

Shari'a As Discourse
Legal Traditions and the Encounter with Europe
Edited by Jørgen S. Nielsen and Lisbet Christoffersen
ISBN 978-0-7546-7955-4

Legal Practice and Cultural Diversity
Edited by Ralph Grillo, Roger Ballard, Alessandro Ferrari, André J. Hoekema, Marcel Maussen and Prakash Shah
ISBN 978-0-7546-7547-1

The Challenges of Justice in Diverse Societies

Constitutionalism and Pluralism

MEENA K. BHAMRA

Routledge
Taylor & Francis Group
LONDON AND NEW YORK

First published 2011 by Ashgate Publishing

Published 2016 by Routledge
2 Park Square, Milton Park, Abingdon, Oxfordshire OX14 4RN
711 Third Avenue, New York, NY 10017, USA

First issued in paperback 2016

Routledge is an imprint of the Taylor & Francis Group, an informa business

British Library Cataloguing in Publication Data
Bhamra, Meena K.
The challenges of justice in diverse societies : constitutionalism and pluralism. -- (Cultural diversity and law)
1. Justice, Administration of. 2. Multiculturalism. 3. Sociological jurisprudence. 4. Constitutional law.
I. Title II. Series
340.1'15-dc22

Library of Congress Cataloging-in-Publication Data
Bhamra, Meena K.
The challenges of justice in diverse societies : constitutionalism and pluralism / by Meena K. Bhamra.
p. cm. -- (Cultural diversity and law)
Includes bibliographical references and index.
ISBN 978-1-4094-1928-0 (hardback : alk. paper)
1. Culture and law. 2. Cultural pluralism. 3. Justice, Administration of--Sociological aspects. 4. Sociological jurisprudence. 5. People (Constitutional law) 6. Group identity. I. Title.
K487.C8B488 2011
340'.115--dc22

2010046229

ISBN 13: 978-1-138-25452-7 (pbk)
ISBN 13: 978-1-4094-1928-0 (hbk)

For Arya, who grew along with this book

Contents

List of Figures

Acknowledgements

I owe a considerable debt to Professor Werner F. Menski and Dr Prakash Shah. Their work, both scholarship and teaching, has inspired this book and my research.

One of the biggest thanks goes to Professor Alison Diduck, who has at least two brains and a heart that matches their combined size. This book would not have been possible without her numerous contributions and helpful discussions. I am thankful to Colm O'Cinneide who provided invaluable comments. Mention must also go to Arif Jamal, who has often provided me with academic refuge and continues to do so. All errors remain my own.

I have learnt many lessons about diversity from all the strong women in my family. I know I stand on your shoulders to reach these heights, and for that, I am truly grateful. Thank you also to my parents who go above and beyond for me.

Last, but never least, Rav. Thank you for your patience (*Dhiraj*) throughout this process; thank you for your emotional and intellectual support; and thank you for looking after me, and Arya.

Chapter 1
Introduction

Ali v Ali: The Subtlety of the Challenges of Justice

The unreported case of *Ali v Ali* is an example of the subtle nature of the challenges of justice in diverse societies, which form the focal point of this book.[1] Mr and Mrs Ali were Bangladeshis living in London, who both had good careers that afforded them the means to live a comfortable life. As part of the arrangements of their marriage, a dower, or *mahr*, was negotiated. Menski states that this bargaining process 'was not over some kind of sale of the woman, but reflects a contest over the relative status and financial standing in society of all participants to these negotiations' (2002: 48). Menski also explains the meaning and purpose of *mahr* (2002: 48):[2]

> The main point of the Muslim *mahr* clearly is to provide the wife some financial security after divorce or the husband's death. In the classical Muslim law, there is an understanding that *mahr* should be divided into 'prompt' and 'deferred' dower, the first to be paid in connection with the consummation of the marriage, the deferred part being normally due on divorce or death. … In either case, this is an important financial security for the wife.

The final amount settled upon, and included in Mr and Mrs Ali's *kabhinama* (marriage contract) was £30,001. Menski notes that the couple had two weddings: a civil wedding recognised by English law and a Muslim marriage.[3]

---

1 Menski (2002: 47–52) provides the factual background, and analysis of this case. His role as expert witness in this case means that he provides a report of this case that is readily amenable to socio-legal analysis. Although Menski notes that '[s]uch cases, albeit important for legal practice, remain systematically unreported' (2003: n 7), I wonder whether an official report of this case would reveal the dimensions that Menski's case comment and analysis makes visible. It follows that material facts may be excluded in those cases that do reach the official reports, which impacts on their availability for socio-legal scholarship.

2 For further details of *mahr*, Menski refers to Pearl and Menski (1998). See, in particular, Pearl and Menski (1998: 178–81, 190–201, 232–4).

3 This double marriage is a form that many other British South Asians also follow, and Menski has termed these evolving hybrid legal systems *angrezi shariat* (Pearl and Menski 1998). It should be noted that the legal hybridity that Menski has observed goes deeper than double marriages. The idea of hybrid legal systems is considered in greater detail in Chapters 2 and 5.

Mr and Mrs Ali's marriage broke down after a few months, and Mr Ali sought a divorce in the English courts. Mrs Ali cross-petitioned the court, asking them to refuse to allow the divorce unless Mr Ali paid her any financial entitlements she was owed, including the *mahr*. Menski (2002: 48–9) explains that Mrs Ali would have had no financial entitlements under English law, given that this was such a short marriage and that there were no children. Mr Ali sought to claim that Mrs Ali was not entitled to the *mahr*, arguing 'in essence that in England, only English law should be applied' and that *mahr* was a matter of culture, not law (2002: 49).

Called as an expert on Muslim law in this case, Menski clarified that there were two marriages and two divorces: the proceedings before the English court and a Muslim marriage and *talaq*. This hybrid scenario meant that there were also 'two sets of financial arrangements' that the judge needed to consider (2002: 49), namely those under English law and Muslim law. Menski went on to explain the complexities of diversity in contemporary Britain to the judge (2002: 50):

> Not surprisingly, the judge was a little confused. I insisted that if he did not consider the complete multicultural scenario, he would not only be doing injustice to the wife, but he would also damage the standing of English law, because he would drive Mrs. Ali straight into the office of one of Britain's many Shariat Councils, virtual Muslim courts, which have an unofficial internal hierarchy.

Troubled by this description of unofficial legal systems in Britain, the judge awarded Mrs Ali £30,000. Menski analyses this judgment as something more than a judge equitably resolving the dispute before him (2002: 51): '[b]y giving her £1 less, he applied not Muslim law, but asserted the application of English law', and therefore 'protected English law from the unrelenting pressure to accept personal laws, such as that of the Muslims, as part of the new British legal framework'.

I believe the challenges of justice in diverse communities lie in the significance of this missing one pound. It would be simple to dismiss such a small amount of money as meaningless; Mrs Ali got the money that was contractually owed to her, and would surely not complain about the missing one pound, so what does this insignificant sum of money matter? My arguments in this book aim to provide fresh perspectives on justice and law that are able to explain the significance of this missing one pound. I argue that fresh perspectives are necessary so that it is possible to understand the challenges of justice in diverse societies more clearly. In becoming clearer as to the significance of the missing pound, my belief is that this will lead to new, and more just, legal responses to diversity.

The Importance of Contexts

Habermas (1978) expanded the ambit of critical social theory in *Knowledge and Human Interests* by separating it from the Frankfurt School, with its distinctly Marxist framework. He took a broad view of critical theory as a reflexive process that has the ultimate aim of emancipation from domination. It is this emancipatory interest that provides an ideal platform for this book. Moreover, this project follows Iris Marion Young's understanding of critical theory. Young (2000: 10) describes critical theory as a 'socially and historically situated normative analysis and argument' and writes that (1990: 5): 'normative reflection must begin from historically specific circumstances because there is nothing but what is'. This book pursues this method of inquiry by constructing a normative framework that creates spaces in which this reflection upon social and historical realities can take place. This socially and historically contextualised reflexive process has the goal of facilitating new legal responses to diversity. I do not aim to construct a universal and decontextualised theory of justice that proposes ideals, which, by their very nature as ideals, imagine a better society. Instead, I seek to contribute to an ongoing dialogue which endeavours better to understand, and thereby better respond to the challenges of justice in the context of diversity. By making space for reflection upon the social and historical realities of the experiences of diversity, I hope to achieve the emancipatory effect that Habermas identifies as crucial to critical theory. The first, and vital step, towards emancipation is to craft sound normative foundations that can ground these reflexive processes; I hope to take this first step in this book.

Crucial to Young's explanation (1990: 8) of the role of critical theory is that it is not an approach that 'must be accepted or rejected in its entirety. Each [theory] provides useful tools for the analyses and arguments I … make'. There are three interdependent consequences to adopting this methodological stance here. First, by taking up the premises of a particular theoretical approach, it does not follow that I accept the tenets of all theorists that adopt this approach. Indeed, some of the ideas expressed in this project may well conflict with those of other critical theorists. Secondly, in adopting this methodological approach, it does not follow that there is an obligation to confine myself to literature which also adopts this particular theoretical approach. Indeed, it is wholly legitimate to use a variety of literature which touches upon the same themes as this study, regardless of the theoretical and methodological approach that is adopted. For example, whilst Kymlicka's *Theory of Multicultural Citizenship* (1995) may not use the method of critical theorists, it nevertheless provides useful insights and norms which inform this project.

Finally, it also follows that adopting the premises of critical theory does not necessarily mean I align myself on either side of purportedly mutually exclusive discourses. This study does not reject theories which critique critical theory, such as Dworkin's; at the same time, it does reject academic divisions, such as the barrier between sociology and anthropology. It rejects particularly the idea of sociology as the study of the West, and anthropology as the study of the Rest, even if the Rest are studied in their new Western context.[4]

---

4 I am grateful to Arif Jamal for succinctly explaining the difference between sociology and anthropology this way, and borrow the phrase from him.

Moreover, the aim of this book is not to contribute to hardening such divisions, since they are antithetical to the progress of discourses in these relatively new fields of inquiry. Dichotomies such as these tend towards dictating one's position on a spectrum of views, and can therefore be counterproductive to the integrity of scholarship. Kymlicka (2001: 18–19) has written of the liberal/communitarian dichotomy in the context of minority rights discourses, which unfolds as individualists versus collectivists. Liberals would concern themselves with prioritising the individual prior to the community, and communitarians would emphasise that individuals are embedded in their social relationships and roles, and that individuals are therefore a product of community. One's position on this political spectrum would then dictate whether one understood minority rights as just or unjust. However, this characterisation distorts the debate, since, as Kymlicka persuasively argues (1989, 1995, 2001), liberalism is not inherently adverse to claims that minority rights are just. Kymlicka's success in shattering the illusion that liberalism is intrinsically antithetical to minority rights serves as a reminder that it is not necessary to be confined by academic battle lines that have already been drawn, or by ideological divides. By adopting the method of critical theory, it does not follow that this book must fit within a preconceived notion of how the challenges of justice in contemporary societies should be viewed.

Which Diverse Societies?

I could quite simply answer the question of which diverse societies that this book focuses upon by replying, 'all of them'. Much time could be spent on defining who comes within certain groups, and agonising over labels and terminology.[5] Often

5 Much British literature in this field employs the term 'ethnic minorities' to describe its immigrant groups and their descendents. For an early example see Krausz (1971). Whilst there is considerable debate about how appropriate the numerical inferences of this term are, I would reject the term on the basis of the reductionist tendency of 'ethnicity' (which I consider in greater detail in Chapter 7), which makes this term unhelpful in locating the challenges of diversity in diverse societies. Tonkin, McDonald and Chapman (1989: 17) eloquently illustrate this reductionist tendency when they explain that majorities and dominant peoples are no less 'ethnic' than minorities. Other countries prefer the terminology 'visible minorities' to refer to people of colour. I find this equally as unhelpful as it is merely a linguistic turn: women are not considered to be visible minorities, although many women are quite visibly female; many people of colour are not as easily identifiable as the idea of visible difference suggests. For a critique of the use of 'minorities' and 'majorities' see Parekh (1990a: 60–63), for emphasis on the importance of numerical influence see Fredman (1997: 595–600), and for explication of the concept of 'ideological minorities' see Asad (2003: 75). Asad's 'ideological minorities' implicitly draws upon Foucault's thesis (1982) that actions occur within power relationships; by focusing on issues of power, Asad illustrates that the numerical nature of these minority groups is an accidental and tangential feature of their composition, although there is no *need* to abandon this numerical

a simple division is made between immigrant groups and Aboriginal peoples. I do not find this division helpful for two reasons. First, I question how easy it is to assign different analysis to these two separate groups when both contain intense internal plurality. Secondly, I do not find the tendency to categorise immigrants as perpetual immigrants helpful, when there are many instances of these groups including people who have not migrated anywhere and were born and bred in countries that are considered as their 'hosts'.

My concern in this book is non-dominant groups and individuals who are excluded from civil society. I am refraining from elaborating upon why this exclusion is my focus here, but do so in Chapter 2. Furthermore, I choose not to draw the boundaries around these groups and individuals any tighter for a number of reasons. First, when individuals and groups are excluded from civil society, it is rarely on account of one easily identifiable characteristic. Diversity and plurality are complex factors which we often make judgments about, and act upon, in equally complex and subtle ways. If I am excluded from civil society, I am first likely to question the fact that I can be sure I have suffered an injustice. If I decide that I have suffered such an injustice, I am even less likely to be certain of the grounds of my exclusion: is it because I am a different colour; or is it because of my gender; or is it because of my class; or is it because of my religion, or lack thereof; or is it because I do not like modern art? The reality is that the list of characteristics is endless, and an answer is not likely to be forthcoming. It is more likely that my exclusion is based on a complex variety of factors, as our identities are intrinsically intersectional; it is almost impossible to draw neat boundaries and create satisfactory groups this way. However, I can be sure that there is something about me, or my behaviour, that is deemed unsuitable or unacceptable. Since my arguments in this book do not turn on the nature of this unacceptability, I see no need to become involved in constructing inherently unsatisfactory boundaries.

Secondly, the ways in which we understand and theorise diversity are continually evolving. Vertovec (2007) writes about the multi-dimensional nature of diversity and argues that diversity is a complex phenomenon that occurs along many different intersecting axes. His shorthand term to encapsulate this complexity is 'super-diversity'. He also challenges theorists to develop new ways of understanding diversity so that we can begin to unpick these complexities. Although I develop a conceptual tool in this book to help ease the discomfort that is caused by writing about diversity in very abstract and general terms, my aim here, and with this conceptual tool, is not to undertake an empirical analysis of the complex pluralities that we find in today's diverse societies. Rather, my aim is to develop a tool that can expand and adapt as our understandings of diversity evolve.

(and accurate) description in order to convey the importance of this power relationship. 'Diasporas' is also a contested term (Kalra, Kahlon and Hutnyk 2005). Eriksen states (2002: 153) that a 'diasporic identity implies an emphasis on conservation and re-creation of the ancestral culture'.

Finally, it appears as if plurality around the globe is increasing. As globalisation, in its many and varied forms, continues to gather pace, we are becoming ever more aware of differences. I suspect that this awareness stems both from a better understanding of pre-existing diversities, as well as the development of new and interesting differences. Regardless of the reasons behind this seemingly relentless turn in plurality that is our modern condition, it simply becomes increasingly unsatisfactory to draw hard and fast boundaries around the condition of being different.

It is for these reasons that I leave the concept somewhat up in the air and, for the moment at least, choose to focus on the fact that individuals and groups that suffer injustices are my concern in this book. However, I readily admit that my reference to empirical examples of the social realities of diversity draw from traditional categories of diversity. The reason behind this is simply due to the availability of socio-legal literature in the field. I further readily admit that many of these examples focus upon British South Asians in particular. Again this is due to the fact that far more research has been done in this particular area than others. It is interesting to note that emerging literature which focuses upon South Asians diasporas in other countries tends also to reference the same literature.[6] Where it has been viable to draw upon broader examples, I have taken the opportunity to do so.

Scheme of the Book

This book is organised into four parts. Part I (Chapters 2 and 3) sets out a global normative framework that informs my arguments that new legal responses to diversity are necessary, as well as forming part of my fresh perspectives on justice and law. Part II (Chapters 4 and 5) draws upon the conclusions from Part I and locates the role of law in its responses to diversity. In Part III (Chapters 6, 7, 8 and 9) I supplement my global normative framework with a local normative framework. This latter framework is crafted with the aim of making room for the expression of the specificities of diversity. My normative framework, with its global and local dimensions, presents fresh perspectives on justice and law. These fresh perspectives ground my proposal for a new vista of constitutional pluralism, which I set out in Part IV (Chapters 10 and 11). This vista is intended to lead to new legal responses to diversity.

I anchor my claims in this book by outlining a diversity-conscious form of justice in Chapter 2. My aim in introducing justice at this early stage is to place it at the heart of my consideration of the implications of diversity for law. Since the injustices suffered by diverse groups and individuals prompt the inquiries in this book, it follows that justice is the primary motivating force driving the search for better, or more just, ways for law to shoulder its burden in responding to diversity.

6 See, for example, Zaman (2008) and Fournier (2001–2002, 2006).

I argue that when the citizenry of a nation-state significantly changes shape, so too must our conception of justice. Therefore, I outline a diversity-conscious form of justice that reflects these changes. Whilst my conception of justice is heavily associated with law, it is not exclusively tied to it, and also has social and political affiliations. My focus in this book, however, is to consider the consequences of a diversity-sensitive form of justice in legal domains. The form of justice that I outline represents the idea of justice that I reference throughout this study.

In Chapter 3 I build upon this diversity-conscious form of justice by arguing that pluralism also has significant implications for the ways that nation-states are theorised. In this chapter, therefore, I consider an extra-legal dimension of my fresh perspective on justice. I claim that the changes in the way that nation-states are theorised must be explicitly stated, as they orient the way that we engage with diversity. I highlight three cardinal principles that impact my approach to diversity, and which are broad enough to be applicable to any study of diversity and law. The idea of a diversity-conscious form of justice, together with these three cardinal principles, make up the global dimension of my fresh perspectives on justice and law.

I begin my case for new legal responses to diversity in Chapter 4. I provide a social, historical and political account of the evolution of Britain's anti-discrimination legislation, and argue that its underlying narrative limits its capacity to meet the challenges of justice in the context of British diversity. I then illustrate that recent amendments to this legislation, both actual and proposed, are not equipped to dislodge this limiting narrative. I go on to consider Canada's constitutional test for Aboriginal rights at common law and argue that it displays further limitations in our current legal responses to diversity.

In Chapter 5 I complete my case for new legal responses by demonstrating that human rights do not fully meet the challenges of justice in diverse societies. I do this by emphasising the tension between the universal ambitions of human rights and the local and specific nature of the demands of justice in diverse societies. I then go on further to support my claim by critically analysing Sebastian Poulter's (1998) use of human rights as a framework for the legal accommodation of British Afro-Caribbean and South Asian diversity, and demonstrate the difficulties of his approach.

Having made a case for new legal responses, I begin to complete my fresh perspectives on justice and law in Chapter 6. I start constructing a local normative framework that will ground my own proposal for a new vision of constitutional pluralism. I argue that official law functions in a manner where it acts as a type of normative shorthand, but that these underlying norms need to be restated and modified in order to take into account the changes effected by diversity. Therefore, I set out a triad of norms that aims to rework this underlying normative framework, and respond to the specific localities of diversity by making space for the expression of the local realities of diversity.

I continue setting up this local normative framework in Chapter 7, where I illustrate that the current analytical tools used to understand diversity do not capture the realities of contemporary diversity. I do this by, first, identifying the blurred boundaries between ethnicity, culture, religion and race, and then demonstrate that they exacerbate a tendency to singularise identities, so that we categorise ourselves according to only one of these concepts. I then consider identity as a substitute for these analytical tools, and conclude that it also has its drawbacks in the form of its determinist tendency. My analysis in this chapter demonstrates that any fresh perspectives on justice and law must go beyond the limitations that I identify in Part II.

The claims of Chapter 7 culminate, in Chapter 8, in my proposal for a new analytical tool, that I term 'identity markers'. I flesh out this proposal by considering what I mean by identity markers, and how this tool overcomes the difficulties of the current analytical tools in use. My goal is to propose an analytical tool that permits a more accurate, and therefore more just, understanding of diversity.

I complete my arguments for identity markers by illustrating their relations to law in Chapter 9. This requires a plural understanding of law, and I use Masaji Chiba's model of law to demonstrate these relations. Chiba's model of law also provides occasion to demonstrate, through consideration of traditional constitutional theories, that the plurality of law is not antithetical to dominant jurisprudential theories. Given that the focus of this study is the role of law in achieving a diversity-conscious form of justice, I then lead into an account of the conceptualisation of law that grounds my proposal for a new vista of constitutional pluralism. Here, I précis Werner Menski's (2006 and 2009) global working definition of law and flying kites of law, and present this as a model of law that fits the realities of diversity. This pluralist account of law concludes my local normative framework, and my fresh perspectives on justice and law.

In Chapter 10 I propose a new vision of constitutional pluralism. I argue that constitutional pluralistic discourses, that are grounded by my normative framework, have the potential to lead to new, and more just, legal responses to diversity. I first briefly explain what I mean by constitutional pluralist discourses, and situate this proposal with a concise idea of what the British Constitution entails. I focus on the British Constitution because its unwritten nature provides a wealth of academic analysis that serves my purposes well. I then justify my proposal by illustrating why this new vista should entail constitutional pluralist discourses, as opposed to legally pluralist discourses. Moreover, I further elaborate upon the nature of these constitutional pluralist discourses by assessing them against Neil Walker's criteria for constitutional renewal.

I conclude my new vista in Chapter 11 by considering what a constitutional pluralist discourse might look like. I do this by returning to consider *Ali v Ali*, and argue that my proposals for fresh perspectives on justice and law, and my new vista of constitutional pluralism, provide a clearer picture of the significance of the missing one pound in this case. I then discuss, through a constitutional pluralist lens, the difficult issue of prohibitions on religious forms of dress in public spaces. This enables me to demonstrate further that this vista provides the potential for new legal responses to diversity. This application of my proposal for constitutional pluralist discourses allows me to highlight its relations with my normative framework, and thereby tie together the arguments and claims in this book. I end this project by considering whether the new vista I propose is nothing short of a form of relativism. I use this as an example further to highlight why I propose discourses, rather than new legal responses or a new constitutional blueprint.

This book attempts to address the question of how we can develop our legal responses to diversity without, it must be admitted, actually providing any new legal responses. Whilst it may feel wholly unsatisfactory to some that there are no answers to the tricky and controversial issues raised by diversity in the 21st century, this is intentional. The arguments and claims in this book respond to a need to ensure that our normative foundations are sound before we provide answers that solve the problems of diversity. The urgency with which challenges related to diversity demand the attention of legal professionals, policy-makers, scholars, think tanks and others within and outside of legal circles, often lead us to skip this vital first step. This is detrimental to how we manage the intense pluralities that span our globe, and merely compounds the challenges that we face. Although I believe there are sound and good reasons to adopt the normative framework that I argue for in this book, my primary intention in this study is to demonstrate to all those involved with, or interested in the challenges of justice in diverse societies, that this first step of becoming clear about our normative foundations cannot be overlooked in our rush to find answers. Once we are clearer as to the questions raised by diversity, we stand a far better chance that our answers will achieve the justice that we so desperately seek in diverse societies.

PART I
A Global Normative Framework

Chapter 2
Justice and Diversity

Today's globe is replete with infinite forms of diversity and plurality. Increasing consciousness of the challenges that this diversity presents, together with an acute awareness of contemporary struggles over identity and difference, has given rise to a body of scholarship by political philosophers that focuses upon this field.[1] This body of scholarship is driven by an urgent need to understand these struggles, but takes the perspective of examining the political obligations fostered by diversity. Within this broad field of political obligations, these philosophers have addressed questions about diverse identities in many ways.[2] Yet, at the core of all of these studies is, I believe, the question of justice.

Giving justice such a central focus is necessary because, as the structures within which justice does its work evolve, ideas about how best to define and achieve justice, and the challenges these questions raise in nation-states that are home to intense pluralities, must also change. When the citizenry of a nation-state changes, so do the demands these citizens make upon justice. Our conception of justice, therefore, must respond to the changing demands made of it, and developments in the way that we theorise these demands. Fraser (2006) explains that when the nature of injustices change this disorients past core assumptions creating a 'disensus' on the basic parameters of justice.

The intense pluralities and diversities that can be seen around the globe have effected this sort of change and have, in turn, disoriented core assumptions about justice. Nation-states have responded to this disorientation in a variety of ways.

---

1 There are a great many scholars involved in this field of study, the key scholars being: Kwame Anthony Appiah, Seyla Benhabib, Joseph Carens, Rainer Forst, Nancy Fraser, Amy Gutmann, Jürgen Habermas, Axel Honneth, Will Kymlicka, Tariq Modood, Susan Okin, Bikhu Parekh, Anne Phillips, Michael Sandel, Amartya Sen, Charles Taylor, James Tully, Michael Walzer and Iris Marion Young. Whilst this political philosophical endeavour spans more than one country, it is possible to identify a Canadian school of thought in this area comprising of the work of Charles Taylor, Will Kymlicka, James Tully and, more recently, Ayelet Shachar. For a more comprehensive list of scholars see Laden and Owen (2007).

2 See, for example, Kymlicka (1989, 1995, 2001) who sees the persistence of ethnic conflict as an imperative to secure minority rights within liberalism; Habermas (1996) who responds to the plurality of views in the modern world with a diversity-conscious theory of democracy and law; Taylor (1994) who argues that diversity leads to a political obligation to recognise these differences; Fraser (1997, 2005) and Young (1990, 2000) who both theorise diversity as an issue that directly relates to justice; and Tully (1995) who argues that theorising constitutions is an essential component of responding to diversity.

Examples include stand-alone anti-discrimination legislation,[3] exceptions for non-dominant groups,[4] and human rights legislation and/or entrenched equality clauses.[5] Yet there has been no explicit realignment of the parameters of justice in response to this diversity. However, a broad idea of the form of justice that informs, motivates and shapes the arguments in this book is crucial. The body of political theory that considers diversity and plurality can provide useful insights that permit this diversity-conscious form of justice to be sketched out here.

In this chapter then I outline a diversity-conscious form of justice that forms an integral part of the foundations of the fresh perspectives on diversity that I argue are vital if we are to begin to meet the challenges of diversity. This diversity-conscious justice sits at the heart of my arguments in two related ways. First, in clarifying what the challenges of justice are in the context of diversity, the ideas here act to guide the arguments which sustain my claim that new legal responses to diversity are needed. Secondly, a diversity-sensitive justice contributes to my fresh perspectives on justice and law, which, in turn, lead to my proposal for a new vista of constitutional pluralism. The first purpose of this outline of a diversity-conscious justice means that it roots this project, and therefore must take centre stage and precede any explanations why fresh perspectives on diversity are necessary.

It is not necessary to craft a comprehensive theory of justice. Justice is concerned with matters that go well beyond the remit of diversity, making the parameters of a comprehensive theory of justice too wide for the purposes of my arguments. Furthermore, many political philosophers have already concerned themselves with questions related to diversity, whether in terms of ideal theories

3 Britain introduced its first Race Relations Act in 1965, and this was closely followed in 1968 and 1976 by two further attempts to improve prohibitions on discrimination in Britain. These statutes responded to increased migration after the Second World War largely from South Asia and the Caribbean.

4 Britain has passed a number of statutory exceptions that make room for non-dominant ways of life. For example, s 6 of the Motor-Cycle Crash Helmets (Religious Exemption) Act 1976 exempts turban wearing Sikhs from the laws that require motorcyclists to wear crash helmets, and the Slaughter of Poultry Act 1967 and the Slaughterhouses Act 1974 allows Jews and Muslims to slaughter animals according to their religious practices. For further details, see Jones and Welhengama (2000). However, these exceptions are not limited to countries without written constitions. See, for example, the federal lifting of the ban on Sikh turbans in the Royal Canadian Mounted Police on 15 March 1990.

5 Whilst there are many equality clauses that could be highlighted, one particularly interesting approach can be seen in the Schedules of the Indian Constitution. In an attempt to redress past imbalances amongst castes and other disadvantaged groups in India, its Constitution was drafted to require special treatment, or positive discrimination, for these groups. These provisions were intended to provide Scheduled Castes, Scheduled Tribes and other backward classes with access to employment in government institutions and higher education facilities. These provisions have been highgly controversial in India, with many resenting them on the grounds that they provide these groups with privileged status. For further details, see Menski (1992).

or more contextual approaches,[6] and this provides rich material and insights that allow me merely to sketch out a diversity-conscious form of justice. My aim here is not to provide a comprehensive or rigorous analysis of this body of scholarship. Rather, I wish to draw upon these works in a selective manner, in order to craft a form of justice that responds to the intense pluralities of diverse societies.

In order to locate this conception of diversity-conscious justice, I use Fraser and Honneth's (2003a, 2003b) philosophical conversation on the relations between recognition and redistribution, to explain the links between justice and diversity. By explaining these links I show why justice sits at the heart of my arguments. I then turn to outline a diversity-conscious form of justice. I argue that this conception of justice has two interdependent pillars. The first pillar of justice encapsulates the value of identity in contemporary societies. I show that justice must involve the encouragement of the self-actualisation of authentic identities, if it is to reflect contemporary understandings of diversity. I do this by referring to philosophical arguments and empirical evidence of the value of identity. In the second pillar, I set out a general idea of justice as the free and fair participation in and access to civil society. I argue for a broad understanding of civil society that includes Habermas's (1996) idea of the unorganised public. These two pillars of justice are, in fact, intimately connected. However, I separate them out in order to demonstrate more clearly the two areas that make up this diversity-sensitive form of justice.

The Relations Between Diversity and Justice

Political theories that focus exclusively upon contributing to a world that is more hospitable to diversity, in all its forms, are relatively contemporary in their occurrence.[7] In contrast, the dominant framework of political theory has been concerned with the redistribution of resources and wealth to create a more just society. However, as the struggles over identity and difference have increased,

6 Examples of ideal theories of justice include Fraser (1997, 2005), Habermas (1996), Rawls (1993) and Young (2006). This type of study sets out the arguments for a comprehensive theory of justice which explicitly takes into account our contemporary diversities, and often makes plurality a focal point of the study. Examples of contextual approaches to diversity include Modood (2007), Parekh (2000, 2008), Taylor (1994), Tully (1995) and Sen (2006). These studies consider diverse identities as the key component of their work, although this does not lead to a comprehensive theory of justice. This produces works of great variety: for example, Parekh's works (2000, 2008) have produced theories of multiculturalism or diverse national identities, whereas Sen's study (2006) considers the nature of identity, the way identity is used and its links to contemporary forms of violence.

7 I make a distinction between earlier political philosophy that aimed, *inter alia*, to treat 'foreigners' fairly and endow them with (human) rights, and more contemporary theories which endeavour to ensure that people are not treated as 'foreigners' in the first place.

and in some cases become violent enough to tear nations and communities apart,[8] political philosophers have turned their minds to the complexities of justice in these situations.[9] Whilst the body of scholarship in this field is rapidly increasing, a number of theorists have already dedicated a considerable portion of their research efforts to this topic. These include Charles Taylor, Jürgen Habermas, Will Kymlicka, Nancy Fraser, James Tully and Iris Marion Young. It is from amongst the work of these theorists that I will sketch the shape of a diversity-conscious form of justice.

I have linked the legal problems raised by diversity to justice, and placed the idea of a form of justice that is conscious of and sensitive to diversity at the core of my arguments without much justification. However, further exploration of this link will provide a solid background to this outline of diversity-conscious justice. Nancy Fraser makes clear the link between the issues raised by plural societies and the requirements of social justice. Fraser's insight (1997: 16) that the questions and difficulties presented by diversity are rooted to justice seems trite when she explains that marginalisation on the basis of culture, religion, race, ethnicity, gender, and so on, are injustices. Once said, this seems like an obvious point, yet it often remains unmentioned in much legal literature that is concerned with diversity.

It is not just that we live in a world of immense pluralities and diversities, and pragmatism requires that we adapt to this new terrain. The terrain may be new, but it is more than pragmatism alone that drives and encourages legal developments; the goal of justice is a key imperative behind the need to understand our new diversities and pluralities. This point is often lost when the dialogue focuses upon whether a particular group has been provided with a special advantage by the state. Underlying such arguments is the notion that an *unjust* advantage has been provided. It is crucial to the correct casting of my project that this point is emphasised. Theories that respond to the struggles of identity and diversity do so with the aim of justice in clear sight. My hope is that explicit recognition of justice as a driving force behind my claims and arguments will provide them with a different hue and subtly adjust the nature of the dialogue that will follow.

---

8 The list of incidences of identity-based violence is disturbingly long. However, the more publicised incidents have occurred or continue to occur in the Darfur region of Sudan, the Former Republic of Yugoslavia, post-independence India and Pakistan, Israel, Palestine and the Occupied Territies, Kenya, Rwanda, South Africa, Sri Lanka and the Democratic Republic of Congo.

9 Fraser (1997: 1–3) links the rise of such theories with the 'post-socialist condition'. The collapse of socialism, she argues, gave rise to serious doubts about and exhaustion with the utopian ideals that underpinned socialist emancipatory reforms. This coincided with a change in the nature of political claims, which began to be formed in terms of the recognition of group difference, moving away from redistribution claims. The final element of the post-socialist condition is rapid and aggressive marketisation giving rise to sharp material inequalities, which in turn have thrown redistribution claims off-centre.

Nancy Fraser and Axel Honneth are amongst a minority of theorists that have considered the relationship between redistribution and recognition as elements of social justice.[10] Social justice has been described as encompassing two categories of claims, namely redistribution and recognition. Redistribution encompasses those theories that aim to redistribute resources and wealth to create a more just society, and such theories have, over a considerable period of time, become the dominant model of political philosophy.[11] In contrast, theories within the category of recognition aim to make the world more hospitable to diversity in all its forms. Although such theories are reclaiming the Hegelian notion of recognition,[12] they are firmly rooted in a contemporary phase of political philosophy, which is motivated by a desire and need to understand our very contemporary struggles over identity and difference.

There is an assumption that these two forms of political philosophy are not only distinct but also sit at opposite ends of a political spectrum. Redistribution theorists are universalists, anti-sceptics and liberal individualists, whereas recognition theorists are relativists, communitarians and sceptics; the former are concerned with class and socio-economic disadvantages and the latter with gender, sexuality, ethnicity, race, culture (or any other terms used to express aspects of our identities) and the disadvantages these identities can cause. These assumptions, however, merely serve to set up a false dichotomy that is more of a hindrance than help. Class and identity are not separable in the way that this dichotomy suggests; the two domains are, in fact, related and they interact. Poverty, low-pay, menial work and unemployment are disproportionately found amongst certain identities. Redistribution theories will have some impact upon identity disadvantages that are apparently the concern of recognition theories; and recognition theories, which seek to address and destroy the association between certain identities and notions of inferiority, will also have an impact on socio-economic status.[13]

In addition to this, the separation of the political spectrum into the opposing schema of liberal and communitarian, individualists and collectivists, anti-sceptics and sceptics/critical theorists, universalists and relativists, is misleading and inaccurate. This is precisely the issue that Kymlicka was concerned with when he introduced the term 'liberal culturalists'. A paradigm has developed which is

---

10 This is an under-theorised area, but see Fraser and Honneth (2003) and Fraser (1997).

11 Fraser (2003b: 7) estimates this period of time to be around 150 years.

12 In fact, such theories do not just reclaim Hegelian recognition, they also reconstitute it. In its Hegelian form recognition is the antithesis of liberal individualism, although the same cannot be said of the politics of recognition. For example, Taylor (1994) attributes some of the modern condition, which necessitates recognition, to liberal individualism. It is, in significant part, liberal individualism that has precipitated a new attachment to the development of our own authentic identities.

13 For more detail on the ways that these two domains interact, see Fraser (2003b: 11–16). See also Vertovec (2007) on 'super-diversity' and Chapter 7 on the difficulties of theorising diversity in absolute terms such as ethnicity.

no longer useful or accurate in describing diversity claims. Group claims have historically been concerned with the preservation of an existing *status quo*, or the resurrection of lost past practices.[14] In this way they have come to be seen as inherently incompatible with liberalism, with its emphasis on challenging the *status quo* and freedom of choice.[15] However, this paradigm fails to capture the developments that have taken place in this arena; yet, the strength with which this paradigm prevails has shaped debates in this field to the extent that those promoting diversity issues have been automatically placed in the communitarian camp. In turn, this means that they are also cast as collectivists, sceptics, and so on. This facile division does a disservice to the debates in this field, which are actually far more complex.

Although the suggestion that those writing in the field of diversity occupy positions all across the political spectrum is not controversial, it is in fact the case that diversity debates have developed according to this old paradigm. For example, Charles Taylor has been, and still is, seen as a communitarian, whilst the substance of his work on the politics of recognition and identity is predicated upon the rise of the individual, her sense of self and her freedom to choose and revise her conception of the good life. Taylor's work, therefore, is based upon the fundamentals of liberalism. It is correct that Taylor recognises the importance of community too, but this element of his work has been magnified, and he has been unhelpfully placed in the communitarian camp.[16] In fact Taylor's work is a mix of both liberal and communitarian ideals, but this reading does not fit neatly into the polarised paradigm that currently exists.[17] My point is that this paradigm is inaccurate and actually presents obstacles to the furtherance of debates in this field, precisely because there is no solid basis behind the creation of these polarised camps. Additionally, there is no real need to make a choice between redistribution and recognition theories. One does not have to align oneself on either side, especially as both concern themselves with social justice and both provide important insights that ought not to be easily cast aside.

14 For example, see the old minority rights regime under the League of Nations, prior to the United Nations.

15 Kymlicka's (1989) original concern with minority rights was motivated by the aim of exploding this myth and showing that minority rights are not only compatible with liberalism, but that liberalism also intrinsically requires a sympathetic position to minority claims.

16 Fraser (2003b: 10) notes that this automatic assumption of communitarian politics may also owe something to the use of the Hegelian concept of recognition; Hegel's work focused upon consciousness in contrast to liberal thinking which was based upon reason, thus a polarisation naturally occurred and has been replicated.

17 Kymlicka (2001: 17–38), in his most recent complete text on minority rights, notes that there is a 'new debate' and revises his initial assessment of Charles Taylor as a communitarian, casting him instead as a 'liberal culturalist'. He includes himself in this new category of writers in the field of diversity. I return to this issue later in this chapter.

My belief that recognition and redistribution are complementary is based upon an understanding of identity as two-dimensional.[18] This notion of two-dimensionality follows from Nancy Fraser's explanation of gender and race (2003b: 22): identities are a 'compound of both status and class' in that they are constituted by both class divisions and status differentiations. The two-dimensional nature of identities sheds light upon the relation between recognition and redistribution. The vital point to note is that redistribution is not derivative of recognition, or vice versa. The two categories of political philosophy represent the two dimensions of social justice. The challenges of diversity, in the sense that I am concerned with them, require resolution by both theories of recognition and redistribution. However, recognition and redistribution do not cover identical ground; they overlap and are interconnected, but they are also independent of each other; redistribution cannot hope to remedy all the difficulties of misrecognition, and vice versa.[19] What I mean to reject here is Axel Honneth's (2003a, 2003b) theory that recognition includes and subsumes all aspects of redistribution. This is too reductive an explanation of recognition and redistribution, and identity.

Brief consideration of the relation between recognition and redistribution is crucial as it highlights that recognition-based projects, such as this, are not intended to replace or encourage abandonment of theories that promote redistribution, and the legal tools that they give rise to. This point will become clearer as the arguments here progress, but I do not put forth any arguments with the notion that they will do the work that human rights and anti-discrimination laws are designed to do. Instead, my conclusions are intended to be complementary to redistribution-based theories. The normative base of my work is the politics of recognition. This encapsulates the notion that with the modern rise of individualism, failure by the nation-state to recognise identity is an injustice different from, although intimately connected to, the injustice of maldistribution.

A Diversity-Conscious Form of Justice

Having provided a background to the link between diversity and justice, I turn to the elements that create my diversity-sensitive conceptualisation of justice. This form of justice is best understood as involving two main pillars: (1) the value of identity in contemporary societies; and (2) the significance of access to and

18 See Fraser (2003b: 22–6), where she explains that all axes of subordination are, in the real-world, two-dimensional. See also Vertovec (2007) who argues that societies are not just diverse, but are super-diverse. He argues that theorising along one axis, such as ethnicity, is insufficient to understand the complexities of the plurality that exists in contemporary Britain.

19 Similarly, these challenges demand legal and non-legal answers; one or the other cannot be expected to shoulder all the responsibility of meeting these challenges.

participation in civil society. In many ways the ideas of the second pillar relate to, and even encompass the ideas of the first pillar.[20]

I illustrate the first pillar of justice by referencing Taylor's work on identity (1994), and Kymlicka's (1989, 1995) philosophical defence of diversity. I corroborate these normative conclusions by drawing on anthropological works that analyse the evolution of behaviour and practices amongst British South Asians.[21] I use these studies to illustrate that the normative conclusions of political philosophers align well with social realities of diversity. Having outlined the first pillar of justice, I turn to consider a more general meaning of justice in the second pillar. By referencing studies by Charles Taylor (1994), Nancy Fraser (2005) and Jürgen Habermas (1993, 1996), I conclude that justice, in its general sense, means free and fair access to, and participation in civil society. I consider two separate elements of this general sense of justice. First, I look at the idea of free and fair access to and participation in social life. Secondly, I consider the conceptualisation of civil society beyond the bounds of official action, and thereby extend the general idea of justice beyond familiar notions of electoral suffrage, and having a voice in democratic processes.

The First Pillar: The Value of Diverse Identities

Charles Taylor rightly notes that 'our ancestors of more than a couple of centuries ago would have stared at us uncomprehendingly if we had used [recognition and identity] in their current sense' (1994: 26). He therefore sets about understanding how recognition and identity came to be such significant discourses, indentifying the contemporary 'collapse of social hierarchies' (26) and the consequent search for new sources of authenticity and dignity, as the sources of this paradigm shift (26–37). He explains that a world where identities were intimately tied to state hierarchies and state honour systems has given way to a democratic society based upon the inherent dignity of all citizens. In light of this increased importance of identity, Taylor argues that 'misrecognition shows not just a lack of due respect. It can inflict a grievous wound, saddling its victims with a crippling self-hatred. Due recognition is not just a courtesy we owe people. It is a vital human need' (1994: 26). The idea of due recognition as a critical human need reflects, I believe, a gradual change in the importance of individual identity processes. Furthermore,

---

20 They are separated here in order to emphasise the importance of these two elements to a diversity-conscious approach to justice, and not to recognise two wholly independent domains of justice.

21 Much of the socio-legal research on diversity and law has been undertaken in reference to British South Asians. Although literature outside of Britain is beginning to discuss legal hybrids and take socio-legal perspectives, this literature refers back to concepts that have evolved in the literature that considers British South Asians. See, for example, Zaman (2008) and Fournier (2001–2002, 2006).

Taylor's due recognition thesis emphasises the link between the value of identity processes in our contemporary environment and justice.

Having shown the initial link between identity and justice, it is important to delve deeper and establish a sound philosophical explanation of the value of our identities. To do this, I use Kymlicka's (1989 and 1995) philosophical defence of culture, on the basis that it also works as a defence of identity. Kymlicka (1989: 166) readily admits that expressions such as 'cultural community' and 'cultural structure' are extremely hard to define, and so clearly sets out the cultural structure that is relevant to his argument. He is not concerned with isolating the character of a community at any one moment in time, so that any changes to this community would be considered a loss of culture. Rather, his focus is upon culture as a context of choice (1989: 166–77), with such a structure persisting even if its members should decide to modify the character of the culture, should it no longer find those ways worthwhile. Kymlicka defines his focus as 'societal culture' (1995: 76). Societal culture 'provides its members with meaningful ways of life across the full range of human activities, including social, educational, religious, recreational, and economic life, encompassing both public and private spheres' (1995: 76). Societal cultures involve more than just 'shared memories or values' and must include 'common institutions and practices' (1995: 76).

On Kymlicka's account it is difficult to separate the importance of societal cultures from the importance of identity processes, and although I later go on to consider why Kymlicka might choose societal cultures over identity,[22] the lack of clear boundary is sufficient, at the moment, to introduce his philosophical defence of societal cultures as an explanation of the underlying value of identity.

Kymlicka's philosophical explanation of the value of culture forms an integral part of his defence of minority rights as compatible with liberalism. There are two parts to his arguments supporting culture. First, he (1995: 82–93) explains the importance of culture and, secondly, he explains why we need our *own* cultures, as opposed to being satisfied with leading a life that involves the culture of the host society, or indeed anybody else's culture. For Kymlicka, cultural structures, in a general sense, are valuable (1995: 83): '[p]ut simply, freedom involves making choices amongst various options, and our societal culture not only provides these options, but also makes them meaningful to us'. Understanding cultural narratives is vital to our capacity to make judgments about how we should lead our lives. Thus, culture not only provides us with options in life; it also makes those options meaningful. Culture 'provides the spectacles through which we identify experiences as valuable' (Dworkin 1985: 228, quoted in Kymlicka 1995: 83). Cultures, therefore, are not an end in themselves, but they provide us with meaningful 'contexts of choice'.[23] Thus, the very value and worth of our lives

22 I consider the issue of the boundaries between concepts such as culture, religion, race, ethnicity, nationality, gender, and so on in Chapter 7, and also consider their relation to identity.

23 I have borrowed this phrase from Kymlicka (1995: 82).

is derived from access to culture. Culture acts as a guide to how people act and react, it orients choices, it defines what people consider to be desirable, and what is unacceptable; as such, it provides colour to our lives and is therefore an integral element of our identities.

What Kymlicka convincingly argues is that culture has value because of its character as a meaningful context of choice, and in so doing emphasises the value of identity processes. However, this norm does not support the claim that we need to choose our *own* cultures, and that our own agency in these identity processes is vital to its authenticity and meaning. Kymlicka addresses this point by asking why we need to protect minority societal cultures, because as long as we have access to a culture, including majority societal cultures, what does it matter which culture provides colour to our lives? This second element of Kymlicka's normative claim seeks to explain why we each need to choose our own cultures, and therefore why it is not legitimate to allow minority cultures to disintegrate. He does this by stating that we have strong bonds with our choice of cultures, and by explaining that the depth of this bond means that agency in processes of culture is more than something that we enjoy and like, but that it is actually a human need.

It is worth noting that Kymlicka writes in terms of the bond we have with our 'own' cultures. However, I do not interpret from this that he means that we possess a culture as a pure matter of heritage. Rather, I believe he means to refer to authentic cultures in the sense that Charles Taylor uses the term 'authentic'. Taylor isolates individual endeavour and agency in identity processes as key to their authenticity. This interpretation of Kymlicka is congruent with his dynamic definition of societal cultures, which emphasises evolutionary processes and distinguishes itself from static notions of cultures that are inherited. As a consequence, I favour Taylor's idea of authenticity, with its connotations of individual agency, in my presentation of Kymlicka's argument, as it is more consistent with the broader parameters of his study.

In order to illustrate the value of authentic societal cultures, Kymlicka challenges Waldron's (1992) claim that 'examples of successful 'cosmopolitan' people who move between cultures disprove the claim that people are connected to their own culture in any deep way' (1995: 85):

> On [Waldron's] view, an Irish-American who eats Chinese food and reads her child *Grimms' Fairy Tales* is thereby 'living in a kaleidoscope of cultures' ... But this is not moving between societal cultures. Rather it is enjoying the opportunities provided by the diverse societal culture which characterizes the anglophone society of the United States.[24]

---

24 To explain briefly Waldron's argument, he (1992: 762) sees the Herderian argument for the importance of cultural contexts collapsing because this cosmopolitan Irish-American illustrates that there is no distinctive human need for culture. It is this distinctive human need for culture that formed the basis of Herder's claim that we need our own cultural contexts.

Kymlicka is willing to concede that Waldron raises a legitimate point and we must address the question of whether people should, on balance, assimilate into the host society. However, he points out that whilst it is a possibility to leave one's culture, such a choice must be viewed as 'analogous to the choice to take a vow of perpetual poverty and enter a religious order' (1995: 86). Just because it is a physical possibility to leave one's own culture, it does not follow that it is desirable or legitimate to require individuals to abandon their own culture. The deep bond we have to our own cultures is 'normally too strong to be given up' (1995: 90). The key to this argument is that the *requirement* of abandonment of culture denies individual agency and thereby threatens the authenticity of one's cultural contexts.

Agency and authenticity are also evident in Kymlicka's further justification of this conclusion. He does this by demonstrating wide acceptance of this view amongst liberals. In particular, he considers Rawls (1993) and Margalit and Raz (1990), and explains that the importance of agency is consistent with liberalism (1995: 88–93). If a liberal society is one where individuals are free to choose their own conception of the good life and engage in a process of open-ended revision of these choices,[25] then it follows that a liberal society is not one where cultures or ways of life are imposed upon individuals. Thus, a liberal society is consistent with a society which respects individual agency and the idea of authenticity.

Whilst Kymlicka provides a compelling philosophical account of why the self-actualisation of authentic identities is integral to any theory of justice, it is crucial to refer to some anthropological and legal anthropological works to provide contextual validity to this pillar of justice. Roger Ballard (1994) provides an anthropological study of South Asian diasporas in Britain that is instructive in understanding the value of identity processes. He notes that South Asians in Britain continue to draw inspiration from their cultural, religious and linguistic heritage and are actively engaged in a process of reinterpreting and rebuilding 'their lives *on their own terms*' (1994: 5, emphasis in original). This process of reconstruction on their own terms stands in opposition to the official expectation that South Asian diasporas would assimilate to mainstream identities. Ballard observed that migrant families were, in fact, recreating around themselves familiar cultural structures. Although familiar in nature, these structures varied from the original structures in the migrants' country of origin. This reconstruction was intended to take into account the changed circumstances of Britain. Indeed, Ballard describes this process as an 'adaptive strategy' born of a need to cope with a new environment (1994: 4).

This creation of what Ballard has termed *Desh Pardesh* can be understood in more concrete terms when one considers the celebration of life-cycle rituals

25 It is beyond doubt that this is Kymlicka's interpretation of a liberal society. See, for example, Kymlicka (1995: 80).

amongst South Asian diasporas, such as those of marriage and death.[26] Menski (1988b, 1993) and Pearl and Menski (1998: 74–7) have written of the two marriages that take place amongst these communities – there will be, for example, a Muslim, Sikh or Hindu marriage as well as a civil marriage that complies with the requirements of English law. Moreover, the religious marriage is sometimes adapted (reconstructed) to accommodate the elements required by English law. For example, Menski (1991) has written of the incorporation of the English registration ceremony into the Hindu wedding with the development of new ceremonies, inspired by traditional forms, to suit the occasion; a sort of Hindu-isation of the English registration ceremony, in order to incorporate it as part of the Hindu wedding ceremony.

Menski goes further and also writes of this reconstruction beyond the bounds of just life-cycle rituals, and explains this phenomenon as the creation of hybrid laws by which day-to-day life is to be lived; he has termed these hybrid laws *angrezi shariat*, *angrezi dharma* and so on.[27] In many ways Menski's work on cultural diversity in a legal context parallels Ballard's conclusions in social contexts – one writes of legal hybrids, the other of cultural hybridity.

Ballard's work also provides the helpful concept of 'skilled cultural navigation'. Later generations of South Asian migrants (including those who migrated to Britain at a very young age, as well as those who are born in Britain) are active in wider social orders beyond those of their own culture, and these other social orders can, in fact, contradict the conventions of their inherited culture. Ballard (1994: 30) asks whether this code-switching between different social orders will create psychologically confused individuals. He concludes (1994: 31) that the ability to switch conceptual codes does not result in cultural confusion anymore than being bilingual confuses speech. Those individuals who develop an accomplished capacity to switch codes are 'skilled cultural navigators'. It is this notion of 'skilled cultural navigators', together with an understanding of culture as an agency-laden process of 'reconstruction on their own terms' that provides tangible examples of the value of self-actualisation and authenticity in identity processes.

Waldron (1992) describes an Irish-American who eats Chinese food and reads German folk stories to her child as an individual who is not rooted in any particular culture, an individual with a cosmopolitan identity. However, armed with the concepts of skilled cultural navigators and identity as a continual process

26 *Desh Pardesh* is Urdu, meaning 'home from home' or 'home abroad', and Ballard uses it to describe 'the embodiment of the self-created worlds of Britain's South Asian settlers' (1994: 29). Given the linguistic proximity of Urdu and Punjabi, Ballard's use of *Desh Pardesh* resonates with the Punjabis that are actually the subject of his own chapter in this edited collection of papers; in Punjabi the same phrase would be *des pardes*. The term has also been adapted and translated into Bengali to denote a similar process amongst British Bangladeshis: see Gardner (1993), cited in Shah (2005: 126), who writes of *Desh-Bidesh*.

27 See, for example, Menski (1988b, 1991, 1993) and Pearl and Menski (1998: 74–7).

of reconstruction and renegotiation undertaken on the agent's own terms, this Irish-American can be explained in a very different way; she is an exemplary skilled cultural navigator who is actively engaged in rebuilding and reinterpreting her culture on her own terms. By virtue of incorporating aspects of other cultures into her life, it does not follow that she does not have an authentic identity. In fact, the incorporation of Chinese food and German folk stories can be said to illustrate a dynamic and fluid reconstruction and renegotiation of Irish-American identity on one's own terms that is typical of diasporic minorities.[28] Intrinsic to the nature of identity is that it is neither reified nor absolute in the way that Waldron's explanation of this Irish-American suggests, so that it is not possible to abandon one's own identity by simply skilfully navigating the diverse identities that exist within various social orders. It does not follow that people lose their authentic identities merely by virtue of this capacity to navigate.[29]

Ballard's study especially evidences the value of authenticity in identity processes. The reinterpretation and reconstruction of identities by members of diasporic minorities takes place 'on their own terms' (1994: 5). Vital to identity processes is the individual agency that it involves, and I would tentatively suggest that this individual investment not only assists in explaining the depth of the value of authentic identities, but also sheds some light on why Kymlicka theorises matters in terms of the bond to one's *own* culture. I reference both Ballard and Menski's work here to reinforce, in terms of social realities, the significance of authentic identity processes in our lives, and therefore to illustrate that it is a vital plank to a diversity-conscious conception of justice. Kymlicka's philosophical defence, together with its corroboration in social realities, leads to the conclusion that a diversity-conscious justice must acknowledge the importance of authentic identities and facilitate their realisation.

It does not implicitly follow from this conceptualisation of justice that I am also arguing that all aspects of our identities have a worthwhile impact upon our lives. In acknowledging our agency in identity processes, and the meaning that identity gives to our lives, it does not mean that all aspects of our identities take on a valuable role in our lives, nor that we will only engage with them if they have a positive impact in our lives. British policy on 'forced marriages' provides an example here. Britain has a policy of intervening abroad when its citizens are forced to marry against their will.[30] Consular services will stage an intervention

28 See Kymlicka (1995: 104–5) for an elaboration of the dynamism of societal culture.

29 Arguably Waldron's interpretation of one's own culture is that of a static entity that one inherits, rather than something that one actively engages with, reviews, assesses and chooses. Admittedly, there is a spectrum of engagement that one can have with one's own culture or identity processes, and some will be more engaged than others.

30 Britain has passed legislation that provides the English courts with powers in cases of forced marriages: Forced Marriages (Civil Protection) Act 2007. For further details on the Forced Marriage Unit see http://www.fco.gov.uk/servlet/Front?pagename=OpenMarket/Xcelerate/ShowPage&c=Page&cid=1094234857863 (last accessed 21 September 2010).

and take these individuals out of the situation they find themselves in and return them to Britain.

A *Guardian* newspaper report on this policy followed two girls in this situation and noted that after the intervention they had attempted to reconcile with the parents who had forced them to marry against their will (Walsh 2005). Whilst these girls were clear that they did not want to marry against their own will, it did not follow that they wanted to abandon their parents. This is the consequence of being attached to one's own identity; to live outside and without this context is an impoverished existence. It is entirely possible, therefore, to be attached to one's identity, and also for that identity to have a detrimental and damaging impact upon parts of one's life. The deep bond that we have to our own identity is a complex relationship that cannot simply be understood as implying that all of our affiliations will lead to worthwhile and valuable experiences, or that where there are (personally acknowledged) detrimental practices, this will drive us to cut out those parts of our identities.

In this particular example, the injustice of forcing these girls to marry against their will stems from a denial of their individual agency in their identity processes. Moreover, nobody could force them to give up some sort of a relationship with their parents, although they would be free to make this choice themselves. Let us suppose these girls freely consented to having their marriages arranged in this way. As autonomous individuals with free will, their choice ought to be respected, regardless of the fact that a significant number of individuals would choose to find their partners in a different way.

Alternative examples illustrate the other ways in which identities can give rise to damaging life experiences. Consider, for example, the gender inequality in pay around the world. There is evidently an injustice in this situation based upon gender identity. Whilst it is important to address the challenges of justice in this situation, abandoning one's identity is not considered a viable option, perhaps, in this case, because we feel that gender is not a matter of choice and cannot be abandoned. My point, however, is that it is incorrect to assume that the identities that we are deeply bonded to must only provide us with valuable, life-enhancing experiences, or that we are deeply bonded to our identities only because they provide nothing but empowering, life-enhancing experiences. Instead, our identities expose us to a wide spectrum of experiences, some more positive than others; they provide context to our lives, and although this context is not always empowering or positive, it gives meaning to our lives, and it is this aspect that explains the bonds we have to our affiliations. Furthermore, we ought not to assume that where our identities are a source of detrimental, agency-denying or oppressive experiences we will want to move completely outside of that context. I argue here that we have strong and deep bonds with our own authentic identity processes which means that a life where we are denied these contexts would be impoverished, not that our affiliations only provide life-enhancing and emancipatory experiences; the two are separate norms and I mean to reference only the former here as an integral element of this diversity-conscious justice.

Earlier, I set aside the difference between Kymlicka and Taylor's studies as irrelevant, and asserted that in essence they both related to identity. This conclusion, however, merits some explanation. I believe the difference in these two studies is a consequence of the creation of the ideological dichotomy in the field of diversity studies that I referred to earlier. This dichotomy has mischaracterised the nature of the debates within this field. In one of his later works, Kymlicka himself explains the creation of this liberal-communitarian dichotomy when he identifies a 'new debate over minority rights' that has three stages (2001: 17–38). The first stage was the pre-1989 liberals versus communitarian debate, which played out as individualists versus collectivists. Liberals saw the individual as being prior to the community, and communitarians saw people as being embedded in their social roles, thus encouraging minority rights; because the debate revolved around these two poles, one's position on the political spectrum dictated how one viewed minority rights.

Movement into the second stage of the debate was facilitated, in part, by the fact that commitment to individual autonomy is something that Kymlicka concludes has become widespread in modern society, and has crossed ethnic, religious and linguistic lines. Since it has become an imperative to accommodate a plurality of groups in these liberal spaces, theorists began to think about the possibility of accommodation within a liberal framework. This is not to say that all liberals fall into this category of 'liberal culturalists'; critics continue to argue over the merits of common citizenship, but the debate of minority rights is no longer one between the two camps of communitarianism and liberalism. Indeed, Kymlicka no longer describes Charles Taylor as a communitarian, preferring instead to see his work as a form of liberal culturalism. He summarises that 'minority rights are consistent with liberal culturalism if (a) they protect the freedom of individuals within the group; and (b) they promote relations of equality (non-dominance) between groups' (2001: 22–3). However, he argues that this stage needs to be challenged because it misinterprets the demands that a liberal state places on minorities.

The third stage, which is what Kymlicka argues for in this study (2001), is one where theorists shed the assumption that in its default position the liberal state is ethnoculturally neutral: this assumption insists that the state is indifferent to its citizens' ability to reproduce their culture, so that culture is in the same position as religion, namely, it is something that individuals are free to pursue in their private lives. This model of liberalism involves, as Walzer states, a 'sharp divorce of states and ethnicity' (1992: 100–101, quoted in Kymlicka 2001: 23).

Whilst Kymlicka's concern is to give his arguments for a new debate on minority rights a background, my claim uses his explanation of the stages of this debate to shed light upon the focus of his work on the value of culture, and therefore identity. My argument is that the liberal-communitarian dichotomy that was set up in the early stages of the debate colours the nature of Kymlicka's early arguments. Having decided that there is a strong imperative to show that minority rights are compatible with liberalism, Kymlicka placed himself on one side of this ideological dichotomy. In so doing, his arguments reflect a need to engage with liberalism on its terms and, just as important, a need to distinguish his work from that of communitarians. However, as Kymlicka acknowledges, when he places Charles Taylor in the liberal culturalist bracket with himself, his work does not oppose that of Taylor's: where Taylor concerned himself with the manifestation of meaning or value in our lives, namely identity, Kymlicka concerned himself with the contexts that give meaning to our lives, and termed them societal cultures. Societal cultures encompass all aspects of our lives. They provide their 'members with meaningful ways of life *across the full range of human activities*, including social, educational, religious, recreational and economic life, encompassing both public and private spheres' (Kymlicka 1995: 76, emphasis added). As a consequence, Kymlicka's philosophical defence of societal cultures also serves as a defence of the value of identity.

To clarify further the claim that this ideological dichotomy has distorted the nature of diversity debates, I wish to explain how Taylor's recognition thesis cannot so easily be squared with communitarianism.[31] Taylor's thesis is, I believe, grounded upon the contemporary rise of individualism. His communitarian label comes from his acknowledgement that this project of individual identity, which is so salient in contemporary societies, has reinvigorated our links to communities, associations, groups, or whatever term best describes collections of individuals. The link that Taylor makes between individualism and community places his work at odds with the orthodoxy of liberalism, which prioritises the individual over the community. Within the framework that diversity debates have been taking place, accepting the continued relevance and impact of group affiliations placed Taylor's work within the communitarian bracket, thereby shifting the spotlight away from its emphasis upon individualism in the modern world.

The liberal-communitarian framework has, however, been counterproductive. I have shown how it has led to a mischaracterisation of Taylor's work. On a broader scale, it hampers debates in this field by making studies by those in the opposing bracket inaccessible, because each side is presumed to be pursuing conflicting aims. This is a difficulty that I hope to bypass by introducing pertinent elements of Kymlicka's liberal defence of minority rights to a book that does not deny the importance of group affiliations. Group affiliations do not necessarily lessen the importance of individual endeavour, nor are such affiliations incompatible with prioritising the autonomous individual.

The Second Pillar: Access to and Participation in Civil Society

In the first pillar of justice I outlined a normative argument justifying the value of authentic identities, and thereby argued that justice militates in favour of the promotion of diverse identities. In this pillar of justice I showed how our group

31 One example of a study that falls squarely into the liberal bracket is Franck (1999). He prioritised individual endeavour in identity processes, denying the relevance of our group affiliations in our personal journey; he concluded that ours is 'the Age of Individualism'.

affiliations are vital to these identity processes, and argued that this conclusion is indeed compatible with prioritising the individual. However, in this second pillar of justice I want to concentrate on isolating a general meaning of justice. In so doing, I hope to outline the basic parameters of this book, in the sense that this general idea of justice must guide any new legal responses to diversity, and can also be used to measure current legal responses to diversity. My concern is not to craft a complete theory of justice, and consequently the general idea of justice that I present here is relatively superficial. Since I am not crafting this idea of justice from scratch, I borrow from the work of Charles Taylor, Nancy Fraser and Jürgen Habermas.[32] I use their consideration of justice in plural societies to set out this second pillar of a diversity-sensitive form of justice and explain that, at its core, justice must be concerned with free and fair access to and participation in civil society.

The notion of misrecognition as an injustice is only a partial explanation of what I hope to refer to when I use the concept of justice. Whilst Fraser explains that recognition and redistribution are two complementary, sometimes overlapping, non-conflatable dimensions of justice,[33] she also considers its abstract meaning (2005: 73–5), which she describes as participatory parity. Participatory parity is a term she employs to express the ideal of free and fair participation of peers in all aspects of social life. Habermas (1996) incorporates a similar, although by no means identical, ideal in his discourse theory and deliberative democracy. The mechanics of Habermas's conception of this ideal permits a deeper exploration of this pillar of justice.

Habermasian discourse (1993) requires that competent speakers must satisfy a set of ideal conditions if they are to reach a reasoned consensus.[34] These discourse ethics ensure that principles such as equality, justice and solidarity are inherent in the process of discourse. For example, they ensure that argumentation excludes no-one, that no assertion is immune from criticism and that there is no coercion, just the unforced force of the better argument. Entering into the process of discourse involves, therefore, accepting presuppositions which relate to the aim of the discourse (the attainment of a rationally reached consensus) and the means of the discourse (the equality, solidarity and justice of the conditions of discourse).[35]

---

32 Referencing the work of more than one political theorist serves to highlight that the notion of justice is somewhat fluid and dynamic, with manifold interpretations, and that it must be adapted to suit the particular specifities of diversity. This is a point that I consider in greater depth in Chapter 6.

33 Fraser later adds a third dimension to her interpretation of justice, namely representation. She explains (2005: 69–73) these three dimensions as the what (recognition), how (redistribution) and who (representation) of justice. In our post-Keynesian-Westphalian world the how and who of justice are now also up for grabs.

34 See Habermas (1993: 65, 66, 93); the rules are taken from Alexy's 'The Rules of Reason' (1990, 165–7).

35 This formulation is similar to the Kantian notion of acceptance of the end necessitating acceptance of the means to this end.

Although these conditions are ideal and real discourse cannot hope to conform to them, failure to satisfy these conditions is known as a 'performative contradiction' that results in a violation of the rules that they implicitly include.

Norms derived through this process of discourse are universal since each participant freely accepts the consequences of a norm, and in each case the norm is accepted to the satisfaction of everyone's interests, not just the participant's own interest. Thus reasons are tested from all perspectives. This universalisation principle (U) suggests, therefore, an end-point to moral inquiry, where those norms which satisfy the interests of all, would be settled upon; in so doing it represents an impartial judgment. However, in contradistinction to Kant and Rawls, participants are not required to move away from their own interests and take a third-party perspective, instead impartiality is obtained through the process of discourse where everyone's interests are considered in order to reach consensus.[36] This process is not just an epistemic check on whether one can universalise the norm in question, but opens one's views and interests to the critical interpretation of others.

Discourse ethics, and more precisely, the discourse principle, forms a crucial background to Habermas's theory of the legitimacy of law and its relationship to morality and democracy. It is important to appreciate the role that U plays in Habermas's theories, as this appears to be a key site of concern in relation to issues surrounding the plurality of worldviews, and explains the idea of free and fair access to and participation in civil society. The critical aspect of Habermas's radical democracy lies in the validity of positive law. Legitimate validity of positive law is achieved when such statutes 'meet with the assent (*Zustimmung*) of *all* citizens in a discursive process of legislation that in turn has been legally constituted' (Habermas 1996: 10, emphasis added). U, therefore, is the crucial legitimising force to legislation; it ensures that a plurality of worldviews are considered and that a diverse citizenry has access to law-making processes.

Achieving an uncoerced consensus with processes open to participation by all, and crucially, with each participant attempting to take on and understand the standpoint of all others affected, without adopting a veil of ignorance, lies at the heart of Habermasian radical democracy. Similarly, Fraser promotes an abstract understanding of justice as participatory parity, this being the free and fair possibility of participation by all, as equals, in civil society. As much as these two interpretations overlap, they are also very different and sometimes diverging theories. I make reference to both here in order to highlight how, having established on a normative level that diverse identities must be promoted, plural societies must impact on our interpretations of the demands of justice. If each member of society is to receive her dues, it seems to follow that the diversity within our societies must impact the deliverance of justice.

---

36 Habermas has dismissed the criticism of the problem of dissociating the self that considers these interests and the self that has those needs and interests, since his form of impartiality involves a process where the participant attempts to occupy the standpoint of all others affected by a norm and to identify their needs and interests.

Having outlined the idea of the possibility of free and fair participation in social life, it remains to consider what is meant by civil society. To elucidate this idea I draw upon Habermasian (1996) radical democracy. Habermas's institutional version of deliberative democracy has two-tracks, namely an organised public which consists of formal political institutions, including a legislative body, and an unorganised public which encompasses a broader notion of civil society, where citizens use a great number of techniques to participate in political debate (such techniques include the media and more formal political associations). The 'organised public' focuses public opinion and translates this public opinion into legal form, whereas the unorganised public, or civil society, has a far more chaotic nature and is engaged in identifying political concerns.[37] The significance of this distinction lies in Habermas's desire to construct a theory of deliberative democracy which recognises and accommodates the plural and heterogeneous nature of civil society, and does not create a homogenous public sphere. Moreover, it is the twin-track nature of this form of deliberative democracy that enables legitimate law to be created in a diverse and plural society. The anonymous nature of civil society does not detract from its awesome communicative power, which is used to achieve an uncoerced consensus and mutual understanding.

It is a tension within this twin-track model, which Habermas himself identifies, that provides an important insight for this book. Since administrative power is the only mechanism of employing communicative power, the power of the unorganised public is wholly dependent upon the power of the organised public for effect. This paradox is, for Habermas, a manifestation of the tension between facticity and validity (the core concern of this particular book). Crucial to this tension is Habermas's identification of law as the medium through which communicative power is transformed into administrative power; law and the fate of representative democracy are, therefore, inherently linked. By illuminating this function of law, Habermas highlights, from within a philosophical framework, the burden that law shoulders in complex pluralistic societies. It is rare to see acknowledgement of the gravity of law's role in plural societies. This book is grounded upon an acceptance of this role for law; acceptance of this role has enormous repercussions for the burdens that law *must* take on in plural societies and is, therefore, a central driving force for this project.[38]

---

37 It is worth noting that Habermas avoids giving civil society a tangible quality, as is implied by the well-known concept of 'the people'. Indeed, Habermas talks about civil society being subjectless. The emphasis on the anarchic and anonymous nature of civil society appears to be a signalled dissociation from a long line of political philosophy which relies on a unitary notion of popular sovereignty that resides with 'the people'.

38 It seems to me that the field of multiculturalism and law must be based on similar philosophical foundations, namely that law has an important and useful role to play in promoting harmony in plural societies. In these circumstances, my reference to plurality includes the whole spectrum of difference, from race, ethnicity, religion and culture through to nationality, gender and disability. My isolation of nationality as a reference point for

In Taylor's recognition thesis, Fraser's participatory parity, Habermas's discourse ethics, universalisation principle and interpretation of civil society it is possible to sketch out a general idea of justice. It is all the elements of these theories that I mean to encapsulate in the phrase 'free and fair access to and participation in civil society'. Moreover, this general idea of justice, which values and therefore encourages the self-actualisation of authentic identities, grounds this book. It provides the tools with which legal responses to diversity can be measured, as well as representing the focal point in my fresh perspectives on justice and law.

Whilst this project is concerned with the challenges of justice in the context of diversity, an important point about its boundaries must be made. The fresh perspective on justice that I have presented here is intimately tied to law. This association is evident in Habermas's explanation of the vital role the law plays in democratic societies. However, my conception of a diversity-conscious form of justice is not tied exclusively to law. The breadth of the notion of civil society demonstrates that this form of justice has implications in social and political domains, as well as in legal arenas. In spite of this, for the purposes of this book I focus upon these implications in relation to law.

difference here has scenarios such as the divisions between the English, Welsh and Scots in mind.

Chapter 3
Nation-states and Pluralism

In her study on liberalism and nationalism, Yael Tamir counsels us that '[t]he era of homogenous and viable nation-states is over (or rather, the era of the illusion that homogenous and viable nation-states are possible is over, since such states never existed), and the national vision must be redefined' (1993: 3). Tamir's cautionary words serve as a reminder that a diversity-conscious form of justice is a blunt instrument without an understanding of the role of the national vision in encouraging, or discouraging, diversity.

I have argued that my fresh perspective on justice requires an emphasis upon valuing the self-actualisation of authentic identities, and understanding the significance of free and fair participation in and access to civil society when recognising diversity. However, this perspective on justice loses some meaning without an account of the role that the national vision plays in engendering or prohibiting diversity. In this chapter, therefore, I add to my fresh perspective by drawing attention to three principles that support my diversity-conscious justice. These principles focus upon the links between nationhood and diversity. Within the social sciences there is increasing interest in theorising the relations between nationality, nationhood and diversity.[1] The burgeoning study of these areas permits for greater depth and clarity in my perspective on justice, which in turn allows for sounder foundations to my new vista on constitutional pluralism.

The aim of this chapter is not to set out arguments in support of a thesis that explains the relations between diversity and the nation-state. Rather, the intention is to clarify some of the presuppositions upon which my fresh perspective on justice rests, and thereby also explore the non-legal dimensions of this diversity-conscious justice. Many of these presuppositions would normally be tacitly assumed. This, however, is unsatisfactory as it leads to a lack of clarity and consequently creates a confusion that often goes unnoticed, and is therefore all the more damaging. Without explaining and justifying these underlying presuppositions, there is a significant risk that this book engages with others at cross-purposes. A lack of clarity with regard to these presuppositions compromises the potential contribution of this book to a much larger and ongoing dialogue in this field. The primary aim in this chapter, therefore, is to clear away that uncertainty and explicitly set out the presuppositions upon which the arguments in this study are predicated.

---

1 See, for example, B. Anderson (1991), Brubaker (1996), Fraser (2005), Gellner (1983), Habermas (1994, 2003), Held et al. (1999), Kymlicka (2001), Miller (1995), Sandel (1982), Soysal (2000), Tamir (1993), Taylor (1994), Tully (1995) and Walzer (1983).

This chapter begins by providing a background to the idea of theorising nation-states and diversity. By considering aspects of Will Kymlicka, James Tully, Yael Tamir and Benedict Anderson's work, it is possible to sketch out a case for the significance of the connections between theorising nation-states and theorising diversity. From this starting-point, I landmark three cardinal and interrelated principles that inform my perspective on justice. First, I explain Anderson's idea of imagined political communities and illustrate how this approach to understanding nation-states can affect the way that diversity is understood. Secondly, I propose that *all* nation-states engage in an ongoing project of nation-building, and illustrate that this project is inherently biased towards one single and dominant conception of the good life. This, I suggest, has profound implications for how diversity is theorised. Finally, I move to consider why today's diversity presents novel and unique challenges for justice, by arguing that globalisation has created an unprecedented confidence in difference. I argue that when these three principles are taken together, as they must be, they make the challenges of justice, in its quest to manage diversity, clearer. They therefore form an integral part of my fresh perspective on justice. I do not present a comprehensive theory of nation-states and diversity, but instead landmark those principles that significantly alter the course of my arguments in this book.

Understanding Nations and Diversity

Will Kymlicka's treatment of minority rights within a liberal framework includes inquiries into the relations between nation and diversity in at least two different ways. First, he proposes differential citizenship based upon whether one is a 'national minority' or a member of an 'ethnic group'. National minorities are found in multination states where cultural diversity is the consequence of the incorporation of previously self-governing, territorially concentrated cultures into a larger state. Ethnic groups are found in polyethnic states, where cultural diversity is a consequence of familial and individual immigration (1995: 6). It is perfectly possibly (and likely) that a country is both multinational and polyethnic (1995: 17).

Immigrants are entitled to a group of rights that Kymlicka terms 'polyethnic rights',[2] and he concedes that they may also be granted 'special representation rights'; in contrast, national minorities are entitled to 'self-government rights'. These three categories are the forms of 'group-differentiated rights' identified by Kymlicka (1995: 26–33); they represent the range of mechanisms through which

2 In his later refinement of his theory of multicultural citizenship Kymlicka suggests (2001: 51) that polyethnic rights could be more accurately labelled as 'accommodation rights' by virtue of the fact that they seek to accommodate diverse ethnic backgrounds into one coherent whole. He does not, however, alter the structure of the differential citizenship that he initially argues for in this later work.

diversity can be accommodated within a nation-state. Self-government rights involve some form of political autonomy or territorial jurisdiction which enables the development of the culture in question. At one extreme of the spectrum of self-government rights is secession, but only as a last resort where other forms of self-determination are impossible within the larger state (1995: 27). A less extreme point on this spectrum is the federal division of power; however, this 'can only serve as a mechanism for self-government if the national minority forms a majority in one of the federal subunits' (1995: 29).[3] As Kymlicka states (1995: 30):

> Self-government claims, then, typically take the form of devolving political power to a political unit substantially controlled by the members of the national minority, and substantially corresponding to their historical homeland or territory. It is important to note that these claims are not seen as a temporary measure, nor as a remedy for a form of oppression that we might (and ought) someday to eliminate. On the contrary, these rights are often described as 'inherent', and so permanent (which is one reason why national minorities seek to have them entrenched in the constitution.)

'Polyethnic rights' are group specific measures which aim to help 'ethnic groups and religious minorities express their cultural particularity and pride without it hampering their success in the economic and political institutions of the dominant society' (1995: 31). They are also not temporary, but are intended to encourage integration into the larger society. In polyethnic societies it became clear that it was necessary to combat discrimination and prejudice. However, the efforts made in this regard are aimed at ensuring common rights of citizenship and therefore do not come within Kymlicka's bracket of group-differentiated rights. Examples of polyethnic rights are public funding to ensure cultural expression, and to enable ethnic groups to counter the dominant European-derived forms of cultural expression; and the demand for exemptions from laws and regulations that disadvantage these groups on account of their religious beliefs and practices (1995: 30–31).

'Special representation rights' embody a growing area of interest for both national minorities and ethnic groups, together with other 'non-ethnic social groups' (1995: 32).[4] This interest reflects the increasing concern that the political

---

3 The situation that Kymlicka has is mind here must be the federal division of powers between the provinces of Canada. Within Canada Francophones are a minority; however, within the Canadian province of Quebec they form a majority. Federalisation allows Quebec some level of self-government, and some believe it therefore accommodates the cultural distinctiveness of this minority group.

4 Kymlicka's non-ethnic social groups must aim to include groups which organise themselves along non-ethnic lines, but have a subordinate position in modern day power balances. Examples of such groups are women, the elderly, homosexual individuals and the disabled. Kymlicka's division between groups raises the question of how accurate and just

process in democracies is unrepresentative of the plural interests in a society, and therefore fails to serve diverse societies adequately and appropriately. In most Western democracies, those that sit in the legislature are white middle-class able-bodied men, and they fail to represent other interests within society, for example, women, the poor, the disabled, and ethnic and racial minorities. There are a number of responses to this inadequacy, and the arguments are complex and intricate. However, whatever the precise resolution sought, the main issue is that national minorities and ethnic groups are increasingly seeing the unrepresentative nature of democracy as a barrier to the full realisation of the rights they feel entitled to. The main distinction between ethnic groups and national minorities, with respect to this form of rights, is that they are a necessary corollary to self-government rights (for example, to ensure that self-government powers cannot just be revoked by the dominant group). In contrast, ethnic groups seek such rights to ensure proper and just political representation, rather than as an adjunct to self-government rights (1995: 31–3).

This brief outline of Kymlicka's differential citizenship serves to highlight how his work on multiculturalism, of necessity, involves engagement with the relations between nation and diversity. Whilst this extract from Kymlicka's *Multicultural Citizenship* has the concepts of nation and diversity, and their relations, as an underlying narrative to differential citizenship, in one of his later works Kymlicka explicitly approaches the idea of nation-building processes and their relevance to diversity. He does this (2001: 1–9) in his identification of three themes that tie together his refinement and elaboration of his earlier defence of multicultural citizenship.

He first identifies a dialectic of nation-building and minority rights, arguing that minority rights must be understood within the context of nation-building in liberal democratic societies, which promotes citizens to integrate into dominant institutions in various ways. Secondly, he notes that nation-building processes in these liberal states have taken place 'with an almost complete absence of militancy, terrorism, violence, or state repression' (2001: 3).[5] Finally, Kymlicka argues that there is a gap between theoretical and practical approaches to multiculturalism. He attributes this to the overwhelming acceptance by theorists of the ethno-cultural neutrality of the state. In practice, he explains, the ethno-cultural neutrality of liberal states is a myth because nation-building involves the promotion of one

it is to view national minorities, non-ethnic social groups and dominant groups as devoid of ethnicity, and ethnic groups as identifiable only along the lines of ethnicity. This question is considered in greater depth in Chapter 7.

5 It is worth noting that the second theme that ties Kymlicka's work together also exposes it as prior to the 'war on terror', and the possibility that political policies can act to radicalise certain sections of a nation's population; the former head of MI5 in Britain, Eliza Manningham-Buller, when giving her testimony to the Inquiry into the Iraq war on 20 July 2010, clearly stated that Britain's foreign policy, with its perceived anti-Muslim sentiment, had a role to play in radicalising Muslim youth in Britain. See Sparrow (2010).

dominant framework, therefore this process creates a structural bias that acts to subordinate the ways of life of non-dominant groups.

These three unifying themes evidence the importance of understanding nations in the context of diversity. Moreover, the pre-9/11 tenor of Kymlicka's second theme, and the onset of what can arguably be seen as violent responses to liberal nation-building processes, only serve to underscore the importance of clarifying the interactions between the ongoing processes of building a nation and the diversity of its citizens. It is not only Kymlicka that serves as a reference point for the interactions between nation and diversity; James Tully's work on constitutionalism also evidences my claim that theorising nation is intrinsically linked to theorising diversity.

Tully's (1995) work on constitutionalism in the context of diversity led him to argue for a fluid understanding of constitutions, so that it is possible to go beyond the traditional conceptualisation of constitutions as a set of relatively entrenched rules. Given the diverse nature of our societies, Tully argues for a form of constitution that permits an ongoing dialogue where citizens are able to negotiate and renegotiate the terms of their membership in accordance with their evolving needs. As a reference point for this dialogical constitutionalism, Tully drew inspiration from Bill Reid's sculpture, *The spirit of Haida Gwaii* (1995: 23–4):[6]

> No matter from which direction you approach the canoe, the crew members manifestly seem to say that, after centuries of suppression, they are here to stay, in their own cultural forms and ways. Hence, if there is to be a post-imperial dialogue on the just constitution of culturally diverse societies, the dialogue must be one in which the participants are recognised and speak in their own languages and customary ways. ... *The spirit of Haida Gwaii*, I would now like you to imagine, can be seen as just such a constitutional dialogue, or multilogue, of mutual recognition. The passengers are squabbling and vying for recognition and position each in their culturally distinct way. They are exchanging their diverse stories and claims as the chief appears to listen attentively to each, hoping to guide them to reach an agreement, without imposing a meta-language or allowing any speaker to set the terms of the discussion.

6 Tully describes *The spirit of Haida Gwaii* as follows (1995: 17–18): 'It is the wonderful sculpture by Bill Reid, the renowned artist of Haida and Scottish ancestry from the Haida nation of *Haida Gwaii* (the Queen Charlotte Islands) off the northwest coast of Great Turtle Island (North America). The sculpture is a balck bronze canoe, over nineteen feet in length, eleven feet wide, and twelve feet high, containing thirteen passengers, *sghaana* (spirits or myth creatures) from Haida mythology'. The sculpture is displayed outside the Canadian Embassy in Washington, D.C. A second casting, entitled *The Spirit of Haida Gwaii, The Jade Canoe* is currently displayed at the international terminal of Vancouver International Airport. *The Black Canoe*, and original casting, adorns the Canadian 20 dollar bill.

From his starting point of political philosophy, James Tully's work led him to consider constitutional arrangements and to stray into areas traditionally reserved for constitutional experts. This, in itself, speaks to the intrinsic links between diversity and the constitution of nations. Moreover, it follows from this that when one engages with the subject of diversity, regardless of whether the perspective taken is legal, philosophical or a combination of both, it contributes to the clarity of the study when one explicitly sets out the presuppositions that explain the underlying relations envisaged between nation-building and diversity. These presuppositions may well be implicit in the arguments of this study, but there is merit in clarifying these, not least because they contribute to the normative foundations upon which my new vista of constitutional pluralism rests.

It is not only the work of political philosophers concerned with diverse societies that can be usefully referenced to demonstrate the relations between theorising diversity and theorising the nation. Tamir's study of liberalism and nationalism seeks to 'demonstrate that the liberal tendency to overlook the value inherent in nationalism is mistaken, and to explore ways in which nationalism might contribute to liberal thinking' (1993: 4). She is driven by a desire to reclaim nationalism from its stronghold within conservative ideologies. In so doing, she reconciles the ideas of personal autonomy and choice, which occupy a central place in liberal ideology, with those of community, loyalty and solidarity, which are associated with nationalism. Tamir does this by emphasising the element of individual choice in our cultural contexts, whilst also recognising its communal dimensions.

Tamir does not paint an absolute and concrete picture of the liberal nationalism in her study, preferring instead to focus on the value of highlighting 'the irresolvable collision between worthwhile values', thereby making a 'plea to liberals to be attentive to the nature of national claims, and to seek ways of taking them into account alongside traditional liberal values' (1993: 11). Liberal ideology has tended to champion the cause of subordinate groups, but Tamir questions this commitment by illustrating that the claims of these groups must be considered in light of the processes of the nation-state.[7] This unique study permits us to see the imperative in understanding and clarifying the relations between a liberal conception of justice, whatever specific form that might take, and processes of building a nation and a national vision. In constructing a platform for this imperative, Tamir implicitly asks liberal states to reflect upon their obligations to their citizens, and to do so with consideration for any qualitative changes necessary to nation-building processes as a consequence of the diversity of its citizens.

One final example of the proximity between theorising nationhood and theorising diversity is Benedict Anderson's (1991) well known work on the nature

7 This seems remarkably similar to Kymlicka's argument that minority group claims can only be understood within the context of the hegemonic tendencies of nation-building policies. It is also noteworthy that Tamir argues for a form of differential citizenship, much like Kymlicka. Whilst the two scholars pursue their claims within similar frameworks, there remains considerable difference in the detail of their claims.

of nationhood. Anderson articulated a claim that, perhaps because of its self-evident nature, seemed to have been bypassed in other studies on nationalism; he explained (1991: 5–7) that the communal nature of nationalism and 'nation-ness', a term I borrow from Anderson, must rest on our imaginings of a political community, since we cannot possibly meet or even know of all our fellow-members. With this enlightened, yet seemingly obvious, claim, Anderson builds a path that leads towards the inquiry of nationalism as an imagined commonality between these fellow-nationals that goes beyond common membership of a nation-state. In so doing he draws in issues relating to the social reality of diversity within almost every nation-state, in present terms, and as historical social realities.

Whilst it is not my intention to explore in any depth these studies, cursory reference to them corroborates an intrinsic relationship between theorising nation and theorising diversity. My claim is that one cannot theorise one of these fields without at least clarifying where one places oneself in the other field, in general terms at the very least. This is precisely because one's perspective on diversity is influenced and informed by one's affiliations to theories of nationhood and nationality; and vice versa. In the remainder of this chapter, therefore, I landmark the key presuppositions I subscribe to in the field of theorising nationhood. My aim is to clarify, in general terms, my fresh perspective on justice and, to a modest degree, explore the non-legal dimensions of this diversity-conscious form of justice.

Normative Clarification

Nations as Imagined Political Communities

Anderson defines nation as 'an imagined political community', explaining that '[i]t is *imagined* because the members of even the smallest nation will never know most of their fellow-members, meet them, or even hear of them, yet in the minds of each lives the image of their communion' (1991: 6). They are communities because these imaginings conjure up 'a deep, horizontal comradeship' (1991: 7). He is careful to ensure that the nature of this conclusion is not coterminous with the underlying theme of falsity, and clarifies that the powerful imaginings that bind communities does not necessarily precipitate inauthenticity. This is a particularly important clarification because it validates actions based upon various forms of nationalism; the idea of the imagined nature of this political community does not detract from the authenticity of these choices and decisions, and does not lead to the conclusion that they are based upon myths and therefore meaningless. Indeed, whilst nations are imagined political communities, the communion that Anderson writes of has a tangible quality, making the loyalty and allegiances that it evokes especially potent, as evidenced by the continued and unabated willingness of individuals to sacrifice their lives for their nation.

Of particular interest to this study is Anderson's explanation that '[t]he nation is imagined as *limited* because even the largest of them, encompassing perhaps a billion living human beings, has finite, if elastic, boundaries, beyond which lie other nations' (1991: 7). The rising consciousness of plural identities within territorial political units sheds new light upon Anderson's insights. The nature of these imagined political communities, which Anderson describes as one of deep solidarity, is profoundly impacted by diversity. The importance of taking this perspective on nations (and nationalism) is best illustrated by assessing Thomas M. Franck's (1999) approach to nation-states, in light of Anderson's imagined political communities. Applying Anderson's notion to Franck's explanation of the nation-state brings into sharp relief the significance of this perspective when conceptualising diversity within nation-states.

In contrast to Anderson, Franck claims (1999) that the nation-state is almost obsolete in today's world. His claim is predicated upon an understanding of nations as encompassing a pure ethnicity.[8] Franck argues that it follows from this that a nation-state must be a state that contains a people of one single ethnicity. He provides (1999: 7–8) an historical narrative of a world that begins with states that form from tribes that relinquish their nomadic lifestyles. In this beginning, 1000 years since gone, states were more akin to nation-states than they are today, precisely because kinship bound their members (1999: 7). This purity of kinship could not, however, be maintained as states became larger and their populations became increasingly diverse (1999: 8): 'kings and queens came to rule several distinct communities, often made up of persons who were of different stock'. States came to encompass many tribes, and even fused non-tribal peoples. Franck marks the American and French revolutions as the final death of ethnicity as a binding force within states. On Franck's account, it was after this point that we became 'citizens of a state' and no longer looked to our genetic heritage to bind us to others on a territorial basis.[9] He points to Europe between 1200 and 1400 AD to find the archetypal nation-state, where 'newly sedentary communities congealed as states' (1999: 7).

Franck's narrative appears to be accurate; he recounts how loyalty referents evolved from tribal and kinship bonds, and had to move towards feudal lords, monarchs, religious leaders, and so on, in order to bind populations effectively as they became increasingly diverse, rendering tribal and kinship bonds increasingly ineffective. However, this account conflates loyalty, whether this was to tribes, lords or monarchs, with nationalism, and is therefore difficult to square with Anderson's explanation of our imagined communion as having a direct causal link to our feelings of loyalty towards a nation, and the nationalism that follows from this.

Anderson's explanation of nationalism, and nations, as the product of modernity provides a more feasible account of modern day loyalties than Franck's linkage

---

8 I prefer to use 'ethnicity' where Franck uses 'ethnie', since the former is more widely used and understood than the latter. He provides no definition of 'ethnie' and his use of the term suggests meanings no different to that commonly attributed to ethnicity, so nothing turns on my preference.

9 I consider the fluid social science understandings of ethnicity in Chapter 7.

of nations with genetic purity. Anderson's purpose in his study is to explore why 'since World War II every successful revolution has defined itself in *national* terms', and bears in mind that '[t]here is nothing to suggest that this trend will not continue' given that new nations continue to seek membership of the United Nations (1991: 2–3). On the other hand, Franck's declaration of the end of the nation-state, which he attributes to ever-increasing diversities, fails to recognise that nationalism, and therefore nationality and nations, continue to be salient in today's world.[10]

When one puts Franck's claims in close proximity to Anderson's theory of nationalism, the divergence in their approach to this field of inquiry is starkly apparent. On empirical grounds Anderson's theory is more compelling: Franck's prophecy of the increasing irrelevance of the nation-state simply does not seem to be coming to fruition. However, my unease with using Franck's approach to conceptualise the nation-state and diversity goes deeper than just this empirical objection. The difficulty with Franck's conclusion, and its relevance to this project, is that it is divisive and damaging in its characterisation of diversity (although this is almost certainly an inadvertent side effect of his work). Using his historical narrative, Franck positions plural identities as something new and unique that threatens the fabric of nationhood, and the role of the nation-state as a strong and real point of reference for loyalty and communion. On Franck's account, our contemporary diverse societies sit in direct opposition to the strong sense of solidarity and loyalty that existed in times now long since past. However, this, I believe, mischaracterises nationalism and its relations to diversity. The strength of nationality as a loyalty referent is underestimated by this account, since millions continue willingly to sacrifice their lives in the name of their nation. Franck's claim sensationalises diversity by constructing a group who act as scapegoats when fortunes ebb: 'if only *those* people were not here, then *we* would not be facing these difficulties, *we* would be a cohesive and harmonious nation'. This process of othering in turn feeds the powerful imaginings of political communities, which, by their very nature, are constructed as limited. The 'we' of this imagined community is conjured up as those people that are not perceived to be different, and it is around this group that the boundaries of nationality are constructed.

Franck's perspective on nationness, to borrow Anderson's term, is, therefore, flawed on two counts. First, the idea that the nation-state is becoming obsolete cannot be supported by our social realities. Secondly, this perspective actually feeds into a destructive conceptualisation of the relations between nationality and diversity. Nevertheless, the manner in which Franck links increasing diversity to the decline of nations does serve to illuminate the close association between

10 There are some that would argue that we largely live in cosmopolitan societies and are all citizens of the world. Whilst our national allegiances might be considered 'looser' today than ever before, the nation-state and notions of nationality still retain significant importance in our societies. See, for example, Bradney (2009: 16–20) for a discussion of cosmopolitan societies and their relations with religions.

nationality and uniformity. This association is of particular importance because it draws out a tendency within our imaginings of our political communities that significantly contributes to the construction of their boundaries or limitations. Anderson eloquently argues that our political communities are imagined because their members will never know the vast majority of their fellow-members, 'yet in the minds of each lives the image of their communion' (1991: 6). Franck's claims reveal that uniformity and commonality are heavily implicated in this image of communion. Furthermore, the trajectory that Franck's claim takes, predicting an irreconcilable clash between the continued relevance of nations and increasing diversity, highlights the implications of this association in plural societies: an image of communion that creates group boundaries upon imaginings of commonality and uniformity sits uneasily within nations that are visibly plural in character.

The powerful imaginings that are vital to political communities, whether these are labelled as nations or nation-states,[11] have implications for justice in these communities; if communities are imagined as inherently limited, the nature of these boundaries impacts access to and participation in civil society. A diversity-conscious justice, therefore, requires realignment of the ways in which we imagine our communities. More precisely, it requires the disassociation of unity, communion and solidarity from commonality and uniformity. Our powerful imaginings of communion, which are strong enough to conjure up feelings of loyalty upon which lives are willingly sacrificed, need to embrace diversity as an integral element of nationalism, and therefore of nationality. Imaginings that exclude those deemed to be too different inflict an injustice upon those excluded citizens by erecting barriers to their access to civil society.

Habermas's explanation of the unorganised public sphere emphasises that civil society is broader than just formal and organised elements. Thus, the exclusionary effect of our imagined communities spreads further than formal institutions, such as the legislature and electoral processes, and reaches into areas that upon first sight appear not to be limited. For example, if one is excluded from a political community, then how relevant are its newspapers, its history and its literature to that individual? In short, if your sense of belonging to a community is compromised, and that community forms the dominant core community of the territory in which you reside, not only is your loyalty to that community undermined but your involvement in that community also becomes less feasible as a consequence of this rejection.

This may seem remarkably similar to Norman Tebbit's infamous 'cricket test', and therefore requires further clarification. In 1990 the British Conservative politician, Norman Tebbit, suggested that the loyalty of British South Asians could

11 Anderson favours the use of nation, whereas Franck writes of nation-states. This difference reflects the broader subject of inquiry of each scholar. Anderson is concerned with dissecting nationalism, whilst Franck's work concentrates on political dimensions to our current geographical territorial units. Little turns on this distinction for the purposes of this book.

be measured by considering whether they were supporting the English cricket team or the cricket team of their country of origin.[12] It may, therefore, seem like cricket is an example of one way of assessing participation in civil society, and that this was all that Norman Tebbit was suggesting with his cricket test. However, the difficulty with Tebbit's cricket test, and the difference between this and the perspective upon nation-building taken here, is that it assumes that non-dominant groups must integrate into a dominant framework.[13] In contrast, the perspective I am proposing here takes the approach of embracing diversity by abandoning notions of integration and assimilation, with their connotations of uniformity, in favour of coupling unity and stability with difference, diversity and plurality. To put this another way, it follows from the perspective of nationhood taken here that the challenge of justice, when there is a plurality of identities within a territorial unit, is to ensure that the boundaries of nationality are inclusive in a manner that is consistent with the idea of free and fair access to and participation in civil society.

Nation-building as an Ongoing and Unequal Project

A key presupposition of the preceding discussion requires further mention. Thus far, it has been implicitly assumed that nation-building is an ongoing project engaged in by all nation-states, even constitutionally 'mature' ones such as Britain, France, the United States and Canada. Traditionally the idea of nation-building has been associated with newly independent states that have the task of creating a viable and stable political unit. Examples can be found amongst the period of decolonisation; these include India, Pakistan, Kenya and Zimbabwe. Additionally, identity-based struggles and conflicts have also led to the formation of new states which have been engaged in nation-building projects. Examples of such states include Kosovo, East Timor, Bosnia, Afghanistan and South Africa. South Africa, in particular, is an instructive example of the ongoing nature of nation-building

---

12 He has since declared that his test could have stopped the 7/7 bombings in London, because it is an indication of how well communities have integrated into British society. See Davie (2005).

13 Although Lord Tebbit may be using integration in the manner interpreted by Roy Jenkins whilst he was the Labour Home Secretary, namely 'not a flattening process of assimilation but equal opportunity accompanied by cultural diversity in an atmosphere of mutual tolerance' (Lester 2006: 24), this does not, I believe, move far enough away from the processes of assimilation. Roy Jenkins's definition of integration was progressive for its time in the 1960s, particularly because it heralded an official rejection of assimilation. The notion of integration is, in many ways, peculiarly British; many European countries have an active dialogue based on the idea of assimilation. See, for example, France's policy of *laïcité*. Canada has always been the home of the multicultural mosaic and the United States was the country of immigrants who all entered its melting pot. This latter take on diversity has more recently given way to notions of the multicultural salad which houses the tomato and the cucumber, yet each ingredient retains its own characteristics.

projects because, although the abolition of apartheid signalled a rebirth for this nation, in this particular case there was no redrawing of boundaries upon maps as a consequence of decolonisation or identity-based conflict. A viable nation of South Africa required, and continues to require, significant nation-building techniques intended to bring the people of this nation together and create the 'deep, horizontal comradeship' that Anderson identifies as the cornerstone of nationhood (1991: 7).

As an example, South Africa does not neatly fit into the categories most obviously associated with the idea of nation-building, and therefore is a fitting illustration of the point I am making. Nation-building projects are not confined to newly independent states, or even nations that are emerging from violent identity-based conflicts. Rather, I argue, they are ongoing projects that all nations are engaged in, and to which there is no final end point. If, as Benedict Anderson cogently illustrates, nations are imagined political communities, then these imaginings must be ongoing if that nation is to continue as a viable and stable political unit. Indeed, states are *inadvertently* engaged in this ongoing project of contributing to an imagined political community.

Consider, for example, the recent official apologies to Aboriginal communities that have taken place in both Australia and Canada.[14] Both apologies form part of a healing process in which Aboriginal communities are officially seen to be treated with the respect and acceptance that equal citizens deserve. They work towards an inclusive imagining of a political community where injustices are remedied. Furthermore, state policies that are viewed as more mundane, in the sense that they do not contribute to a specific and tangible moment in a nation's imagination in the same way as these apologies, also form part of this ongoing nation-building project. One such example can be seen in equality-based policies that aim to put diverse groups on a level playing field, such as diversity policies in employment practices that work towards creating an employment scenario where all citizens have equal access and are therefore included within civil society. My point is that, despite traditional interpretations of nation-building, it must be understood as an ongoing project that all nations are engaged in regardless of the age of a nation.

Equally as important is the presupposition that this nation-building project has no specific end point and is ongoing. Kymlicka makes a convincing case for understanding nation-building in liberal democratic societies as an ongoing project. He explains that the very claims made by minority groups are the product of policies that seek to assimilate all members of liberal societies into a dominant framework. He asserts that liberal democratic societies encourage their citizens to 'integrate into common public institutions operating in a common language' (2001: 1).[15] Access to civil society is dependent upon one's capability to operate

14 For details of these apologies see BBC News Online (2008) and CBC News Online (2008).

15 Whilst Kymlicka terms this type of policy as integration, I prefer to view it as assimilation, for two reasons. First, liberal understandings of integration suggest that it should be viewed as a two way process of give and take between dominant and subordinate

within this privileged, and therefore dominant, framework. There are a variety of ways in which liberal democratic societies encourage this type of assimilation, some implicit and some explicit; one example of explicit forms of assimilation can be seen in the discourse which associates the segregation of non-dominant communities with the assumption that this occurs because they are unable to speak English. It follows from this that one of the policy solutions is to require, through citizenship tests and the like, fluency in English, on the basis that this situation of segregated communities will not persist if everyone speaks the same language.[16] The fallacy of this line of thinking was most evident in the videos of the British suicide bombers, all of whom explained the reasons behind the bombings in London in English, and in strong Northern British accents.

One example of the implicit push towards assimilation can be seen in the very structure of formal institutions, and in particular legal systems, which embody and express the dominant value system. This enables these dominant norms to reach into our lives with a tentacle-like quality, and in a variety of different ways. Some of the most accessible examples of the dominance of one single value system can be found within the area of family law. This area of law is prominent, I believe, because the terrain covered by family law overlaps with our day-to-day way of life more often than other areas of law and public policy – most value systems

---

groups. However, few liberal democratic societies pursue such policies in this manner. At best, their end of the bargain tends to involve allowing subordinate groups to maintain some superficial element of their chosen way of life – the saris, samosas and steel bands approach. Such an approach merely reflects a liberal comfort with each individual pursuing his or her own conception of the good life, but only so far as is does not interfere with the dominant conception of the good life. The underlying ethos behind this integrationist agenda is, therefore, not coterminous with integration as a two way process. Secondly, liberal policies such as this offer no incentives if one's idea of the good life does not match with the dominant form. Indeed, conforming with the dominant conception of the good life is rewarded with the enhanced possibility of success in life. As such, there are significant incentives for conforming with the dominant model. This, I believe, is a form of implicit assimilation.

16 Use of the idea that these communities are 'segregated' from the dominant parts of society trades on the insidious connection between segregation and racism made as part of the civil rights movement in the United States. Kymlicka (1995: 58–60) considers whether this association resonates beyond this particular scenario and argues that in some situations segregation addresses the harm caused by the systemic injustices intrinsic to dominant frameworks. One example he provides is the reservation system in Canada, where native Canadian youths have better educational success in reservation schools than in the general public school system. Although this is a form of segregation, the harm caused by systemic injustices seems to be lessened, and therefore it seems inappropriate to dismiss this system as unjust on the basis that it segregates communities. Indeed, Kymlicka argues that the *ratio decidendi* of the American landmark case of *Brown v Board of Education of Topeka* 347 US 483 (1954), is that one must identify the harm caused and redress that by whatever means are appropriate; this case has, however, contributed to a powerful ideologly, no doubt in tandem with the evils of apartheid South Africa, in which segregation is without exception assumed to be a sign of division, damage and deep danger within society.

concern themselves with the cycle of family life: birth, marriage, children, divorce and death.[17] Prominent examples of internal conflicts of law can be seen in English law's response to marriages that take place within a non-Church of England religious framework.[18] Whilst there are some examples of English law drawing on its equitable jurisdiction to recognise religious weddings outside the dominant Church of England conception of marriage,[19] the degree to which this conception of marriage occupies judicial imaginings in this field is evident in *Gereis v Yagoub*.[20] Here the courts recognised a Coptic Greek Orthodox marriage that did not comply with the legislative requirements on the basis that it 'bore all the hallmarks of an ordinary Christian marriage' (759).

Furthermore, consider the recent decision of the European Court of Human Rights on the issue of same-sex marriage. In *Schalk and Kopf v Austria*,[21] the Strasbourg court recently rejected the applicants' claim that their inability to enter into a same-sex marriage in Austria violated their right to marry under the European Convention for the Protection of Human Rights and Fundamental Freedoms (ECHR). The court felt that there was no consensus amongst member states to the ECHR on the issue of same-sex marriage, therefore Austria should be given a wide margin of appreciation in its interpretation of the right to marry. In essence the court could not find enough movement within the dominant framework of Council of Europe member states to justify including same-sex marriage within the definition of marriage in the ECHR. Although the Strasbourg court cannot often be accused of judicial activism that verges on nation-building, the court's

---

17 Hamilton (1995: 37) indicates that marriage, divorce and the family unit are areas that are central to the majority of religions, and therefore, they regulate these areas in ways that differ from dominant models. In turn this creates a discrete area where conflicts are more visible.

18 I borrow the idea of internal conflicts of law from Werner Menski, who has used this concept in his course entitled Ethnic Minorities and the Law at the School of Oriental and African Studies. Internal conflicts of law describe the situation where the normative frameworks of Britain's ethnic minority groups clash with the dominant normative framework, as expressed through English law. The idea of internal conflicts of law must be contrasted with the traditional legal field of conflicts of law, or private international law, where the central concern is to decide which nation-state's legal system applies to a fact situation that has a transnational component.

19 See, for example, *Chief Adjudication Officer v Bath* [2000] 1 FLR 8, where the court utilised the presumption of validity to recognise a lengthy Sikh marriage that had taken place in a Sikh temple, Gurdwara, despite there being no evidence that the requirements of the Marriage Act 1949, particularly of registration of the temple as an approved place of solemnisation of marriages, were met. It is worth noting that the courts view the question of recognition and non-recognition of marriages as one of 'policy', which seems to relieve them of the responsibility of taking a consistent approach to all religions – there are good policy reasons to recognise some, and not recognise others.

20 [1997] 3 FCR 755.

21 Application no 3014/04 (24 June 2010).

decision, and more broadly its approach to the margin of appreciation, evidences the importance of dominant frameworks in casting the idea of which conceptions of the good life are considered acceptable or part of the norm in any nation.

There are many other examples of this implicit form of ongoing nation-building; however, the example of implicit assimilation under English law is especially instructive because it serves a double purpose. First, it demonstrates that established countries such as Britain are engaged in an ongoing nation-building project; and, secondly, it reveals the intrinsic bias of these nation-building projects. It is telling that Aglionby J, in *Gereis*, did not just liken the Coptic Orthodox marriage to a Christian marriage, but saw it as the same as an *ordinary* Christian marriage. The use of the word ordinary here betrays a dominant way of life that is tacitly employed as a reference point in English law. I have previously mentioned that Kymlicka identifies this bias as one of the themes that ties together his refinement of his approach to minority rights and liberalism. He describes (2001: 4–9) this theme as a gap between theory and practice in liberal democracies, which he attributes, *inter alia*, to the fact that theorists have largely bought into the myth of the neutral nature of nation-building; he terms this the 'ethnocultural neutrality' myth (2001: 4).

Whilst the degree to which any nation encourages its citizens to take part in a dominant conception of the good life is contestable,[22] I believe it is possible to agree that these nation-building projects are not neutral. When one incorporates this perspective, the links between imagined political communities, nation-building and diversity come into sharp relief. If a diversity-conscious form of justice requires that the limits to our political communities are imagined in a more inclusive way, we place obstacles in the path of this form of justice if we fail to acknowledge the inherent biases of the nation-building project.

On the written page, acknowledgement of an ongoing nation-building project *and* that this project inherently favours one normative model, appears to be a relatively minor shift. However, the paradigm shift that takes place with this change in perspective is enormous, and the impact and power of such a shift ought not to be underestimated. Consider Trevor Phillips's statement,[23] in 2004, that

---

22 I sit at a relatively extreme end of this spectrum, as I believe that English law and British public policy are influenced by Britain's religious roots in framing a dominant conception of the good life. Although Britain is secular in the contemporary sense that the idea of values and ways of life beyond Anglican Christianity are permissible (Taylor 2007), its history does not permit the idea that the British public sphere is detached from Anglican Christianity. As a liberal democracy it should not be apologetic about its rich religious history. However, pursuit of the myth that Britain's institutions and structures are detached from these religious roots perpetuates a damaging and false picture of the neutral nature of the British public sphere. It is possible that much the same argument could be made with regard to other secular democracies; however, cursory consideration here would not do such arguments any justice.

23 At the time Trevor Philips was the UK's Commissioner of Racial Equality. He is now the Chair of the Equality and Human Rights Commission, – the Commission for Racial

multiculturalism is dead (Andrew 2004). His case was that multiculturalism had gone too far in encouraging individual cultures, and that this had fostered segregated communities. However, in accepting the perspective that Britain has been engaged in a project of tacitly encouraging one conception of the good life, Trevor Philips's claims that we need to consign multiculturalism to the rubbish heap of history seems to misunderstand the *status quo* in Britain; indeed, from this perspective the proper line of inquiry would be to question whether multiculturalism was ever really alive in Britain. Permitting citizens to pursue their own conception of the good life, arguably the core of multicultural policies, takes on a distinctly different hue against a background where state policies implicitly encourage one, dominant way of life. Furthermore, the segregation that Phillips concerns himself with may, from this perspective, be argued to constitute a response to the unequal playing field upon which citizens are free to pursue their own way of life. My goal in introducing Trevor Phillips's comments here is not to engage with the debate over whether multiculturalism has been a divisive force in Britain. Rather, I aim to demonstrate that by explicitly justifying my perspective on nations and diversity, instead of assuming that it is implicitly evident within the other arguments and claims I make, the characterisation of debates significantly change.

Globalisation, Nation-building and Diversity

A diversity-conscious form of justice requires that nation-building techniques must, *inter alia*, focus upon how best to engender an inclusive imagining that couples stability and unity with difference and diversity, and take account of the biases intrinsic to the very idea of nation-building. However, it is important to note that most, if not all, nations have long since been home to a great plurality of identities, along many different axes (religion, culture, race, ethnicity, gender, nationality), and have been engaged in nation-building, even though explicit admission of this ongoing nation-building project has been absent, throughout their histories. This begs the question of whether today's diversities are merely today's set of changes and developments that provide no unique or novel challenges for justice. To put this point another way, today's pluralities and diversities merely sit at the end of a long line of changes, developments and diversities, so why does this contemporary diversity create a unique and novel challenge for justice? If a nation's historical, albeit tacit, nation-building technique has adequately managed its historical pluralities, it is legitimate to consider whether managing today's diverse identities is merely a question of achieving a suitable equilibrium over time, with any injustices representing temporary side-effects that will be ironed out over time.

Equality has been incorporated into this single body – which has the mandate to oversee all of Britain's anti-discrimination legislation. The Equality Act 2010, which consolidates Britain's previous piecemeal anti-discrimination legislation, largely came into force in October 2010.

It is arguable that the unique nature of today's diversity lies in the fact that migratory patterns around the world have contributed to a more visible difference in most countries' citizens. The shift in populations between the South and the North, or the East and the West, could be considered to provide an extra and unique element of difference. In turn, because the chasm of difference is so much wider, bridging the gap between this ideological West and East presents a novel and greater challenge than the historical diversities that most countries have seen.[24] However, although this line of reasoning has appeal, I claim that it is only a partial response to the question of why today's diversity gives rise to unique challenges. I argue that the effects of globalisation must be considered, and that they make a significant contribution to creating an environment that presents a unique set of challenges for justice in diverse societies. The unique nature of these challenges arises from the ways in which globalisation has created a new dynamic between nation-building techniques and the diverse identities that these techniques seek to unite; understanding this dynamic is, therefore, vital for my fresh perspectives on justice.

Franck (1999) argues that technological developments have given rise to a new, and still developing, era of individualism. He claims that greater accessibility across the globe, and a wider knowledge of the world, whether this is cultivated off- or on-line, is liberating individuals from imposed values, traditions, customs and communities of origin. Franck terms our era the 'Age of Individualism' and concludes that across the world individuals are recognising the true and important value of autonomy and individual rights.[25] He explains that (1999: 39):

> What may be on the way out is the monopoly that, together, the state, the socio-cultural group, and certain transnational movements and organizations have had on the shaping and determination of human identity. Insinuating itself amongst these is a new but growing consciousness of individual worth, manifesting itself in the claim to personal autonomy and inherent human rights. Among these new claims, the most fundamental – and most astonishing – is the demand selectively to choose the components of one's personal identity. This new individualism challenges the limits of personal self-determination so long imposed by the traditional objects of allegiance.

On Franck's account, this rise of individualism pierces notions of loyalty referents based upon nationality, and therefore threatens the very future of nationality and nations; Franck prophesises a future of global citizenship, and a world where every one of us is empowered to 'ask who we are and … make the answering of that

24 For an argument along similar lines but focused specifically on Britain's post-war migrants see Spencer (1997).

25 Franck argues that the global spread of human rights, which place the individual subject at their core, not only evidences this development, but also illustrates that the universal truths of autonomy and individualism are protected around the world.

question a central enterprise of our lives' (1999: 3). However, Franck's translation of technological developments as the key source of an age of individualism fails adequately to consider the continued importance of the affiliations that we use as inspiration as we negotiate identity processes. Whilst individuals are undoubtedly taking a more central role in these processes, it overstates the case to conclude that our affiliations and memberships are no longer relevant to these processes.

Post-modern perceptions of identity are closely tied up to the value and importance of personal autonomy. The trajectory of evolution that we subscribe to, in the ideological West at the very least, is one that moves towards a freedom that is defined to include unfettered personal choice as a fundamental element of our identity processes. Limits upon how we pursue our intensely personal life-journeys constrain our free choice, and this is antithetical to the liberal project that values us as autonomous individuals who are responsible for our own lives and our own choices. This can be contrasted with the growing consciousness of the significance of contexts to the many choices we make during our lives. As Kymlicka (1995) argues, contexts give our identities meaning; these contexts are variously described as culture, religion, community, race, ethnicity, nationality, gender, sexual orientation, to name but a few. There is, however, a tension in this understanding of our world; our lives lack meaning and therefore depth without any context, yet these contexts place limits upon our identity processes and therefore threaten our attainment of freedom.

This tension between meaning or context and unfettered freedom is conceptualised in a variety of ways, and consequently is resolved in many different ways. Kymlicka (1995: 83), for example, argues that culture provides us with a context of choice. For him, freedom of choice is achieved when one understands the 'cultural narratives' from within which we make choices and decisions in our lives. He frames (1995: 94–5, 152–72) the tension that I isolate here by considering how illiberal cultures fit into a liberal theory that argues that culture gives meaning to our lives, and thereby places cultural survival and minority rights at its core. Kymlicka provides examples of this difficulty (1995: 153): prohibitions on the right of exit by the Pueblo Indians who discriminate against those who leave their religion; groups that discriminate against women in the provision of education, or electoral rights. He resolves this conflict with the principle that (1995: 152–3): 'a liberal view requires *freedom within* the minority group, and *equality between* the minority and majority groups. A system of minority rights which respects these two limitations is, I believe, impeccably liberal. It is consistent with, and indeed promotes, basic liberal values'.

In contrast, Thomas M. Franck deals with this same tension in a vastly different manner. He argues that we now live in an age of individualism where traditional forms of imposed identity no longer define who we are. This leads Franck to downplay the value of contexts and the associations and bonds we might have to others, when he claims, for example (1999: 39), that '[t]his new individualism challenges the limits on personal self-determination so long imposed by the traditional objects of allegiance'.

At the heart of both of these theses, however, is the same conflict: a full and deep realisation of our identities requires one to be embedded within contexts, without which our lives lack meaning, yet the very contexts that provide meaning to our lives act to create boundaries to our experiences. The importance of responding to this tension derives, I claim, from a change in the dynamic between (tacit) nation-building techniques and their capacity to manage diversity. Furthermore, this change in dynamic is one of the many and varied ramifications of globalisation.

Technological developments have created what Franck terms the Empowered Self and, whilst I disagree with Franck as to the degree of self-determination involved in identity processes and position myself towards Kymlicka's philosophical account of the importance of culture as a context to our choices, I am convinced that he is correct to assert that today, individuals have far more involvement and interest in existential questions, such as 'who am I?', than they have ever had in the past. My claim is that globalisation has created a new dynamic that has implications for how nation-states manage their diverse citizenry. In particular, I believe that once-effective tools of nation-building have been rendered blunt. On my account, nation-building techniques are especially being affected by two developments: first, communication and accessibility across distances, both transnational and national, have become easier; secondly, the strength of self-determination in matters of identity has reached hitherto unknown heights. These two developments have created a confidence in difference that has detrimental ramifications for the efficacy of nation-building techniques that enforce and promote commonality in the form of homogeneity. The entrenched Hegelian form of the nation-state as a collection of individuals who cohere around a common point, whether that be language, ethnicity or values, is being challenged, and it is becoming increasingly difficult for nation-states to aspire to this form by enforcing a level of homogeneity amongst its citizens in the face of this new found confidence in diversity.

Whilst Franck terms these changes 'technological developments', they can equally be understood as part of the complex processes of globalisation. Globalisation is a heavily contested term;[26] however, this does not provide good grounds for avoiding this concept here.[27] On the whole, whatever approach is taken to globalisation, theorists tend to agree that it involves a greater level of

---

26 Held et al. (1999: 2–10) identify three broad schools of thought on the definition of globalisation. Hyperglobalists predict the end of the nation-state and the beginning of a new world order. In contrast, sceptics argue that there is nothing unprecedented in contemporary global trends. Transformationalists occupy the middle ground and argue that something unprecedented is occuring, and that much of this takes place beyond the nation-state, but that globalisation does not render the nation-state irrelevant.

27 Held et al. (1999: 11–14) isolate five areas of contention in globalisation debates, and argue that any coherent account of globalisation must deal with each of these. These five areas are: (i) the method of conceptualising globalisation; (ii) the causes of globalisation; (iii) the period when globalisation began; (iv) the impact of globalisation; and (v) the trajectory that globalisation produces.

interconnectedness than the world has seen before. On this definition, the idea that globalisation is implicated in the new found confidence in diversity that we see today is uncontroversial. The reluctance to see this as a consequence of globalisation comes, I believe, from the assumption that this interconnectedness leads to the flattening of the world (Friedman 2007). The premise is that this increasing interconnectedness provides increasing access across the world to a global economy; in turn, this provides opportunities that were not possible in the past, one often cited example being the growth of call centres in India, and consequently the global playing field is flattened. This approach to globalisation has been contested theoretically, with scholars arguing that globalisation has actually created more plurality, rather than engendering uniformity and universal level playing fields.[28] The claim I make here provides an empirical contribution to this debate: the idea that globalisation leads to global citizenship does not correspond with our social realities; rather, there is a notable shift towards an emphasis upon our differences and this, I argue, is a consequence of our enhanced levels of interconnectedness. Robertson summarises this debate well (2003: 13, quoted in Menski 2006: 15):

> The creation of effective strategies to handle the reality of human diversity is one of humanity's most pressing challenges, as recent wars, ethnic cleansings, genocides, and the restless tides of refugees and displaced persons demonstrate.

This is precisely what I argue for here. My claim is that one of the effects of globalisation is to magnify, rather than obliterate, diversity. There are, today, networks engendered by the internet, global travel and global media that link together new transnational communities of shared ideas and values.[29] In the face of these transnational communities, tacit nation-building techniques that aim towards the assimilation of citizens into one way of life are increasingly ineffective. Moreover, these strategies of assimilation are likely to be divisive, given the new ways in which those pushed into the margins of society can link together with like-minded individuals, and the new confidence in diversity that results from these greater levels of interconnectedness. The need for effective strategies to manage diversity must also take into account the idea of the imagined boundaries of political communities and acknowledge the ongoing project of nation-building with its intrinsic biases.

---

28 Advocates of this approach include Robertson (2003), Doshi (2003), Santos (2002) and Menski (2006).

29 For consideration of these transnational networks within a human rights context see Koh (2000). For consideration of transnationalism and the impact this has had on the structures and practices of migrant communities worldwide see Vertovec (2007: 1042–4); Vertovec (2007) uses the term 'super-diversity' as a shorthand to denote the complex and interconnected axes that we now need to theorise diversity accurately.

Conclusions

I have presented in this global normative framework my conceptualisation of a diversity-conscious form of justice. I have argued that, in order to be sensitive to diversity, justice must be conceived of in a manner that accepts the significance of the self-actualisation of authentic identities. Secondly, in order to address the injustices suffered by non-dominant groups, this form of justice takes the general meaning of free and fair participation in and access to civil society, where civil society encompasses a broad range of areas.

Whilst the development of debates in the field of multiculturalism arguably needed to proceed without engaging with theories on nation-building,[30] I have demonstrated that a fuller idea of my fresh perspective on justice, that goes beyond the purely legal, also requires clarification of the relations between nation-building and diversity. I propose that there are three interdependent cardinal themes that relate to the study of nation-building, which act to orient, and significantly alter, the course of this study. First, nations must be understood as political communities with imagined limits and boundaries. It follows from this that the challenge of justice in diverse societies is to uncouple nationhood from uniformity and homogeneity, and to permit a more inclusive imagining of a nation's boundaries by embracing difference and diversity as natural corollaries to nationality, nationhood and nationalism. Secondly, all nation-states must be understood as engaging in an ongoing project of nation-building. Moreover, current nation-building tactics have to be exposed as inherently biased towards one dominant way of life, and the struggle to maintain a different way of life must be understood within this biased framework. Finally, globalisation has changed the dynamic between nation-building techniques and diversity; the increased interconnectedness that globalisation engenders has negatively impacted the efficacy of nation-building techniques that aim to assimilate all differences into one core way of life.

Together with the two pillars of justice, these three cardinal principles form my fresh perspective on justice. This perspective on justice is largely associated with law, but is not exclusively tied to it. However, for the purposes of this book, I largely focus upon the implications of this fresh perspective for law.

---

30 See Kymlicka (2001: 5–8) for a discussion of why liberal political theories of diversity may have produced better scholarship as a consequence of not engaging with theories of nation-building.

PART II
Locating The Role Of Law

Chapter 4
Meeting the Challenges of Justice

Having argued for a fresh perspective on justice that is sensitive to diversity, in this chapter I locate law's role in meeting the challenges of this form of justice in diverse societies. I do this by critically analysing two current legal responses to diversity. This analysis requires an understanding that law does not exist in a vacuum. Instead, law must be understood and explored within its contexts; this is the case for state as well as non-state laws, because contexts are not the exclusive domain of the study of legal systems beyond state systems of law. The very enterprise undertaken by state lawyers would not continue if state law's contexts, and its relations with those contexts, did not inform, orient and impact its implementation. If one could understand state law simply by looking at a piece of legislation, or the report of a court case, there would be no need to dispute the meaning of the content of those state laws, there would be no demand for alternative forums for dispute resolution and the processes integral to our current understanding of state law would be obsolete. The approach in this chapter rests upon taking this perspective on one aspect of Britain's state laws, namely its anti-discrimination legislation, and one aspect of Canada's state laws as concerns its constitutional set-up and its Aboriginal citizens. A full picture of these state laws requires an understanding of their social, political and/or historical contexts. It is from this vantage point that it is possible to see the limits of these state laws and become clearer as to why they may not fully meet the challenges of my diversity-conscious justice.

In my socio-historical account of Britain's anti-discrimination legislation I demonstrate that the British paradigm of race relations is one that focuses upon immigration, and combines controls on immigration with the promotion of integration.[1] Moreover, I argue that any amendments to this legislation, both actual and forthcoming, are destined to have limited success unless they address the narrative underlying Britain's current legislative approach to diversity. This failure, I claim, illustrates the obstacle that the immigration and race relations linkage creates when responding to diversity, and demonstrates the importance of clarifying normative foundations when designing legal responses to diversity. Nevertheless, I suggest that British anti-discrimination laws have had some successes and these alone are sufficient to justify their continued relevance.

1 I am grateful to Dr Prakash Shah for alerting me to and teaching me about this historical link between immigration controls and race relations legislation in Britain. Although the idea of this approach to diversity belongs to Dr Shah, any errors and omissions made in portraying this linkage are mine.

Instead, my conclusions signal a need for new legal responses to diversity, which start from sound normative premises.

My consideration of Aboriginal rights at common law in Canada takes a different approach to contextualising legal responses. A socio-historical context to white settler colonisation in Canada is not possible, in part because it would go well beyond the parameters of this book, but largely because this is a legacy that is still being unearthed and understood. Instead, I focus upon Canadian state law's interpretation of Aboriginal rights, which involves the Canadian courts adjudicating upon what it means to be Aboriginal. I contextualise this approach by incorporating social contexts as a means to consider and assess the Canadian court's test for Aboriginal rights. I argue that identity processes are too fluid for the certainty required by this official legal test. This tension, between certainty and dynamism, signals another vital area which law must expand into if it is to meet the challenges of justice. Furthermore, I argue that this interpretation of Aboriginal identity bears little resemblance to the perspective that Aboriginals themselves have upon the issues they face in the 21st century. Not only is this an example of the tension I identify, I demonstrate that this form of stereotyping of identity processes produces an injustice because it excludes Aboriginals from access to and participation in Canada's civil society. Again, my consideration of Aboriginal rights in Canada is not intended to provide reasons to reform or abandon this area of state law, especially given the important role that these rights play as *part* of Aboriginal identities. Rather, I use it as an example to demonstrate the key areas into which law must expand its role if it is to meet the contemporary challenges of justice.

Race Relations Legislation in Britain

Prior to 1965 there was no legislation in Britain that controlled discrimination; English law 'neither institutionalised nor prohibited racial discrimination' (CRE 2005: 3).[2] As a matter of common law, racial discrimination in public places is

2 Examples of institutionalised discrimination are Australia's forcible removal of Aboriginal children from their families, and Canada's similar placement of First Nation, Inuit and Métis children in Indian Residential Schools. In both countries legislative measures were used with the aim of assimilating these indigenous groups into the dominant white culture. One of the methods used in Australia was to make Aboriginal children legal wards of the state so that no permission was required to remove them from their families. See, for example, the Aborigines Act 1905; and for further details of these policies and the racial theories that informed them see McGregor (1997). Canada employed similar legislative techniques to assimilate Aboriginal peoples; they disenfranchised these peoples and gave them a legal status inferior to citizenship, making them wards of the state. See the Gradual Civilization Act 1857 and the Indian Act 1876. These children were removed to state-funded church-administered Indian Residential Schools. These schools were located great distances away from Indian reserves so that day attendance was not possible. As part

lawful.[3] The theoretical foundation of this common law position was freedom of contract: individuals were free to regulate their relations as they chose without any state interference, and discrimination was a problem for private parties to resolve between themselves (Thornberry 1965: 74). This position changed in 1965 with the introduction of Britain's first Race Relations Act (RRA 1965). The RRA 1965 was the first legislative prohibition of racial discrimination in Britain. It defined racial discrimination as treating one person less favourably than another on the grounds of colour, race, or ethnic or national origins.[4]

The notion of prohibiting discrimination did not, however, first appear on the political agenda in the early 1960s. Private members' bills tabling legal mechanisms to control discrimination had been introduced in Britain relatively consistently from 1950 onwards (Hindell 1965: 390–91).[5] Indeed, the Labour Party had committed itself to prohibiting discrimination as early as 1958 (Hindell 1965: 390). Yet nothing appeared on the statute books until 1965. It is clear from this that issues of race and racial discrimination were visibly on the political agenda for over a decade before any official legal action was taken. When these private members' bills were debated, no serious arguments were put forward to justify racial discrimination as a measure to counter these bills, suggesting that discriminatory treatment was widely perceived to be unjustifiable. Arguments in favour of maintaining the common law position were based upon freedom of contract, free choice, whether it was desirable for the state to interfere in the private sphere and whether law could appropriately and effectively be used as a tool for social engineering. If the political climate was heavily balanced towards maintaining the common law *status quo*, it is a legitimate question to ask what tipped the balance in favour of outlawing racial discrimination in 1965. I claim that anti-discrimination legislation in Britain is first and foremost a political strategy to address growing anxiety about the presence of non-white immigrants and,[6] at

---

of the Indian Acts 1876–1975 it was a summary offence for Indian parents if their children did not attend an Indian Residential School. For further details see Annett (2005).

3 There are two limited exceptions to this common law rule. First, a hotel proprietor cannot refuse a guest on grounds of colour or race: *Constantine v Imperial Hotels Ltd* [1944] KB 693. Secondly, transport providers (common carriers) cannot refuse to carry persons or their goods on grounds of colour or race: *Lane v Cotton* (1701) 12 Mod 472. These exceptions no longer have any practical purpose since current day anti-discrimination legislation in Britain prohibits discrimination to a far greater extent than this.

4 My intent in introducing the definition of racial discrimination here is to illustrate that this remains the bedrock definition of racial discrimination in Britain.

5 In 1950 Lord Sorensen introduced the Colour Bar Bill and, between 1956 and 1964, Lord Brockway introduced eight bills on the matter of controlling discrimination. In 1952 the Commonwealth Sub-Committee of Labour's National Executive Committee sought the advice of two experts on whether Labour should sponsor anti-discrimination legislation (Hindell 1965: 390–91).

6 I recognise the force of the argument that the label 'non-white' perpetuates an Orientalist approach – why is the dichotomy not black and non-black? Furthermore,

best, only secondly, the legal interpretation of the moral value of equality. This, I believe, better explains the incidence of anti-discrimination legislation in 1965. I also argue that this conclusion has significant ramifications for the way lawyers should approach questions surrounding diversity.

The vast majority of British legislation is a product of political bargaining, negotiation and lobbying, and the RRA 1965 is no different in that regard. In fact, it was the product of intense negotiations in the years prior to its enactment and during its passage through Parliament (Hindell 1965: 392–405). I see this negotiation as an integral part of Britain's legislative process that facilitates a level of scrutiny and consideration that is to be welcomed.[7] Nevertheless, it is neither the substantive content, nor this aspect of the legislative history of the RRA 1965 that form the focal point of my argument. Rather, it is the early and continued twinning of the control of racial discrimination with a political desire to halt Britain's post-war immigrants that I argue is problematic. The primary motive behind the RRA 1965 was to respond to a highly charged political climate that saw the problem, and not the victim, to be non-white immigrants. Moreover, because anti-discrimination legislation has the problem of non-white immigrants intimately entwined within its genesis, I claim it is ill equipped to respond single-handedly to the issues raised by diversity in contemporary British society. This underlying narrative, which does not speak of justice or equality, poses problems for law's role in meeting the challenges of justice in this field. It is worth noting that this underlying narrative was identified as damaging by those that campaigned for and even drafted Britain's race relations legislation. Rather, it is the product of political negotiations and consequent redrafting.

There is no great controversy in linking the advent of the RRA 1965 with post-war non-white immigration in Britain. Indeed, this is something that was openly discussed during the passage of the Act through Parliament, and was a linkage that continued to be made in later race relations legislation. The timing of the RRA 1965 is one of the most prominent illustrations of this causal link between racism and

I sympathise with those who propose abandoning its use. I therefore use it with much reluctance, but on the basis that: (1) it is vital to my argument to be clear that I am not referring to all immigrants, but that I wish to isolate Britain's Afro-Asian post-war migrants; (2) the categorisation of 'black' has been as hotly debated and rejected by British South Asians as unrepresentative of their identities, and therefore comes with its own baggage also; and (3) the 2001 census, which contains the most recent statistical evidence available for analysis, continues to use the label of white, thus implying its dichotomous corollary of non-white, resulting in an important social usage of the label that ensures its continued use. The complexity of this issue, and the way that one feels that one's ideal choices are limited by the social use of label such as this, reflects some of the seemingly intractable questions in debates surrounding race.

7 See Hindell (1965) for a somewhat different interpretation of the legislative process, given the back and forth amendments of the RRA 1965 and its final substantive content. My commendation of legislative process in Britain should not be conflated with the view that such processes are an ideal reflection of democracy.

the presence of immigrants. Those campaigning for anti-discrimination legislation were inspired by the norm of equality; however, it is my claim that it was not the strength of this norm, and arguably not the direct result of the efforts of those campaigning, that prompted government action in 1965. The motivation behind the RRA 1965 was, instead, the increasing numbers of non-white immigrants and the growing and vocal disapproval of Britain's white citizens, which created a social conflict that the political machinery could no longer ignore.

In the early 1950s, when the first controls on racial discrimination were proposed, the numbers of visibly 'non-white' British citizens were limited to a few hundred students. As a consequence, in political arenas, racial discrimination was not perceived to be a problem that required legislative controls, despite strong moral arguments for such legislation on the basis of racial equality, and campaigns built around this principle. However, by 1964 circumstances had radically altered; there were 'hundreds of thousands of immigrants' and Britain had also experienced race related violence (Hindell 1965: 391). Vicious skirmishes in Nottingham and Notting Dale in 1958 were the explosive expression of a growing malcontent between immigrants and non-immigrants. The political right and the media fanned the flames of this malcontent by representing immigrants as a threat to the economic wellbeing of the country, and to the very fabric of British society, with reports of foreigners taking scarce jobs and drugging and abducting young white women. This representation gave the non-immigrant groundswell a sense that their sentiment, that these foreigners should go back home, was supported by a widespread consensus. The violence in Nottingham and Notting Dale was, therefore, perceived to be a response to the presence of non-white migrants (Phillips and Phillips 2000: 158–88). Moreover, these foreigners were portrayed as the problem causing this violence, rather than the victims of violence, perhaps because they did not fit the description of passive recipients. It is only more recent accounts which mention that the teddy boys involved in these violent episodes were busy fighting each other when there were no migrants available to fight (Phillips and Phillips 1998: 161–2). At the time, right wing politicians capitalised upon this characterisation of non-white migration as a problem, by using breaches of public order to sustain their arguments that something needed to be done about the immigrant 'problem', and that racial conflicts such as these were inevitable given the presence of migrants in Britain.[8]

In 1962 the Commonwealth Immigrants Act (CIA 1962) was passed, and its clear intention was to limit migration into Britain. It is worth noting that prior to

---

8 One is led to ask how useful the term 'racial violence' actually is, since the causes of such incidents are far more complex than this description portrays. The label racial violence implies that the conflict was primarily motivated by the bringing together of races that cannot live together peaceably. However, media and political scapegoating, economic conditions and the teddy boy phenomenon all had a role in explaining these particular incidents, yet their causal role is backgrounded by this terminology.

this Britain's (limited) immigration controls focused upon the alien Other.[9] British citizens, including Commonwealth citizens, were not treated as aliens, and prior legislation regulating the status of Commonwealth citizens was done on the basis of nationality legislation such as the British Nationality Act 1948. The CIA 1962, therefore, represents the first legislative treatment of Commonwealth citizens as the excluded alien Other.[10] Indeed, Bob Hepple (1968b: 310), commenting on developments of the law in relation to ethnic minorities, found it to be 'obvious that the cause of the alien has become inextricably bound up with that of the Commonwealth citizen'.[11] Furthermore, given that an overwhelming majority of Commonwealth migrants arriving in Britain in the 1940s and 1950s came from very localised areas of the Commonwealth, namely the Caribbean and South Asia (Ballard 1994: 5–9; Krausz 1971: 12), these controls were clearly aimed at limiting any further influx from these areas. The CIA 1962 limited migration by applying a voucher system to British subjects with passports issued outside of the UK and Ireland. In effect, the vouchers limited migration to skilled and professional workers. If the presence of immigrants in Britain was leading to breaches of the peace, the political solution was to limit this presence to the absolute minimum.

It is telling that the government of the day passed immigration controls before legislating for the control of discrimination, even though at this point anti-discrimination bills were being proposed on an annual basis.[12] In political arenas the consensus view was that the public order incidents of 1958 were a consequence of the presence of non-white migrants, therefore the solution to this problem was to limit immigration as far as was economically feasible. However, this did not address the 'hundreds of thousands' of immigrants that were already present in the country, and the CIA 1962 did nothing to make them feel as if they were less of a despised target following the violence of 1958. The RRA 1965 was part of a package, together with the CIA 1962, that aimed to secure peaceful race relations. Hepple notes that a 'striking feature of the development

9 See, for example, the Aliens Act 1909.

10 I am grateful to Professor Werner Menski's synopsis of the history of immigration in Britain for this point. This synopsis was part of the course on Ethnic Minorities and the Law at the School of Oriental & African Studies, London, run by Professor Werner Menski and Dr Prakash Shah. This idea can also be found in Shah (2000), as well as in Sachdeva (1993).

11 Given that Bob Hepple was one of the many campaigners for anti-discrimination legislation, his comments corroborate my claim that the narrative underlying this legislation was the product of political processes, and was identified by those campaigning as damaging.

12 The timing of the RRA 1965 also reflects concerns at an international level. Decolonisation created a shift in the balance of power. With newly decolonised states challenging the racial hierarchies of empire, condemnation of racial discrimination was necessary for colonial rulers to retain their position in international relations (Füredi 1998). Arguably the Convenant for the Elimination of All Racial Discrimination 1965 is a product of this need to maintain status at an international level.

of the law in England, Wales and Scotland in relation to ethnic minorities is the interaction between immigration control and legislation designed to promote racial integration' (1968b: 310).

There are two points to be made here. First, the RRA 1965 and CIA 1962 represent a dual track approach to race relations: the conflict between immigrants and non-immigrants was managed by limiting the numbers of immigrants entering Britain, and by integrating those that were already here through anti-discrimination legislation. Secondly, the RRA 1965 was structured in a manner that betrayed its primary purpose of averting any further public order incidents, such as those of 1958. Commenting on the RRA 1965, Hepple states that its jurisdiction was 'restricted to those areas of potential racial conflict which were considered by Parliament to constitute the greatest threat to public order' (1966: 306).

The late 1960s are considered to be a turbulent period in race relations history in Britain; on 20 April 1968 the Conservative MP Enoch Powell gave his infamous 'Rivers of Blood' speech. He called for immigration to be reduced immediately and for immigrants who were already here to be repatriated. 'As I look ahead,' he warned, 'I am filled with foreboding. Like the Roman, I seem to see "the river Tiber foaming with much blood"' (quoted in Jones and Welhengama 2000: 13). By 1968 there was widespread criticism of the RRA 1965. Campaigners in this field argued that the Act 'failed to touch the real problems of discrimination – in employment, housing and education. It was also deliberately designed to avoid legal proceedings, and in this it wholly succeeded. The Attorney-General was not called upon even once to take legal action' (Lester, quoted in CRE 2005: 7). The intense and violent politics of 1958 had only increased, despite the legal measures taken to address these problems.

In light of the increasing discontent with the RRA 1965, from all sides of the political spectrum, amendments to this Act were proposed. The approach taken to amending the RRA 1965 reflected a continued political linkage between Commonwealth immigrants and racial conflict. The Race Relations Board (the statutory body set up to administer and oversee the RRA 1965) had concluded that the RRA 1965 ought to be extended to cover more areas. In order to assist Parliament in the amendment of this Act the Race Relations Board joined with the National Committee for Commonwealth Immigrants and appointed a Committee 'to investigate anti-discrimination legislation in other countries, to assess its effectiveness and to consider what type of legislation Parliament might consider suitable' (Hepple 1968b: 311).[13] Further evidence of this linkage can be seen in the then Home Secretary's announcement that the RRA 1965 was to be amended. In the very same announcement he chose to explain that the current immigration controls would continue to operate and, where necessary, be strengthened (HC deb vol 750

13 Professor Harry Street (chairman), Geoffrey Howe QC and Geoffrey Bindman were appointed to the Committee. At the time, both Geoffrey Howe QC and Geoffrey Bindman were legal advisers to the Race Relations Board. All the members of this Committee have become respected equality and human rights experts who have campaigned in this field.

col 747, quoted in Hepple 1968b: 312 n 12). Hepple noted that making the two announcements together 'emphasise[d] that [anti-discrimination] legislation could not in itself increase Britain's capacity to absorb immigrant minorities' (1968b: 311). Racial conflict in Britain was clearly viewed as a product of immigration from the Commonwealth, and consequently something to be tackled with both immigration controls and anti-discrimination measures.

True to this announcement, Parliament set about strengthening immigration controls and in March 1968 the second Commonwealth Immigrants Act was passed (CIA 1968). Whereas the CIA 1962 slowed Commonwealth immigration down, this Act effectively stopped such immigration. Decolonisation in Africa had led to Africanisation policies, which promoted a hostile atmosphere for South Asians in Africa. Since the British had brought many of these South Asians to Africa during the British Empire era, they were British subjects and consequently sought refuge in Britain. Although British nationality laws had become increasingly complex in order to stem the flow of Commonwealth immigration, many East African Asians had retained Commonwealth and United Kingdom Citizen (CUKC) status, as they feared the implications of increasing Africanisation. CUKC status provided a right of abode in Britain, but the CIA 1968 halted this by confining the right of abode to those with close ancestral links to the UK. This move was designed to preserve a right of abode to (white) British citizens born out in the Empire, but with grandparents born in the UK, whilst excluding those (non-white) British citizens with an ancestral heritage outside of the UK. Today it almost seems trite to emphasise that this legislation was racially biased in its inception and application: it is well documented that the CIA 1968 went through both the House of Commons and the House of Lords with great speed and was passed during a period of great anxiety over immigration levels; the passage of the Act also directly followed a period of mass immigration from Kenya with an average of 750 immigrants arriving a week by February 1968 (Bevan 1986: 80–81; Sachdeva 1993: 23–5). Moreover, the European Commission of Human Rights (ECommHR) held that the CIA 1968 was racially motivated, and therefore discriminatory, in *East African Asians v UK*.[14]

By November of the same year the second Race Relations Act was passed (RRA 1968). It maintained the same definition of discrimination, although the ambit of this prohibition was widened to include housing and employment. Together with the CIA 1968, it mirrored the dual track approach taken in the early 1960s to deal with the immigrant problem: halt immigration whilst promoting good race relations for those immigrants already present in the country. When Enoch Powell made his infamous Rivers of Blood speech in April 1968, this speech captured the mood of many non-immigrants who feared radical change to the *status quo*. News reports described the CIA 1968 *and* the RRA 68 as the government's way of being 'tough but fair' on immigration (BBC News Online 1968). Race relations legislation in Britain was a measure designed to address the

14 [1981] 3 EHRR 76.

domestic consequences of immigration. Further confirmation of the connection between race and immigration can been seen in the creation of a Parliamentary Select Committee on Race Relations and Immigration in 1968. The creation of this Select Committee reflected the political characterisation and treatment of social issues in Britain.

Race relations continued to be coupled with Commonwealth immigration throughout the 1970s, and British immigration law continued to focus upon Commonwealth immigration. The Immigration Act 1971 (IA 1971) stated in its preamble that it had the aim of encouraging CUKCs to remigrate, and was passed in response to the fear of invasion of South Asians from Uganda. When Idi Amin expelled South Asians from Uganda in 1972, Britain only took responsibility for those CUKCs that were expelled following international outrage at Britain's insistence that they had no right of abode in Britain and should therefore seek refuge elsewhere.[15]

Having halted primary migration through the CIA 1962, the CIA 1968 and the IA 1971, the remainder of the 1970s was focused upon limiting secondary Commonwealth immigration.[16] The domestic issue of race relations was not neglected during this period, and a further Race Relations Act was passed in 1976 (RRA 1976). This Act followed consideration of American anti-discrimination models, and benefited from insights drawn from the then recent legislation outlawing sexual discrimination (Lester 2006: 21–4).

The RRA 1976, which, with subsequent amendments, is still in force today, extended the RRA 1968 by outlawing discrimination in housing, education, employment, vocational training, residential and commercial tenancies, and in the provision of goods and services. It widened the grounds of unlawful racial discrimination to include nationality, maintained the original definition of direct discrimination, but added indirect discrimination to the forms of prohibited discrimination (Lester 2006: 25). The two forms of discrimination in the RRA 1976 followed the US model of anti-discrimination legislation. Direct discrimination was defined as treating someone less favourably on racial grounds and therefore maintained the definition set out in the RRA 1968.[17] In contrast, indirect discrimination was defined as the application of a requirement which does not

15 International outrage was founded upon the fact that these people had British passports but, through British legislation, were denied a right of abode in Britain. In effect, therefore, British legislation had rendered these individuals stateless, with their British passports functioning as nothing more than travel documents.

16 Primary migration refers to individuals who migrate for voluntary reasons; secondary migration refers to the migration of dependents of primary immigrants. Secondary migration, therefore, covers matters such as family reunification and family creation (that is, transnational marriages where one partner migrates as a consequence of marriage).

17 See RRA 1976 s 1(1)(a), which has now been replaced by s 13 of the Equality Act 2010. The new definition of direct discrimination appears to follow the definition of direct discrimination under the RRA 1976.

itself have anything to do with race, but has a disproportionate effect on a particular racial group, resulting in an adverse effect upon an individual in that racial group.[18] The RRA 1976 also split up the idea of individual litigation and a regulatory/investigatory agency, the latter being the Commission for Racial Equality (CRE). It restructured the role of individuals in race relations disputes, allowing them to initiate litigation without having to go through the Attorney-General, although the CRE was able to intervene in individually initiated legislation, as well as having *locus standi* to commence litigation in its own name, and has, in fact, been involved in many of the key test cases under the RRA 1976.[19]

Whilst substantive progress towards achieving 'fair and equal treatment for all' was being made in the consideration of,[20] and proposed drafts for, further anti-discrimination legislation, the RRA 1976 failed to reflect this conceptual progress by actually separating race from immigration.[21] In a debate in the House of Commons in 1978 Mrs Margaret Thatcher MP (in her role as Leader of the Opposition) said the following (HC deb vol 958 col 240, quoted in Sachdeva 1993: 34):

> People are really rather afraid that this country might be rather swamped by people with a different culture and you know, the British character has done so much for democracy, for law, and done so much throughout the world that if there is any fear that it might be swamped people are going to react and be rather hostile to them coming in. So, if you want good race relations, you have got to allay people's fear on numbers.

Immigration controls continued, therefore, to be an integral aspect of race relations when the final Race Relations Act was passed. By failing to decouple controls

18 See RRA 1976 s 1(1)(b), which has now been replaced by s 19 of the Equality Act 2010. The new definition of indirect discrimination reflects changes instituted by EU legislation on this matter, on which see later in this chapter.

19 Examples include *Mandla v Dowell Lee and Another* [1983] 1 All ER 1062 (HL) and *Commission for Racial Equality v Dutton* [1989] 1 QB 783. See also the Commission for Racial Equality (1990).

20 This aim was expressed in the 1974 White Paper on amendments to Britain's race relations legislation (Lester 2006: 24). Lord Lester of Herne Hill QC (as he is now) was responsible for developing new race and sex discrimination legislation as the Special Adviser to the Home Secretary (Roy Jenkins) in 1974. Roy Jenkins left the Home Office in September 1976, and Lord Lester returned to the bar; the RRA 1976 was passed on 22 November 1976 (Lester 2006: 25).

21 In fact, campaigners for new legislation in both 1968 and 1976 felt that the content of the Acts fell short of what was necessary, and what they had recommended, in their pursuit of genuine equal treatment or opportunity. See Lester and Bindman (1972: 343–74) for an evaluation of the RRA 1968. For an evaluation of all the Race Relations Acts 1965–1978 see McCrudden, Smith and Brown (1991: 92); Bindman (1992: 62); Singh et al. (2003: 42–53); Lester (2006: 24–6); and Hepple and Runnymede Trust (1997: 6–10).

on immigration from good race relations at a political level, legislation that was subjected to political scrutiny before coming into force could only continue to reflect this link, despite the emphasis of scholarship in this field being to justify such legislation along the lines of justice and/or equality.

My aim in considering the socio-historical context of Britain's race relations legislation is to make apparent the lack of congruency and coherence of the racially biased Commonwealth Immigrants Acts and the IA 1971, with the promise of racial equality and justice implicit within the Race Relations Acts 1965–1976. Furthermore, an account of the context within which the Race Relations Acts 1965–1976 were passed demonstrates that, whilst their campaigners might have grounded their necessity within concepts such as justice and racial equality, they came into being as part of a strategy to manage Britain's non-white immigrants.[22] This, I believe, is problematic for the ways that lawyers in Britain approach legal mechanisms that respond to its diverse societies.

The narrative behind Britain's race relations legislation is one of controlling and managing non-white immigration. In a situation where racial conflict occurred following relatively large migration from South Asia, the Caribbean and East Africa, this characterisation is not only understandable, but also arguably appropriate.[23] However, it has had a limiting effect on the policies of multiculturalism that have since followed this legislation. The plural and diverse nature of British society, even in exclusive relation to Britain's Afro-Caribbean and South Asian populations, has gone beyond this immigrant paradigm. Instead, any strategies to manage British diversity require sounder normative foundations that reflect the social realities of the injustices experienced by these populations. The failure of this race relations legislation to respond to the experience of diversity in Britain is reflected, in part, in the continued attempts to amend this legislation; the inefficacy of the current regime is a direct consequence of its failure to grasp the experience of diversity in Britain.

---

22 Lord Lester's disgust and disappointment in this underlying narrative is evident in his commentary on Britain's race relations legislation. See, in particular, Lester (2006: 24).

23 My claim that the Race Relations Acts 1965–1976 are arguably appropriate responses to British diversity is based upon the fact that a contextual approach to this legislation reveals that they were never considered or characterised during their passage through Parliament as mechanisms to reflect the injustices suffered by non-white immigrants in Britain. It was only in the scholarship behind this legislation that norms such as racial equality were used to justify the need for a prohibition on discrimination. The idea that this legislation promised equality and justice was largely, therefore, an assumption that was not reflected in the political perspective on this legislation during its passage through Parliament. It follows from this that to expect this legislation to serve any purpose other than that for which it was intended is the unreasonable claim. The premise that the normative foundations of legal responses do not affect the perspectives and approaches taken by lawyers is flawed; for a more detailed argument about the importance of sound normative foundations for legal responses to diversity see Bhamra (2007).

Recent Amendments to British Race Relations Legislation

There have been three significant changes to Britain's anti-discrimination legislation since 2000 that can be usefully considered at this point in time: (1) the Race Relations (Amendment) Act 2000; (2) the Race Relations Act 1976 (Amendment) Regulations 2003 and the Employment Equality (Religion or Belief) Regulations 2003; and (3) the Equality Act 2006. The last of these is the most comprehensive amendment to anti-discrimination legislation in Britain since 1976, particularly in terms of the change of normative direction that it endeavours to implement. Moreover, it represents the preliminary stages of political action to overhaul anti-discrimination legislation and is a precursor to the Equality Act 2010. The core provisions of the Equality Act 2010 came into force in October 2010. However, it remains too early for any meaningful analysis of this legislation. My claim is that these legislative amendments are driven by a need for legal responses to diversity that are based upon a broader narrative than the control and management of non-white immigration. This, I believe, is evident in the substantive content of this more recent legislation, as well as in the very impetus for change that, in itself, speaks of the unsatisfactory coverage of the previous legislation.[24]

The Race Relations (Amendment) Act 2000 inserts a new section 71 into the RRA 1976, in order to fulfil the recommendations of the Macpherson Report. Lord Macpherson was the head of an inquiry set up following the failure to apprehend and convict the perpetrators of the racially motivated murder of Stephen Lawrence by white youths.[25] In inquiring into how the police handled this murder investigation,[26] Lord Macpherson concluded, *inter alia*, that the police were 'institutionally racist' and defined institutional racism as follows (Cmnd 4262-I: para 6.34):

> The collective failure of an organisation to provide an appropriate and professional service to people because of their colour, culture, or ethnic origin. It can be detected in processes, attitudes and behaviour which amount to discrimination

24 It should be noted that these amendments cannot be understood exclusively as a response to the unsatisfactory coverage of the Race Relations Acts 1965–1976. They also reflect developments and evolutions in our understanding of the role of law in responding to diversity.

25 It is not possible here to convey the enduring lack of official action taken in response to Stephen Lawrence's parents' complaints of negligent police treatment in the investigation of their son's murder. The Stephen Lawrence Inquiry was ordered by the then Home Secretary, Jack Straw, in July 1997, yet Stephen Lawrence was murdered on 22 April 1993. In the intervening period a small group of individuals, including Stephen Lawrence's parents, worked tirelessly to ensure that this case did not fade into the background. For an account of this work see Cathcart (1997: 8–9).

26 Lord Macpherson's mandate was to 'inquire into the matters arising from the death of Stephen Lawrence on 22 April 1993 to date, in order particularly to identify the lessons to be learned for the investigation and prosecution of racially motivated crimes' (Cmnd 4262-I: para 3.1).

> through unwitting prejudice, ignorance, thoughtlessness and racist stereotyping which disadvantage minority ethnic people.

The insertion of section 71 into the RRA 1976 is a response to this finding. The new section imposes a threefold duty upon public authorities, which as a result of this amendment now requires the police to: (1) eliminate unlawful racial discrimination; (2) promote equality of opportunity; and (3) promote good race relations between people of different racial groups.

Lord Macpherson's identification of institutional racism provides an especially vivid opportunity to illustrate the problems of the race and immigration approach taken by British anti-discrimination legislation. In spite of this legislation, spanning back almost three decades by the time of Stephen Lawrence's murder, the police investigating this murder failed to provide an 'appropriate and professional service' in the case of the murder of an Afro-Caribbean boy. This institutional racism, identified to be at the heart of the Metropolitan Police's failures in this investigation, was not expressed as a form of prohibited discrimination within any of the Race Relations Acts 1965–1976 and this, I argue, is directly linked to the socio-political context within which this legislation was framed. The narrative behind Britain's anti-discrimination measures is one of immigration and racial conflict, where non-white immigrants are viewed as the problem, not the victim, and white non-immigrants act from an arena of acute anxiety at the (illogical and unreasonable) prospect that their own way of life may be swamped by the arrival of vastly different ways of life. The socio-political belief that the friction present in British society could be controlled by severely curtailing immigration from South Asia and the Caribbean was integral to this narrative. Within this narrative it is unsurprising that anti-discrimination dialogues did not consider how British institutional structures might, through their cultures, processes and structural set-up, act to discriminate against these immigrants. Instead, the voice of Britain's anti-discrimination legislation is one of integrating immigrants into British society and thereby avoiding future public order incidents.

The boundaries of this paradigm are exemplified in the work of the campaigners behind this legislation. Roy Jenkins famously explained in May 1966, whilst he was the Home Secretary, that integration was to be understood 'not as a flattening process of assimilation but as equal opportunity, accompanied by cultural diversity, in an atmosphere of mutual tolerance' (Lester 2006: 21). The rejection of assimilation within this definition appears enlightened and progressive from within a paradigm where the immigrant is the problem. Yet this definition is easily attacked once one is outside that paradigm and using sound normative foundations to ground one's perspective: what sort of equality, justice and diversity can be encouraged in a society where non-white immigrants are expected to integrate into institutional structures that are not set up to provide a service that takes diversity and differences into account? Indeed, when one takes an expansive approach to justice and factors in the racial hierarchies intrinsic to Britain's Empire, it is unsurprising that institutional structures that have largely gone unaltered since the time of the British Empire are unable to 'provide an appropriate and professional service to people because of their colour, culture, or ethnic origin' (Cmnd 4262-I: para 6.34). In plugging up a loophole in Britain's anti-discrimination legislation, section 71 of the RRA 1976 therefore not only demonstrates the inadequacy of the legislative prohibitions on discrimination, but also illustrates that this inadequacy is linked to the limiting nature of the narrative that underlies the Race Relations Acts 1965–1976.

The Race Relations Act 1976 (Amendment) Regulations 2003 and the Employment Equality (Religion or Belief) Regulations 2003 speak further of the limitations of this narrative. These regulations were passed in order to implement European directives on race, ethnicity and national origins (Council Directive 2000/43/EC) (Race Directive) and on religion or belief and sexual orientation (Council Directive 2000/78/EC) (Employment Directive). The Race Directive covers four main issues. First, it clarifies that the prohibition of discrimination on the grounds of racial or ethnic origin should be an inclusive concept, by which it means to reject the immutable characteristics approach taken in the United States. According to this latter approach, those characteristics that can be chosen, and are therefore not physical attributes, are excluded from the ambit of protection provided by anti-discrimination provisions. For example, travellers, because they can choose to live permanently in one place, do not have an immutable characteristic and would fall outside of the protective ambit of American anti-discrimination legislation. By the time of this amendment English law had already rejected the immutable characteristics route and adopted a somewhat inclusive interpretation of racial grounds.[27]

Secondly, the Race Directive prohibits broader forms of discrimination than those outlawed in the RRA 1976. It obliged EU Member States to implement a definition of indirect discrimination that does not require statistical analysis between racial groups, and instead only required that the complainant show potential rather than actual disadvantage. Furthermore, it introduces harassment as a free-standing form of prohibited racial discrimination. In contrast, the definition of racial harassment under the RRA 1976 is designed to ensure that employers do not mistreat any employees who are already involved in a claim under the Act. Thirdly, the ambit of protection against unlawful discrimination under the Race Directive includes all public and private bodies, with exceptions for immigration

---

27 The courts have interpreted 'ethnic origins' under the RRA 1976 to include certain religious groups, namely Jews and Sikhs (*Mandla v Dowell Lee and Another* [1983] 1 All ER 1062 (HL)) and travellers (*Commission for Racial Equality v Dutton* [1989] 1 QB 783). Muslims and Rastafarians have, however, been excluded from the protective ambit of the RRA 1976: see *Crown Suppliers (PSA) v Dawkins* [1993] ICR 517 and *Tariq v Young* Case 247738/88 EOR Discrimination Case Law Digest No 2. The English courts have held that Rastafarians do not constitute an ethnic group because they do not have a long enough shared history. Muslims, on the other hand, do not come from one geographical location and therefore cannot be considered to be an ethnic group.

authorities. The failure of the RRA 1976 to prohibit discriminatory behaviour by the police was at the heart of the Stephen Lawrence Inquiry. Finally, the Race Directive shifts the burden of proof when proving incidents of discrimination in favour of complainants. Under the Race Directive the complainant need only introduce facts from which discrimination can be presumed; once this presumption has been established, the burden is on the defendant to show that there was in fact no racial discrimination.

The impact of the Employment Directive upon English law lends itself to a far more concise explanation. This directive aims to establish a framework to combat discrimination in the field of employment and occupation that is based upon religion or belief, disability, age or sexual orientation. Since the RRA 1976 does not explicitly cover religion or belief, the implementing legislation extended the scope of prohibited discrimination to include these grounds, but only in the employment context.[28] In contrast, the RRA 1976 prohibits racial discrimination in housing, education, vocational training, residential and commercial tenancies, the provision of goods and services, and employment. The level of protection provided by the Employment Directive is, therefore, comparatively limited.

These EU amendments and extensions to Britain's anti-discrimination legislation put into effect a more contemporary perspective on equality. Indeed, in Britain itself pressure was mounting as to the need to include religion or belief as grounds of prohibited discrimination. The year after the Employment Directive, Weller, Feldman and Purdham (2000) published the results of a Home Office Study into the extent of religious discrimination in England and Wales. They concluded that 'ignorance and indifference towards religion were of widespread concern amongst research participants from all faith groups' and that this could create an 'environment in which discrimination of all kinds (including "unwitting" and institutional discrimination) is able to thrive'; furthermore, they found that '[h]ostility and violence were very real concerns for organizations representing Muslims, Sikhs and Hindus' (Weller, Feldman and Purdham 2000: vi).

Nevertheless, despite these European led moves towards more contemporary perspectives on diversity in Britain, the nature of EU harmonisation mechanisms are such that Member States can choose the route by which they achieve the level of protection set out in directives (Craig and de Búrca 1998: 108). As such, Britain amended its anti-discrimination legislation to ensure that the increased level of protection required under the EU regime was only necessary with respect to those areas covered by EU law. Anything outside of the jurisdiction of EU law is dealt with under the RRA 1976. This hints at an unwillingness to adhere to the greater levels of protection required by EU law.

---

28 Disability, age and sexual orientation used to be covered under separate legislation in Britain, but they now all fall within the ambit of the Equality Act 2010. The primary aim of this legislation is to simplify the law by consolidating all forms of prohibited discrimination in one single statute.

Despite EU efforts to harmonise equality issues across its Member States, Britain, perhaps inadvertently, ensured that the old paradigm, together with its narrative of limiting further non-white immigration and controlling current non-white immigrants, retained its position. Both the Race and Employment Directives reflected a more contemporary approach to diversity, as illustrated by its inclusive definition of racial or ethnic origins and the carefully worded indirect discrimination provisions which attempted to shift some of the burden of proof in favour of the complainant.[29] Yet, the method by which these two directives were implemented effectively stunted the potential progress that they promised for English law. In this context it is revealing to recount that it was at the insistence of the UK that immigration authorities were exempted from liability for racial discrimination under the Race Directive. Immigration authorities continue to function within a race relations structure that is permeated with the ethos that good race relations requires these authorities to discriminate upon racial grounds. It appears as if this narrative is so entrenched that it now requires more than just a shift to equality talk to facilitate legal thinking that goes beyond the coupling of diversity with non-white immigration. The immigration and race narrative has such a tight and enduring hold upon British imaginings of diversity issues that the promise of radical change held out by the Equality Act 2006 and the Equality Act 2010 are likely to be ineffective.

The Equality Act 2006 (EA 2006), in its content and as a precursor to the Equality Act 2010 (EA 2010), represents the greatest overhaul of anti-discrimination legislation in Britain since the RRA 1965.[30] The EA 2006 establishes a single statutory body, the Equality and Human Rights Commission (EHRC), to oversee all equality and human rights matters. The EHRC has taken on the work of the existing anti-discrimination Commissions and has assumed responsibility for promoting equality and combating unlawful discrimination in three new strands, namely sexual orientation, religion or belief, and age.[31] Alongside overseeing

---

29 It is arguable that the Race Directive does not, itself, have sound normative foundations. See Guild (2000: 416), who remarks that the Race Directive went through the necessary legislative procedures with great speed (seven months), and that it was expected to encounter great resistance. Given that the Race Directive was passed in time for the 2001 Durban World Conference against Racism, Racial Discrimination, Xenephobia and Related Intolerance, there is some suggestion that the EU was more concerned with its status in international relations than the normative value of justice.

30 The Act was brought into force by the Equality Act 2006 (Commencement No 1) Order 2006 SI 2006/1082 (7 April 2006). The bulk of the Act came into force on 18 April 2006. Section 83 and the remaining parts of ss 84 and 85 came into force on 6 April 2007.

31 The old Commissions were as follows: the Equal Opportunities Commission (EOC), which was the statutory body concerned with gender discrimination; the Commission for Racial Equality (CRE), which was the statutory body charged with the responsibility of overseeing the functioning of the RRA 1976; and the Disability Rights Commission (DRC), which was concerned with discrimination on the grounds of disability.

the control of prohibited discrimination on all grounds, the EHRC will also have responsibility for the promotion of human rights.

The EA 2006 does not repeal the RRA 1976 (or any of the other primary anti-discrimination legislation in Britain), but does extend anti-discrimination protection, making discrimination on the grounds of religion or belief in the provision of goods, facilities and services, education, the use and disposal of premises, and the exercise of public functions unlawful. It will be recalled that the Employment Directive prohibited discrimination on the grounds of religion or belief in employment scenarios, thus the EA 2006 brings coverage of this prohibition to the same level as the RRA 1976. The EA 2006 also enables provisions to be made to prohibit discrimination on the grounds of sexual orientation in the provision of goods, facilities and services, education, the use and disposal of premises and the exercise of public functions; and creates a duty on public authorities to promote equality of opportunity between women and men ('the gender duty'), and prohibit sex discrimination and harassment in the exercise of public functions.

There are at least three key principles behind the EA 2006 that are important to note since they depart considerably from the narratives that inform the RRA 1976. First, the EA 2006 is intended to embody the norm of equality, rather than just controlling discrimination and fostering the integration of immigrants. Secondly, it brings all grounds for discrimination under one umbrella in order to reflect the intersectionality of identities and, therefore, the reality of discriminatory practices; discriminatory behaviour rarely focuses upon one aspect of an individual's identity and is more likely to involve a combination of racial grounds, religion, beliefs, gender, sexual orientation, disability, age, and so on. Finally, the EA 2006 does not just mainstream equality; it endeavours to recognise its close affinity with human rights. The EA 2006 is the precursor to the EA 2010, which brings together all of Britain's piecemeal anti-discrimination legislation into one coherent and comprehensive code. The EA 2010 was placed on the statute book on 8 April 2010 and the core provisions came into force in October 2010. Given that the EA 2010 largely consolidates existing piecemeal legislation and only strengthens the law in a handful of areas, it is relatively clear what its narrative will be and the difficulties that it will face.[32]

The general principles informing the EA 2006 and the EA 2010 seductively hint at radical changes to the race and immigration narrative that so tightly buttresses the RRA 1976. Yet the reality of the EA 2010 provides no radical change to the regime under the RRA 1976. Although the parallel regimes created by the implementation of the Race and Employment Directives have been merged, and EA 2010 now prohibits discrimination by immigration authorities (with significant exceptions, most notable are those that relate to national security interests), the reality that this will precipitate any great change to the culture in

32 See http://www.equalities.gov.uk/equality_act_2010/archive-_equality_bill.aspx for consultation responses and other documents relating to the passage of the EA 2010 (last accessed 21 September 2010).

which immigration decisions are made is remote. The immigration legislation that formed an integral part of Britain's race relations package will remain intact, and the provision of immigration services will, I believe, continue in much the same vein as before. This situation will persist unless significant changes are made that specifically target immigration services in Britain. The promise of radical change held out by the EA 2006 and EA 2010 are likely to be limited because the underlying narrative of the Race Relations Acts 1965–1976 remains untouched. Arguably the EA 2010 betrays a reluctance to reform the entrenched race discrimination regime at the same pace as other areas of discrimination. Given the strength with which the race and immigration narrative has captured the British legal imagination, it is unlikely that these reforms will have a positive impact upon the limitations of the current regime.[33]

A brief word should be given to research that indicates the level of entrenchment of the 'immigrant as problematic' narrative. In a MORI poll conducted by the Commission on Integration & Cohesion in January 2007, 68 per cent of people agreed with the statement that there were too many immigrants in Britain. More disturbingly, 47 per cent of the Asian and 45 per cent of the Black respondents felt that there was too much immigration in Britain.[34] The force of this link between immigration and the difficulties, both social and economic, experienced within British society, is so strong that terrifying proportions of those with direct and indirect personal experience of migration are subscribing to this narrative. In this context, a shift from dealing with the diverse nature of Britain's citizenry from a matter of race relations to that of equality has little hope of loosening the restrictive grip that this linkage maintains.

The changes made to the RRA 1976 since 2000 reflect a need to update and modernise Britain's race relations regime. Yet, the outdated and incomplete nature of this regime is not a novel conclusion; this is something that has been commented upon and considered for a number of years, and proposals to amend this legislation have been forthcoming for a number of years. What I have attempted to illustrate here is a different conclusion. I have shown, first, that the current regime that aims to respond to Britain's South Asian and Afro-Caribbean diversity is premised upon a dual track approach of halting non-white immigration from these countries and integrating non-white immigrants that were already resident in Britain. The primary goal of this approach was to ensure that both non-white immigrants and white non-immigrants in Britain were placated enough to prevent conflict and public order incidents. If equality was ever a foundational premise of this regime it was, at best, a secondary premise. The primary motive informing this regime

33 This conclusion is also supported by suggestions that the new coalition government in Britain is likely to reduce the impact of the EA 2010, which was passed in the last few days of the Labour Government, by stalling the implementation dates for those provisions that it finds less favourable. The new government has already indicated it is not bound by the timetables set by previous governments.

34 See the Final Report of the Commission on Integration & Cohesion (2007).

is one that casts immigrants as the cause of many of Britain's socio-economic difficulties. Secondly, I have shown that recent amendments to this regime speak of the limitations of this immigration and race relations narrative, and that these amendments have not succeeded in displacing this narrative. This is in part due to the continued voracity with which immigrants are scapegoated for social and economic problems in British society.

At this juncture it is worth further exploring why the race and immigration narrative limits law's potential to respond to Britain's plural societies. I believe it is because the race and immigration narrative no longer speaks of the experience of diversity in Britain. In the 1960s and 1970s racial conflict in Britain seemed exclusively to surround South Asian and Afro-Caribbean immigrants, and the narrative underlying the legislation designed to respond to these problems reflected this empirical reality. This characterisation also had an impact upon the ways in which groups allied themselves – if the issues were understood as those of primarily race and immigration, then the focal points of group solidarities reflected this. The racial tensions of the 1950s, 1960s and 1970s coincided with the highest numbers of immigration from South Asia and the Caribbean that Britain had ever experienced. Thus it seems inevitable, and arguably appropriate, that the narrative behind anti-discrimination legislation developed along this trajectory. However, the contemporary issues that anti-discrimination legislation seeks to address have altered and evolved over the decades. This evolution has been reflected in the dialogues and scholarship that express these issues; they have moved from race relations to multiculturalism, to identity politics. Academic commentary in this area favours terms such as equality, identity politics, the politics of recognition, accommodation, religion, belonging, plurality, diversity, difference and so on, whilst backgrounding terms such as assimilation, integration and race, that featured so prominently in the old narrative. Moreover, my fresh perspective of justice reflects changes in the way that diversity is now understood. Yet these changes in the ways in which such issues are perceived, and consequently expressed, have not been reflected in the narrative that informs British anti-discrimination legislation. At the very least, the discrimination faced by British Afro-Caribbeans and South Asians is no longer an immigrant issue. The victims of this discrimination are likely to have been born and educated in Britain; Stephen Lawrence, for example, was a young British boy with an Afro-Caribbean heritage who was murdered because he wore that heritage on his person, not because he was confused as an immigrant. This stagnating narrative's inability to coincide with and express the empirical reality of contemporary diversity in Britain is responsible (in part, at the very least) for limiting law's potential to respond and adapt to a plural British citizenry.

Canada's Constitution and its Aboriginal Populations

Canada's constitutional arrangements, as they relate to its Aboriginal populations, provide an opportunity to highlight a second major limitation that must be considered when locating law's role in meeting the challenges of justice in diverse societies. In considering law's role it is, I believe, vital to be aware of state law's reifying tendencies, which clash with the fluidity and dynamism of our diverse identities. Identifying and acknowledging this tension between ongoing evolution and the need for certainty and clarity is essential, less to remove the tension completely, and more to allow for expansion in law's role, in order to accommodate these discordant characteristics.

There are distinct advantages and disadvantages to using Canada's constitution to illustrate this tension. Although this is by no means an exhaustive list, by referencing a constitution that is entrenched I am able to introduce the idea that for the purpose of my arguments in this book, little turns on whether a constitution is entrenched or not.[35] Moreover, Canada has relatively recently made significant changes to its constitutional arrangements (a process that culminated in significant changes in 1982), and continues to negotiate and renegotiate these arrangements. As an established nation-state, which is not responding to violent identity conflicts, these constitutional arrangements serve to underscore my earlier argument that *all* nation-states are engaged in ongoing processes of nation-building. Additionally, by referencing the relationship between constitutional arrangements and Aboriginal populations I am able to introduce the idea that the challenges raised by diversity for justice are not usefully compartmentalised into absolute areas that concern immigrants (or their descendents), as a separate issue from Aboriginal populations. Whilst I am not denying that each group has its own specificities that make the challenges to be met unique, I am suggesting that within each group there is an immense amount of internal plurality that urges us to reconsider the labels and compartments we have assigned in the field of diversity. Furthermore, by refusing to allow the cross-pollination of ideas across various axes of diversity, we run the

35 An entrenched constitution is one where there is a supreme law of the land that cannot be contravened. This can be compared with the situation in the United Kingdom, which does not have a set of documents that act as the supreme law of the land. Instead, the constitutional arrangements in the UK rest upon the notion of parliamentary sovereignty. In brief, this means that Parliament is the supreme law-maker in the land and, with the exception that Parliament cannot fetter itself, Parliament may make or unmake any laws. The meaning of parliamentary sovereignty is much more complex than this description suggests: in the UK there remain a variety of views on the effect that membership in the European Union has had upon the doctrine of parliamentary sovereignty, and whether the Human Rights Act 1998 has changed the nature of this doctrine. Furthermore, my own interpretation of the meaning of law in this book, and in particular my alignment with ideas of legal pluralism, raises questions that relate to the meaning of parliamentary sovereignty in countries such as the UK, New Zealand and Finland.

risk of excluding valuable terrain that can be gainfully employed in all matters relating to diversity and justice.

There is one notable disadvantage to focusing upon Canada and its Aboriginal populations: the history of white settler colonisation in Canada, which provides important contextual material, is inaccessible. It would be right to suggest that this is a history that would not be justly represented within the parameters of this book. However, I believe the inaccessibility of this history goes far deeper than this logistical limitation. The place of Canadian Aboriginals in Canadian society is, at present, a very much unknown or fluid quantity. This is not just because Canadian Aboriginals are negotiating and renegotiating their position in society, as is the case with all identity processes. Rather, it is because so much of the details of white settler colonisation, from an Aboriginal perspective at the very least, are only just beginning to surface. One stark example of this can be seen in the Indian Residential School system in Canada. Stories of the experiences of these school children are only just beginning to become available as part of the hearings of the Truth and Reconciliation Commission of Canada.[36]

There is much that could be considered when looking at how Canada's constitution affects its Aboriginal population. However, I want to use this example to demonstrate the tension between the certainty of state laws and fluidity of the social reality of identity processes. I propose to do this by considering one discrete area, namely the test developed by the Canadian courts to identify the existence of Aboriginal rights. Since much of the historical context is inaccessible in any meaningful sense, I have chosen to concentrate on placing this issue within a social context by contrasting it with the social realities that face Canada's Aboriginal peoples in the 21st century.

Although it is not possible to provide an historical context to colonialism in Canada in any meaningful manner, before turning to consider the test for Aboriginal rights, there is one characteristic to this form of white settler colonialism that can be gainfully referenced in order to situate this discussion. The relationship between white European settlers and Aboriginal Canadians may have initially begun with Aboriginal peoples sharing their knowledge with white Europeans on how to live in Canada's harsh climates. However, once legal regulation of Aboriginal peoples began, epitomised by the Indian Acts, and white Europeans adopted a distinct policy towards Aboriginal Canadians, relations became far more asymmetric and the colonisers took a paternalistic stance towards Aboriginal populations, who were considered to be inferior and savages. The white settlers assumed themselves

36 The Truth and Reconciliation Commission of Canada was set up as part of the Indian Residential Schools Settlement Agreement, which was negotiated between former students of the schools, the Canadian Government and Canadian churches. For further details see http://www.residentialschoolsettlement.ca/english_index.html (last accessed 21 September 2010).

not only to be superior,[37] but also as having to shoulder the white man's burden: it was their responsibility, as privileged individuals occupying the higher echelons of all social, economic and political strata, to take responsibility for, protect and civilise these savages (Kallen 2010: 191–2).

Aboriginal Rights under Common Law: the Van der Peet test

Protected Aboriginal rights come in two main forms: first, there are Aboriginal rights at common law and, secondly, there are Aboriginal Treaty rights. According to dominant jurisprudence, the former flow from the fact that Aboriginal peoples historically occupied and used land,[38] and the latter arise from official agreements made between Aboriginal peoples and the Crown during colonisation. In *R v Van der Peet*,[39] Lamer CJ, of the Canadian Supreme Court, set out the test for identifying Aboriginal rights that arise at common law (Monahan 2006: 439–52). In contrast, Aboriginal Treaty rights are identified by referring to the terms of the relevant Treaty.

For ease of explanation, the *Van der Peet* test can be considered to have two elements.[40] First, the precise nature of the claim must be determined. This is done by: (1) looking at the activities that the claimant was engaged in; (2) considering the nature of the government regulation which is being challenged; and (3) examining the custom that is being argued to be an Aboriginal right. Cases have generally identified these rights as those where a specific activity, such as hunting or fishing, is engaged in on particular lands or territories.[41]

The second element of this test is to determine whether the right claimed is a protected Aboriginal right. In order to be protected the right must be a 'practice, custom or tradition integral to the distinctive culture of the Aboriginal group claiming the right'.[42] There are various considerations the court must make

37 This hierarchy was, of course, racially based, with white people occupying the highest rungs in political, economic and social spheres.

38 Lamer CJ elaborated the origins of Aboriginal rights at common law in *R v Van der Peet* [1996] 2 SCR 507. He explained that these rights arise at common law because 'when Europeans arrived in North America, Aboriginal peoples *were already here*, living in communities on the land, and participating in distinctive cultures, as they had done for centuries' (para 30).

39 [1996] 2 SCR 507.

40 In fact, the judgment in this case could be interpreted as elaborating a test that has far more elements, and is therefore more complex than the two element test that I am setting out here. However, for the purposes of my arguments, nothing turns on examining the precise details of Lamer CJ's judgment in *Van der Peet*.

41 See, for example, *R v Sparrow* [1990] 1 SCR 1075 at 1101, where the right in question was 'the Aboriginal right to fish for food and social and ceremonial purposes'; and *R v Côté* [1996] 3 SCR 139, where the court identified a right to fish for food within lakes and rivers in that particular territory.

42 *Van der Peet* [1996] 2 SCR 507 (para 46).

in assessing this 'integral to a distinctive culture' test. For the purposes of my arguments here, I wish to highlight only a few of these considerations. First, in *Van der Peet*, the court elaborated that it must consider the perspective of the Aboriginal peoples, but 'that perspective must be framed in terms cognizable to the Canadian legal and constitutional structure' (para 49).

Secondly, to claim an Aboriginal right successfully, a claimant must be able to show that the practice, custom or tradition existed prior to contact with Europeans. Lamer CJ explained that, because these are rights that arise at common law by virtue of the fact of Aboriginal occupation of lands prior to European contact, this must be the relevant time period. There is, however, some acceptance of the fact that these customs will evolve and develop over time, but there must still be some sort of continuity with a practice, custom or tradition that existed prior to European contact (paras 60–67). In *Bernard/Marshall* the Supreme Court of Canada clarified this approach further by adding that,[43] 'the court must examine the pre-sovereignty aboriginal practice and translate that practice into a modern right. The process begins by examining the nature and extent of the pre-sovereignty aboriginal practice in question. It goes on to seek a corresponding common law right. In this way, the process determines the nature and extent of the modern right and reconciles the aboriginal and European perspectives' (para 51).

Finally, 'the claimant must demonstrate that the practice, custom or tradition was a central and significant part of the society's distinctive culture. He or she must demonstrate, in other words, that the practice, custom or tradition was one of the things which made the culture of the society distinctive – that it was one of the things that truly *made the society what it was*' (para 55). The court was careful to make a distinction between distinct and distinctive cultures; the former requiring comparison with or reference to other cultures, whereas the latter is something that can be proved in isolation.

Borrows (2002: 59–60) analyses Lamer CJ's judgment in *Van der Peet* by questioning just how it might be possible to capture the notion of what it means to be Aboriginal, and how one might adjudicate the nature of and isolate what constitutes Aboriginal identities.[44] By framing his analysis in this manner, Borrows skilfully illustrates the tension that I wish to highlight by referencing the *Van der Peet* test. Canadian constitutional law, like most positive law, requires a set of criteria to be fulfilled, in order to be certain that a right exists in law. In contrast, the very nature of being Aboriginal is not amenable to such certainty. Aboriginality is, as is the case with all forms of identity, a site of intense pluralities that cannot

43 *R v Marshall*; *R v Bernard* [2005] 2 SCR 220.

44 In fact, Borrows's (2002) framework is far more sophisiticated than I am portraying here. He persuasively uses a method of critique found within Anishinabek jurisprudence to analyse Canadian constitutional law. Borrows explains that he has taken this approach because '[i]t is now time for the common law's treatment of Aboriginal peoples to be judged by stories indigenous to [Canada]' (2002: xii). It is also worth noting that he (2002: 3–55) demonstrates that the Anishinabek have an independent legal tradition.

be captured in the manner that the *Van der Peet* test suggests. Moreover, the focus upon identifying customs that existed prior to European contact, and then translating that custom into a modern right that fits into a framework that Canadian constitutional law can comprehend, fails to appreciate truly the dynamism of identity processes and shackles Aboriginal identities to historical practices.

The approach taken to identifying Aboriginal rights, as set out by the Supreme Court of Canada, can be usefully contrasted with the agenda of a recent National First Nations Leadership Conference in Canada. I place these side by side in order to contrast the official legal system's understanding of Aboriginal identity processes with a glimpse at the issues that Aboriginal peoples feel they need to address. My intention is to consider whether this official picture bears any resemblance to the social realities of being Aboriginal in contemporary Canada.

The most recent National First Nations Leadership Conference took place in August 2010, and the first item on the agenda was governance.[45] The short explanation of this item clarifies that Aboriginal Nations must consider ways to exercise their right to make laws. Second on the agenda is the prevention of Aboriginal suicides and consideration of Aboriginal understandings of something akin to the notion of karma, which is understood here as 'what you give you receive'. The third item is a community development and strategic planning seminar. This is explained as a workshop where strategies that lead to self-reliance and self-determination are discussed. Finally, the conference concluded by having a life skills and motivational seminar where there was a discussion of ways that Aboriginal youths, in particular, can motivate themselves to achieve their dreams.

This small glance at the issues that Aboriginal leaders feel need to be addressed make starkly apparent the chasm that exists between the social realities of Aboriginal identity processes and Canada's constitutional framework, which is intended to make room for these processes. This constitutional framework misunderstands the social realities of Aboriginal identity processes in the 21st century in at least two ways. First, being Aboriginal today is always understood by referencing practices and customs that are over 100 years old. In reality, Aboriginal identity processes in Canada today involve the negotiation of familiar issues, such as how to ensure that as a minority one is not discriminated against in a competitive job market or education system, or how to promote success amongst Aboriginal youths. However, the *Van der Peet* test, in its quest for certainty and clarity, confines Aboriginal identity processes to fishing and hunting and other such historical activities. In reproducing this stereotypical picture of Aboriginality, this constitutional position runs the serious risk of stifling the development of Aboriginal identities; if being Aboriginal is so tightly connected to historical practices and a relationship to the land, then identity processes that conflict with this picture, such as running or working for corporations that mine natural resources, are considered un-

45 See http://wavewalkergroup.com/index.php?option=com_content&view=article &id=46&Itemid=55 (last accessed 20 August 2010).

Aboriginal. Moreover, this constitutional process of determining Aboriginal rights robs Aboriginal peoples of opportunities to negotiate their identities *on their own terms*, as it is an alien legal system that adjudicates whether or not something is integral to being Aboriginal.

Secondly, the need to fit Aboriginal identities into a framework that is understood by dominant notions of constitutional law denies the complex and plural processes of law that exist amongst Aboriginal peoples. This pursuit to occupy a position as the only legitimate, and therefore dominant, legal system involves transforming processes of law amongst Aboriginal peoples into mere practices, traditions and customs. In many ways the pursuit of dominance is so complete that our legal imaginings are unable to visualise law and legal systems beyond that which fits into Western models of law, such as the Canadian constitutional system.

By framing Aboriginal legal systems as customs, or part of Aboriginal culture, and so on, the dominant legal system does nothing more than shut its eyes to these developments. Aboriginal peoples will continue to use these non-dominant systems and continue to renegotiate their structure, even if Canadian law refuses to recognise their validity. A pertinent example can be seen in the Truth and Reconciliation Commission of Canada set up as part of the Settlement Agreement that relates to the legacy of Canada's Indian Residential School system.[46] The idea of the Commission is that it provides a voice to survivors of this system. However, these survivors, having been removed from their Aboriginal backgrounds,[47] are renegotiating their Aboriginal identities by, in part, using Aboriginal legal systems, such as healing circles, to understand and voice their experiences. If the Truth and Reconciliation Commission is considered to be 'legal', it is only through our limited legal imaginings that healing circles, and other Aboriginal forums for dispute resolution and healing, are seen as customs and practices, rather than integral parts of legitimate legal systems. More importantly, the pursuit to privilege one dominant legal system is not so effective as to render these forums and models otiose. Indeed, the agenda mentioned above makes it clear that Aboriginal peoples are aware of a need to invoke their right to participate in and continue to produce legal systems on their own terms.

Locating Law's Role

The examples I have provided in this chapter are intended to illustrate that there is a need for fresh perspectives on diversity, and more particularly on law's role as a part of these perspectives. I have chosen these two particular examples because I believe that they demonstrate the key areas into which law's role in responding to

46 See http://www.residentialschoolsettlement.ca/english_index.html (last accessed 21 September 2010).

47 This policy was nothing short of genocide, with a clear intention of wiping out the ways of life of Aboriginal peoples.

diversity ought to be expanding. It is important that I am clear that my analysis of British race relations legislation and Canadian constitutional law is not intended to provide reasons as to why these two areas need to be either radically reformed or abandoned;[48] both areas of law have had considerable successes in providing legal redress and that, in itself, is sufficient to justify their continued usage. My intention is, rather, to demonstrate key ways in which law ought to be responding to diversity, but is currently failing to do so. Law's role, then, is one of expansion, as a natural reaction to our evolving understandings of justice and the nature of diversity.

I have demonstrated that the narrative underlying Britain's race relations legislation limits law's potential and, furthermore, this has limited the ways that lawyers think about achieving justice in the area of diversity. The narrative that legislation in this area speaks of has distracted us from thinking about the changing characteristics of diversity and the ways in which justice must evolve to respond to this. Instead of considering that the RRA 1976 may not be a panacea to all the issues raised by diversity, we have concerned ourselves with tinkering with the RRA 1976 to ensure that it is equipped to respond to these issues. My claim is that we not only need to be clear about the normative foundations of law's responses to diversity, but we also need to reassess and review these foundations in an ongoing manner.

By introducing the *Van der Peet* test, I have illustrated that the limits we place upon law's role can also limit identity processes. The focus upon historical practices amongst Aboriginal peoples in Canada has an equally distracting effect upon lawyers. We become overly concerned with ensuring that there is adequate space for plural values, *as they used to be*. As our gaze looks backwards, in an attempt to redress past injustices, we forget to look around us and consider contemporary injustices and the ways in which plurality and diversity manifests itself in the context of today's societies. Shackling diversity to the past in this manner not only stereotypes diverse populations, it also stifles individual and group agency: our ability to engage in identity processes on our own terms is compromised by an external picture of the way we ought to behave. Law's role must be broad enough to redress past injustices *and* pave the way forward for a more just present and future.

Equally as important, Canada's constitutional response to its Aboriginal citizens highlights an agenda that positive law engages in, to the detriment of the pursuit of justice in diverse societies. Positive law is concerned with securing its own privileged status as the dominant and only legitimate legal system. In pursuing this aim, it distorts the ways of life found amongst diverse societies by making them conform to structures, models and concepts found within the dominant legal system. Moreover, this agenda ensures that other legal systems are given an inferior less-than-law status by being categorised as mere customs,

---

48 There may well be solid argument for the reform or abandonment of both of these areas, but I make no such claims here.

practices, traditions and aspects of culture. This is clearly unjust, as those who choose to participate in these non-dominant legal systems are thereby excluded from access to and participation in dominant legal systems. Furthermore, the continued practice of these non-dominant legal systems only serves to highlight that the dominant agenda has not been entirely successful.

My conclusion is that, instead, lawyers need to take a fresh and broader perspective on diversity and also focus upon the contemporary challenges of justice in light of the empirical reality of a nation's diverse citizenry. In taking a fresh perspective, and considering what contemporary justice requires in this field, we will be led to consider legal responses in a wider sense and go beyond merely controlling discriminatory behaviour, or preserving historical societies. Moreover, we may even be led to consider 'law' in a wider sense than just its positivist meaning.

Chapter 5
Human Rights and Diversity

In this chapter I continue to locate law's role in meeting the challenges of this form of justice in diverse societies, by considering human rights as a legal response to diversity. Although contemporary human rights regimes do not have diversity as their sole concern, they are grounded by three key principles, namely freedom, equality and dignity (Article 1, Universal Declaration of Human Rights (UDHR)), which speak vividly to the injustices based upon diversity.[1] Consequently, human rights are often understood as a legal refuge for claims that arise from the diverse character of the citizenship of nation-states. I argue in this chapter that this is a flawed approach, and that human rights form *one* of *many* necessary legal responses to the challenges of justice in diverse societies. To support this claim, first I consider the historical context of contemporary human rights and show that the twinning of human rights and diversity is a legacy of this history, that the universal claims made by contemporary human rights ignores the local and specific nature of diversity and that contemporary human rights are born of a fear of the extreme consequences of asserting difference. Secondly, I support this claim by critically analysing Sebastian Poulter's (1998) justification of human rights as a benchmark to frame the legal accommodation of Britain's ethnic minorities. Through this analysis I highlight the empirical and conceptual difficulties of employing human rights as the sole legal response to diversity.

The Historical Context of Contemporary Human Rights

It is worth noting that consideration of the history of human rights also benefits from the adoption of a contextual approach. The twinning of human rights with diversity is not a contemporary phenomenon and can be seen in regimes prior to those developed under the auspices of the United Nations. For example, regimes to protect religious minorities can be traced back as far as the Treaty of Westphalia 1648 (Leuprecht 2001: 112). Concern for minorities became particularly prominent after the First World War, when protection was extended to racial, religious and

1 For further elaboration of the relations between the inherent dignity of human beings and the promotion of justice, peace and democracy see the preambles of the UDHR, the European Convention for the Protection of Human Rights and Fundamental Freedoms, the International Covenant on Economic, Social and Cultural Rights and the International Covenant on Civil and Political Rights.

linguistic minorities in the Versailles Treaty of 1919 (Steiner and Alston 2000: 93–103). Human rights as a legal response to diversity are not, therefore, novel.

Prior to the Second World War and the beginnings of our contemporary human rights regimes, the League of Nations responded to diversity with a range of minorities' treaties and declarations. The period following the First World War was one where much attention was given to the protection of minorities, whether they were racial, religious or linguistic. This characterisation of the problems in Europe followed from the nature of the First World War; one of the immediate causes of the First World War was the ethnic nationalism of the southern Slavs, and the end of this war saw the disintegration of the Austro-Hungarian, Ottoman, German and Russian Empires. Thus, the protective treaties and declarations that came after the First World War reflected an acute awareness of the significance of ethnicity, as well as acting as a response to the redrawing of maps within Europe and the consequential increased incidence of minority groups within nation-states. Treaties were put in place to protect minorities in Central and Eastern Europe, including Austria, Bulgaria, Czechoslovakia, Greece, Hungary, Poland and Romania. Similar declarations to secure the rights of minorities in Albania, Estonia, Latvia and Lithuania were also entered into (Steiner and Alston 2000: 94–5). These treaties and declarations had varied contents, although broadly they all sought to ensure equality. Equality was interpreted in *Minority Schools in Albania* to require a substantive form,[2] as opposed to equality in fact and thus special treatment was a legitimate mechanism to achieve this substantive equality.

This pre-Second World War legal response to diversity can be contrasted with the contemporary human rights approach in at least two ways. First, this historical approach to diversity focused upon the power structures that make the protection of minority groups necessary, as opposed to the universal common humanity emphasised by current human rights regimes. Secondly, the minority treaties and declarations were group-specific, and can therefore be described as a particularised approach to diversity. In contrast, on the whole, the contemporary human rights regime does not target specific groups and is, therefore, not particularised.[3]

Contemporary human rights are a product of the post-Second World War climate, and this has significant ramifications for the manner in which they respond to diversity. After the Second World War there was a shift away from the group-specific particularised minorities protection under the League of Nations. The memory of the Third Reich's heinous use of ethnicity as a tool to legitimate

2 Advisory Opinion, Permanent Court of International Justice, 1935, Series A/B-No 64, extracted in Steiner and Alston (2000: 96–102).

3 In some ways the current human rights regime can be described as one that targets specific groups. For example, there are UN sponsored treaties that concern indigenous minorities and refugees. There are, however, no treaties concerned with geographical specificity in the way that the League of Nations approached minority groups. There are, therefore, no treaties concerned with Canadian or Australian indigenous minorities, or political refugees from Zimbabwe.

territorial annexations, together with the racial hierarchies intrinsic to theories that underpinned the genocide that occurred under Hitler's rule, has had a significant impact upon the trajectory taken by the United Nations and the Commission on Human Rights, led by Eleanor Roosevelt. Whereas the League of Nations responded to the presence of minority groups in nation-states by procuring a guarantee of protection and equality from the dominant governments, the United Nations sponsored treaties were premised upon the notion that this level of protection was best achieved by encouraging a more general respect for human rights and by not surrendering these moral standards to national interests.[4] The experience of ethnic nationalism and genocide during the Second World War engendered an urgent and strongly felt need to emphasise common humanity, rather than focus upon difference and diversity, especially if difference could manifest itself in terms of national sovereignty. This has resulted in a regime where the challenges of plural societies are addressed from a global vantage point, from within a spectrum of human rights that apply equally to all, without distinction.

In practice, a small number of the plethora of human rights have come to be used regularly in defence of diversity. These include freedom of religion, freedom of expression, freedom of association and assembly, the right to a private and family life and equality provisions.[5] My argument is that contemporary human rights regimes are creatures of their political climates and therefore reflect a level of anxiety with the assertion of non-dominant identities and difference. This, no doubt, has some impact upon the interpretation of those rights that may be used by those seeking to protect their non-dominant status. Indeed, my claim is that this compromises their status as a complete and comprehensive legal response to the challenges of justice in diverse societies.

A full exploration of this claim requires further explanation of how the climate in which human rights came into being compromises their role as *the* legal response to diversity. The universal claims made by human rights, and the ways in which they overlook the specificity of diversity, mirrors a theme identified in globalisation literature. Klug (2000) identifies a tension between the uniforming tendencies of globalisation and the need for particular and local responses to local issues. Whilst Klug explores this tension in the context of South Africa's political reconstruction, and notes the importance for South Africans to feel that the processes of political reconstruction were a South African response to a

4 Mrs Eleanor Roosevelt expressed this opinion when discussing minorities before the UN General Assembly in 1947. See UN Doc A/C 3/SR 161 at 726, quoted in Poulter (1998: 77).

5 This is not an exhaustive list. The purpose of my treatment of human rights is not to inquire into the coverage of human rights in their approach to diversity. There are now a great many treaties in this field, and other enumerated rights, that would have to be considered in detail in any analysis of the substantive content of human rights regimes *qua* diversity. Instead, my purpose is to substantiate the claim that human rights cannot be the sole legal response to the challenges of justice in diverse societies.

South African problem, other scholars have also theorised the relations between globalisation and local specificities. Robertson (2003) argues that in order to understand globalisation, it is necessary to go beyond its homogenising tendencies and appreciate it as a force for local specificity and hybridisation; this he terms 'global localization'. Furthermore, Menski (2006: 12) identifies this tension in the context of crafting a globality-conscious comparative framework through which to analyse the legal systems of Asia and Africa, stating that 'as globalisation becomes stronger and more mature, the inherent contradiction between unifying ambitions and plurifying realities becomes more apparent'.

This contradiction, between the uniform and plural local specificities, goes to the heart of the difficulty of human rights as comprehensive responses to the problems that arise in diverse societies. Human rights pull in the direction of uniformity because they are founded upon the principle that the 'recognition of the inherent dignity and of the equal and inalienable rights of *all members of the human family* is the foundation of freedom, justice and peace *in the world*' (UDHR Preamble; emphasis added).[6] Whilst the 'unifying ambition' of contemporary human rights is grounded in sound normative foundations and has clear merit,[7] to take them as a comprehensive answer to the challenges of justice in diverse societies ignores our 'plurifying realities' and the very real need to tailor legal responses to local needs and specific diversities within nation-states, not least because this hybridisation is the consequence of the specific climate within each nation-state.

Sebastian Poulter's Human Rights Framework

Sebastian Poulter devoted a considerable portion of his academic work to the topic of law and Britain's ethnic minorities, as he termed British diversity.[8] He maintained from a very early stage that English law could accommodate ethnic minority customs, as he termed them,[9] to the extent that they did not encroach upon 'certain core values in English society' (Poulter 1986: v–vi). He later

---

6 I believe this tension sits at the heart of a number of familiar debates within human rights. In particular, I mean to refer to the debates over collective and individual rights, the ethnocentric and imperial nature of human rights and cultural relativism/universalism debates, sometimes referred to as the Asian Values debate.

7 The UN's Commission on Human Rights worked for three years before the framework of the UDHR was adopted. During this time, many scholars, jurists and humanitarians debated the idea of human rights, and in so doing created a clear philosophical foundation for the ideas sketched out in the UDHR.

8 As well as numerous journal publications on these issues, he published three books devoted to this topic: Poulter (1986, 1990, 1998).

9 By labelling these practices as ethnic minority customs, Poulter devalued these practices, in contrast to English *law*, which was accorded a superior status merely by not being labelled as a set of customs.

explained that maintaining these core values would allow the 'cohesiveness and unity of English society as a whole ... to be preserved intact' (Poulter 1998: 391).[10] Throughout his earlier works in this field Poulter failed to provide a list of the core values he referred to, preferring instead to highlight those ethnic minority customs that transgress them (Poulter 1986). However, in his last work he identified basic civil liberties, which by implication include 'democracy, the rule of law, natural justice, freedom of expression and religious toleration', as forming the 'bedrock of British values' (Poulter 1998: 23). He even went on to express the dynamic nature of these core values (1998: 25):

> On the other hand, ethnic traditions, beliefs, and values must not be denied the opportunity of influencing the future content of the shared institutional values of the country as a whole. These values are not immutable and just as women's perspectives have profoundly affected their development during the course of the twentieth century, so the viewpoint of the ethnic minority communities can be expected to achieve similar results during the course of the next century.

Indeed, Poulter provided greater substance to his core values formula by using international human rights law as a benchmark by which English legal responses to ethnic minorities ought to be assessed. It should be noted that although Poulter uses other comparative frames of reference, international human rights law forms the 'major comparative frame of reference' in his last publication in this field (Poulter 1998: 68).[11] In using international human rights law as a frame of reference Poulter is led to set out his justifications for this choice, and these reasons present an opportunity to outline further the difficulties of using human rights to respond to diversity, and to demonstrate the importance of locally relevant arguments.

Poulter's Five Justifications for Adopting a Human Rights Framework

Poulter provides five reasons to support his use of international human rights law as a comparative framework (1998: 69–71):

1. Poulter states that the issues arising from the subject matter of his book fall into the broad category of civil liberties, making human rights the obvious comparator, having earlier summarised his subject matter as the examination of 'the reaction of the English legal system to the presence of these four groups [Muslims, Hindus, Sikhs and Rastafarians]' (1998: v).
2. He notes the increasing judicial reference in the English courts to the ECHR and the judgments of the ECommHR and European Court of Human Rights

10 For more detail on the connection between the maintenance of core values and the cohesiveness of British society see Poulter (1998: 26).

11 In fact, as Menski (1999: 139) states, Poulter (1998) was his final publication of any extended length, as he passed away in April 1998.

(ECtHR). Although there is no explicit reason put forth that explains the relevance of this, the implication is that increasing judicial reference makes them increasingly relevant to the English legal system.[12]

3. Poulter appealled to the wide acceptance of the moral standard enshrined within international human rights frameworks by emphasising the number of European countries that are parties to the ECHR.[13] He goes on to argue that these standards are universal (or very nearly so) by virtue of the large numbers of signatories to the international treaties that form the human rights regime. His reference to international treaties extends well beyond the International Covenant on Civil and Political Rights (ICCPR) and the International Covenant on Economic, Social and Cultural Rights (ICESCR), and includes the International Convention on the Elimination of All Forms of Racial Discrimination (CERD), the Convention against Discrimination in Education, the Convention on the Elimination of All Forms of Discrimination against Women (CEDAW) and the Convention on the Rights of the Child (CRC).
4. Poulter argued that a human rights dimension could be justified by virtue of the lack of written constitution with an entrenched bill of rights in Britain. Prior to the incorporation of the ECHR into English law, he explained, there were no guarantees against religious discrimination and persecution in Britain, and given that the English legal system developed when there were very few non-Christians, it is a system that can sometimes treat non-Christian religions unequally.
5. Poulter claimed that this comparative framework could be justified on the grounds that human rights protect minority groups. Majorities are protected by democratic process, whereas minorities are in a more vulnerable position. In support of this claim, he quotes Dworkin who argues, *inter alia*, that rights are crucial as they enshrine 'the majority's promise to the minorities that their dignity and equality will be represented. When the divisions among groups are most violent, then this gesture, if law is to work, must be most sincere' (Dworkin 1977: 205, quoted in Poulter 1998: 71).

Comments on Poulter's Five Justifications

In my consideration of these five justifications, I aim to provide further support for my claim that human rights have a valuable role to play in law's responses to

12 The regional human rights regime in Europe is the relevant framework in the context of English law since the UK has submitted to its jurisdiction.

13 In 1998 there were 40 European countries that were party to the ECHR; however, there have been some significant additions to the list of signatories since then, and by August 2010 there were 47 European countries that were party to the ECHR. See http://conventions.coe.int/Treaty/Commun/ListeTableauCourt.asp?MA=3&CM=16&CL=ENG for a list of signatories (last accessed 21 September 2010).

diversity, but that they are not the only dimension that lawyers need to consider when thinking about law and diversity. Moreover, I hope also to demonstrate the saliency of my claim that law's role in meeting the challenges of diversity must include consideration of local specificities.

Poulter's first, second and fifth reasons for employing a human rights framework are unconvincing owing to a lack of any detailed explanation of these claims. Turning to Poulter's first justification, he argues that civil liberties are the natural home for the issues raised by diversity, but provides no explanation of why this is the case. It is true that in many legal systems the problems of difference and diversity have been characterised as civil liberties claims. For example, in the United States, African Americans fought segregation on the basis that it infringed basic civil liberties and, in Britain, the increasing diversity brought by post-war migration was responded to with increasing controls on racially discriminatory behaviour which alluded to the ideal of equality. However, this represents one legal characterisation of the issues raised by diversity, and Poulter provides no arguments to sustain the claim that civil liberties are the definitive legal characterisation of the problems of diversity. By drawing upon the empirical reality of the British Muslim experience, Pearl and Menski (1998: 74–7) conclude that British Muslims are agents in the creation of hybrid laws, which they label *angrezi shariat*, and their occurrence results from the competing demands of ethnic minority laws and English law. The very concept of hybrid laws and legal systems beyond the dominant system in a nation-state, as well as the legal issues that arise when there is a conflict between these legal systems, demonstrates a dimension to diversity and law that is not captured by the exclusive civil rights characterisation that Poulter adopts. Whilst civil rights have a vital role to play in understanding the relations between diversity and law, it does not, however, allow for the conclusion that they ought to be *the* framework when constructing the boundaries and limitations to the English legal system's accommodation of diversity.

Poulter's second argument, that increasing judicial reference to the ECHR and the judgments of this treaty's judicial organs (the ECommHR and the ECtHR) justifies a human rights dimension when defining Britain's core values, merely reproduces a framework that English law already employs in its adjudication of such disputes. As such, perpetuating the current *status quo* will provide no greater insights into the relations between diversity and law. By using the same frame of reference as English law,[14] on the grounds that English law uses this framework, Poulter's work goes no further than providing a descriptive analysis of the *status quo*. This second reason, therefore, provides no sound justification for the human rights dimension employed in Poulter's study.

---

14 My criticism here carries strong tones of the Humian problem of deriving an *ought* from an *is*. However, I am somewhat sceptical that the is-ought division should have blanket application since I believe empirical realities can provide us with useful and important philosophical insights that can, and should, influence prescriptive statements.

Poulter's fifth justification, namely that human rights exist for the protection of minorities, is also weak. Poulter quotes Dworkin to support his argument; however, he misconstrues Dworkin's claims. Dworkin makes (part of) his case for 'taking rights seriously' on the premise that rights, not just human rights, have the potential to protect minority groups in democracies that are based on a form of majoritarianism. As part of this justification, Dworkin's claims, therefore, do not ground a focus upon human rights in exclusion to other legal rights.

Although Poulter's first, second and fifth justifications do not stand up to scrutiny, neither do they give us reason to exclude a human rights dimension. Instead, they lead to the conclusion that human rights have *a* role, not *the* role, to play in the consideration of the English legal system's responses to diversity. Whilst I do not believe Poulter's third and fourth justifications provide sound reasons for adopting a human rights framework, in considering these two justifications in greater detail it is possible to see in greater depth why human rights cannot be the exclusive reference point when framing legal responses to diversity, but that they have an important role to play.

Human Rights, Morality and Legal Pluralism

Poulter argues that international human rights provisions hold significant moral weight. He evidences this by pointing out the considerable numbers of signatories to the main regional and international human rights instruments. In contrast, I argue that the value of human rights as a comparative framework for law lies in its codification of (some) moral values, and not in the universal nature of these moral values. If one understands morals as the regulation of the way individuals and groups should interact with one another, human rights law certainly has moral content. Yet, there is a crucial difference in valuing human rights law because of its moral content, and valuing it because it embodies a universal moral code. Poulter's reference to the considerable number of countries that are parties to human rights instruments suggests that, for him, their appeal lies in the near universal moral code that they represent.[15] Valuing human rights in this non-universal manner follows from a plural understanding of law. In contrast, Poulter's approach betrays a state-centric understanding of law that I believe limits the potential of law's role in meeting the challenges of justice in diverse societies.

There are many varied theories of legal pluralism. However, the focus of my perspective in this project is based upon Professor Werner Menski's 'global working definition of law' (2006: 173–90) and his later additions to this definition

15 Conflating the signing of an international treaty with a nation-state's approval of the content of that treaty oversimplifies international relations. There are a complex variety of factors that a country considers when deciding to commit itself to international obligations, including the impact that failing to sign will have on the international status of a country and its ability to participate in a global economy.

(Menski 2009).[16] I provide a full account of this model in a later chapter, but for the purposes of my argument here it is crucial to note that this model involves an understanding of law as the product of a variety of sources and processes that go beyond the nation-state. Menski isolates four main sources of law: (1) the state; (2) society; (3) religion/ethics/morality; and (4) international human rights law. These sources broadly correlate to the three main schools of dominant jurisprudence; the state corresponds with positivism, society corresponds with socio-legal theories, and religion/ethics and morality together with international human rights law correspond with natural law theories. Moreover, these sources represent the four main factors that influence lawyers' decisions and choices. Menski likens these push-pull factors to flying a kite: the skill lies in negotiating all of these influences and keeping the kite in flight (2009). It is important to note that these four sources, together with their jurisprudential counterparts, are internally plural and varied, and are not as easily delineated as this categorisation suggests (2006: 183–6).

Menski's kite-like model of law provides a neat illustration of why human rights, with their moral content, have a role, rather than the role, to play in the examination of law and diversity. If we take Poulter's approach and view the rules, principles and norms within ethnic minority communities as customs and traditions rather than laws, this places them in a subservient position to law. In this characterisation, positive law takes on a dominant, privileged position and the boundaries of toleration and accommodation are drawn according to the terms of the dominant player, namely state law. An assimilationist approach, where incoming immigrants are expected to learn the ways of the dominant groups, follows from Poulter's perspective. However, this assumption of assimilation does not correspond with social realities and therefore fails to explain the persistent occurrence of these minority customs and traditions amongst non-dominant groups. In contrast, Menski's model, which posits these customs and traditions as laws, sheds light upon this persistent occurrence because it conceptualises a scenario where laws are competing against each other and pulling in various directions. Menski's perspective reveals a greater intensity of conflict and tension than Poulter's approach permits. Moreover, by viewing the issues that diversity raises for state law through Menski's prism, we are driven to ask how these conflicts and

16 There are innumerable different categorisations applied by different legal pluralists to the various different models of legal pluralism, but helpfully Anderson (2005: 45–9) divides the history of legal pluralism into three chronological phases, which he terms 'classical legal pluralism', 'post-colonial legal pluralism' and 'globalization and legal pluralism'. Classical legal pluralism is epitomised by the work of Hooker (1975), Pospísil (1975), Roberts (1979) and Moore (1978); examples of post-colonial legal pluralism are found in the work of Macaulay (1963) (whose work was largely ignored until the mid-1970s), Greenhouse (1982), as well as feminist scholars such as Manji (1999) and Boyd (1997); globalisation and legal pluralism is the concern of scholars such as Teubner (1997). Anderson suggests that a fourth phase of 'critical legal pluralism' may also be identifiable (2005: 49). This phase, he claims, can be seen in the work of Santos (2002). For further overviews of the theories of legal pluralism see J. Griffiths (1986); Merry (1988); and A. Griffiths (2002).

tensions can be resolved so that justice is done, rather than asking how far state laws can tolerate ethnic minority customs, as Poulter does (1986: v–vi).

In showing that human rights have *a* role, rather than *the* role, to play in furthering law's role in meeting the challenges of justice in diverse societies, I have also illustrated the crucial impact of the underlying premises of the conception of law for my arguments. Moreover, I have argued that a plural approach to law, as taken in Menski's model, facilitates a characterisation of the challenges presented by diversity that explains the social realities in diverse societies. This allows us to be clearer about what conflicts and tensions exist within these communities, and in turn may provide a greater opportunity to fulfil law's potential in meeting the challenges of justice in diverse societies. Poulter's fourth justification also permits the introduction and consideration of arguments that are significant to this book.

Human Rights, Diversity and Constitutions

Poulter's fourth justification for focusing upon human rights when framing English law's response to diversity is based upon Britain's lack of written constitution and entrenched bill of rights. He argued that English law contains an inherent bias towards Christian religions on account of its historical evolution in a time when the numbers of non-Christians were insignificant. Human rights, and in particular the ECHR, represent, therefore, a back door route for the enforcement of religious equality. Not only do I argue that Poulter is wrong to suggest that the ECHR can neutralise any religious bias there may be in the British Constitution, or bias in any constitution, I believe his claim highlights the significance of the constitutional dimension of law's role in meeting the challenges of justice in diverse societies.

There are, therefore, two points to be made about this claim. First, Poulter's claim suggests that the ECHR regime provides a mechanism to redress the religious bias inherent in the British Constitution. This, I believe, is an overambitious claim that fails to take into account the delicate political balance maintained by the supranational judicial organs of the ECHR that attempt to ensure that some measure of state sovereignty is retained. The case of *Choudhury v UK* is illustrative of my point here (and is one that Poulter references to sustain his fourth justification (1998: 71)).[17]

Choudhury forms part of a series of legal challenges connected to the Rushdie affair; thus, a brief note about the Rushdie affair is necessary by way of context. In 1988 Salman Rushdie published his novel, *The Satanic Verses*, and Muslims across the globe felt its contents were disrespectful and insulting to Islam and the Prophet Mohammed.[18] Abdul Choudhury began proceedings, arguing that the relevant British authorities ought to prosecute Salman Rushdie and his publishers for the offence of blasphemy. In the domestic courts, his judicial review proceedings failed

17 (1991) 12 Human Rights LJ 172.

18 Modood (1990) provides a more detailed account of the Rushdie affair.

and it was held that the offence of blasphemy under English law only protected Christianity, and therefore did not cover any other religions.[19]

Having exhausted his domestic remedies, Choudhury took his complaint to the ECommHR, alleging that the UK had breached its obligations under Articles 9 and 14 of the ECHR. He claimed that the UK had failed to ensure the freedom of religion (Article 9 ECHR) of Muslims as a consequence of its discriminatory blasphemy law (Article 14 ECHR). The ECommHR held that freedom of religion under Article 9 of the ECHR did not include the right to bring specific forms of legal proceedings when religious feelings are offended. In essence, Article 9 ECHR does not require a state to make blasphemy an offence under state laws. Since the issue fell outside of the ECHR, the non-discrimination provisions in Article 14 were not engaged, and given that this part of the claim was therefore inadmissible the ECommHR did not consider it.[20] *Choudhury* illustrates that the human rights regimes cannot be relied upon as substitutes for national constitutional guarantees of non-discrimination.

The second point to be made relates to this argument that human rights regimes cannot act as substitutes for national constitutions. If diversity raises issues of constitutional significance, these matters need to be addressed directly, rather than the only recourse being supranational constitutional rights in the form of human rights.[21] It is insufficient and inappropriate to paper over lacunas in our legal responses to diversity by substituting them with written documents that can act as national constitutions, or neutralise the biases within national constitutions, not least because they were not adopted with this purpose in mind. Furthermore, given the richness of the scholarship that focuses upon the British Constitution itself, lawyers should not be wary of approaching these issues merely because they will need to grapple with an unwritten constitution. This is not to say that the ECHR has no constitutional significance in Britain, or that human rights regimes have no significance for diverse nation-states; rather, I argue that these regimes cannot fulfil a role that was not part of their design at the time of drafting. The nature of Poulter's fourth justification does, however, suggest that there are constitutional dimensions to law's responses to diversity, and that these dimensions merit considered analysis.

---

19 See *R v Chief Metropolitan Stipendiary Magistrate, ex parte Choudhury* [1991] 1 QB 429.

20 The non-discrimination provisions in Article 14 ECHR are not freestanding. In order for a claim to be admissible, one of the substantive rights in the ECHR must be engaged. It is not necessary for a state to be found in violation of a substantive right under the ECHR for Article 14 ECHR to become operative. Thus it is possible that a state permissibly interferes with a right under the ECHR, but that it is in violation of Article 14 ECHR, because it has applied that permissible interference in a discriminatory manner. See, for example, *Belgian Linguistics Case (No 2)* (1968) 1 EHRR 252.

21 I address the constitutional dimensions of diversity in Chapter 10.

Conclusions

In my consideration of Canada's constitutional test for Aboriginal rights, I evidenced a tension between the need for certainty in dominant legal systems and the inherent fluidity of identity processes. A lack of awareness of this tension limits law's potential in its responses to diversity and produces sites of injustice, precisely because it inhibits and distorts identity processes, which are so central to our contemporary sense of the authentic self. Furthermore, a contextual approach to the Race Relations Acts 1965–1976 revealed an underlying narrative that twinned halting non-white immigration to Britain with race relations amongst Britain's existing non-white immigrants. The focus of this narrative, I argued, limits law's potential to do justice (in its diversity-conscious meaning) in response to diversity. This limited potential is evident in the amendments to the RRA 1976. However, I argued that these amendments have had and will have little impact upon law's potential, precisely because they fail to alter the underlying narrative of this legislation. The inability of these amendments to change law's potential speaks, I claim, of the significance of sound normative foundations for legal responses to diversity. However, my analysis of human rights demonstrates that sound normative foundations alone do not provide law with the potential to fulfil its promise of justice. Instead, through consideration of human rights as a legal response to diversity, I have argued that it is also vital to balance the global or universal ambitions of such responses with the local or specific demands that these responses aim to meet. I demonstrated that this requires the inclusion of accounts of our social realities as a key element of any legal response to diversity. It follows from this that the ways in which the idea of law is conceptualised has ramifications for the perspective taken on by both of these issues. Finally, in considering the role of human rights when responding to diversity, I argued that it is vital to recognise that there are many dimensions to these legal responses, one of which is constitutional, and that there can be no substituting of these dimensions, as each has an important role to play. This analysis of human rights and its role in relation to diversity, has enabled me to demonstrate further the need to expand law's role if it is to meet the challenges of my diversity-conscious justice in the context of diversity.

PART III
A Local Normative Framework

Chapter 6
A Triad of Norms

Analysis of contemporary legal responses to diversity and human rights led to the conclusions that: (1) sound normative foundations provide a starting point for expanding law's role in meeting the challenges of justice; (2) there is an inherent conflict between the certainty required by dominant legal systems, and the dynamism of identity processes: awareness of this tension might aid law in its avoidance of the injustices caused when this contradiction is overlooked; and (3) the universal ambitions of dominant legal systems need to be balanced with the local and specific nature of diversity. Using this analysis, I also made a case to expand law's role if it is to meet the challenges of justice.

In this chapter I pick up where I left off with my earlier global normative framework and begin constructing a local normative framework that aims to address these conclusions, and further the idea of expanding law's role. The norms that I argue for in this Part II of the study seek to build upon the normative foundations that I set out in Part I so that room is made for the specificities and dynamism of diversity, and law's universal ambitions can be tempered. This local normative framework provides a fresh and expanded perspective on law's role in meeting the challenges of a diversity-conscious justice.

In this chapter I first illustrate that dominant legal systems function as a form of normative shorthand. I argue that it is insufficient for the norms promised by legal responses to diversity to be implicit or assumed. Moreover, given my fresh perspective on justice, these norms need to be reworked. Therefore, in the second part of this chapter, I turn to set out a triad of norms that contribute to my fresh and expanded perspective on law and diversity. This triad consists of the norm of heterogeneity, expansive justice and post-coloniality, and they are designed to support law in meeting the challenges of a diversity-conscious justice.

Law as Normative Shorthand

Law has plural sources and functions, but the focus of my commentary here is positive law in the sense of legislation and case law, and its function as a form of normative shorthand. Chiba (1986) terms the form of law that I am focusing upon here 'official law'.[1] He defines official law as 'the legal system sanctioned

1 Before introducing Chiba's terminology I have been using labels such as 'positive law' or 'dominant legal systems'. These alternative terms are intended to be understood as being the same as Chiba's 'official law'.

by the legitimate authority of a country', and therefore his definition is more inclusive than just state law, although this is the typical form of official law (1986: 5). Official law acts as normative shorthand because legal claims rest upon legal rights, which, in turn, invoke normative frameworks that underpin these rights (Anderson 2005: 4–6). There are two interdependent levels to official law's norm invoking character: first and second order norms.

First order norms are invoked by using a particular piece of legislation, or by framing a claim in terms of a particular human right, and so on. For example, a claim under anti-discrimination legislation appeals to the normative priority of a society of equals,[2] whilst a freedom of religion claim is grounded upon the idea, inter alia, of liberal individual autonomy and the open choice of each individual's conception of the good life. It is assumed that these first order norms are largely already settled in their content. For example, human rights claims invoke solid normative platforms in the form of the discussions and academy that gave rise to various international and regional human rights instruments. Furthermore, legal claims framed by reference to an official law passed in accordance with the protocol in a nation-state invoke the normative framework laid out in the various official discussions that take place before that law is passed. Whilst these first order norms are assumed to be *largely* settled, there are, however, instances where they require interpretation or clarification, and it is notable that there are usually rules regulating how and when this can be done. If, for example, the wording of an Act of Parliament in the UK is unclear, the English courts have ruled that reference can be made to the relevant discussions in Parliament by virtue of Hansard (*Pepper v Hart*).[3]

The final (uncontroversial) source of official law in most nation-states is case law. It is far more difficult to separate out first order norms from second order norms in this form of official law. However, I believe the first order norms in case law can be found in the landmark judgments of the upper courts. By this I mean those judgments that have become strong precedents and which capture or clarify the spirit behind official law in that particular area. I do not mean to suggest that the *ratio decidendi* of such a case represents first order norms; rather, that such judgments move from these first order norms in order to reach their factually specific conclusions.

Law also clarifies second order norms, although they remain more open to argument and dynamic than first order norms, at least within forums legitimated by the official legal system. In the context of official laws, these second order norms take shape during legal arguments and involve discussion of the correct interpretation of official laws. Claims to the right to life, for example, invoke the

---

2 In the case of the RRA 1976, I argued in Chapter 4 that the assumption that this legislation is based upon ideas of equality and justice is misplaced given its socio-political context. However, I stressed that whilst this assumption is misplaced, legislation such as the RRA 1976 nevertheless holds out the promise of such norms.

3 [1993] AC 593.

first order norms of liberal individual autonomy, rational dignified woman and the good life, but consideration of when life begins, or whether life includes dignified death, involves the discussion of second order norms. My concern in this chapter is not these second order norms; in fact their availability to discussion accommodates a dynamism and evolutionary nature that provides official law with some of its much coveted ability to respond to the changing nature of our worlds. It is, instead, the first order norms that inform legal responses to diversity that I believe need to be restated and reconsidered. Before adding to and modifying these norms, in order to provide the fresh and expanded perspective on law that I have made a case for, it is necessary to restate those main norms that official law promises, implicitly or explicitly, in its responses to diversity.

Three main first order norms can be isolated from official law's responses to diversity, although I should add that I do not claim to provide an exhaustive list of these norms. It is vital to clarify that the first order norms I set out here do not necessarily form the actual normative foundations of official law's responses to diversity. Rather, official law holds out the promise of these normative principles, and this promise is often implied from the content of these official laws. This is a subtle distinction that was illuminated by earlier arguments, where it was shown that the narrative underlying the Race Relations Acts 1965–1976 does not correspond to the promise of equality that this legislation holds out. It follows from this that these norms do not act to ensure that official law's responses to diversity form a coherent whole. In fact, official law's responses to diversity appear to be far more piecemeal than this, as if law is somehow muddling through in the face of intense plurality.

The first norm that official law promises is equality, and one such example of this can be found in the UDHR. Not only does the preamble recognise the 'inherent dignity' and 'equal and inalienable right of all members of the human family', but Articles 1 and 2, which enshrine the foundations of the UDHR, speak of the concept of equality. Article 1 states:

> All human beings are born free and equal in dignity and rights. They are endowed with reason and conscience and should act towards one another in a spirit of brotherhood.

Article 2 states:

> Everyone is entitled to all the rights and freedoms set forth in this Declaration, without distinction of any kind, such as race, colour, sex, language, religion, political or other opinion, national or social origin, property, birth or other status. Furthermore, no distinction shall be made on the basis of the political, jurisdictional or international status of the country or territory to which a person belongs, whether it be independent, trust, non-self-governing or under any other limitation of sovereignty.

Whilst the UDHR provides an eloquent example of official law's promise of equality, consideration of the case law which interprets prohibited direct racial discrimination under English law demonstrates how the notion of equality has evolved over the years. The definition of prohibited direct racial discrimination was elaborated in section 1(1) of the RRA 1976:[4] 'A person discriminates against another … if (a) on racial grounds he treats that other less favourably than he treats or would treat other persons …'. It is clear that this legislation attempts to promise equal treatment regardless of race,[5] but equally clear is the evolution of the concept by the courts in England and Wales in a manner that echoes changes in societal attitudes of what constitutes acceptable behaviour. Thus, in *De Souza v Automobile Association* the courts did not accept that a secretary overhearing her manager referring to her as 'the wog' when speaking with another employee constituted discrimination prohibited by the RRA 1976, since the secretary was never meant to hear this name-calling.[6] Such a case would surely not be followed today, and the courts are far more liberal in their interpretation of anti-discrimination legislation. See, for example, the *Burton v De Vere Hotels* case, where the comedian Bernard Manning was performing and making racist jokes in a hotel where the complainant was working as a waitress;[7] the employer of the waitress was held to be vicariously liable for the racist working environment that the claimant had to endure, even though the comedian was not an employee of the firm.

Of late, anti-discrimination measures, in the UK at the very least, have been grappling with the increasing confidence in difference that I argued is one of the implications of globalisation. I also mentioned earlier that Lord Macpherson concluded that the police were institutionally racist in their investigation of Stephen Lawrence's murder. Lord Macpherson's finding evidences a perceptible need to tailor services in accordance with people's diversities, rather than treat everyone alike.[8] This, I believe, is a response to the increasing confidence in difference that globalisation has brought about. Moreover, the new Equality and Human Rights Commission (EHRC), established by the EA 2006, evidences the importance of equality as a key normative principle in this field.

The second norm promised by official laws' responses to diversity is the value and merit attributed to religion, culture and ethnicity. Official law implicitly

4 The definition of prohibited direct racial discrimination can now be found in the EA 2010. However, since the case law relates to the RRA 1976, I continue to use that definition here.

5 Racial grounds are defined to cover 'colour, race, nationality or ethnic or national origins', s 3(1) RRA 1976.

6 [1986] IRLR 103.

7 [1996] IRLR 596.

8 Arguably the addition of s 71 RRA 1976, which is intended to address the problem of institutional racism identified by Macpherson, misses this point. This section places a duty upon public authorities to eliminate unlawful discrimination, promote equality of opportunity and promote good race relations; nowhere in this duty is there any mention of providing services in accordance with culture, colour or ethnicity.

suggests that these aspects of our identity add value to our lives and should therefore be treated as Rawlsian primary goods. This implication can be seen, for example, in the inclusion of freedom of religion as a fundamental right in the ECHR,[9] and the inclusion of the right to freedom of religion, thought and conscience in Article 18 of the UDHR. The value of religion can also be seen in the interpretation of secularism under India's constitution. India's secular constitution is seen as enshrining the doctrine that all religions are equidistant from the state (*sarva dharma sambhava*) (Engineer 1998: 1). The importance of culture can be seen in Canadian constitutional law, which protects the distinctive culture of its Aboriginal peoples.[10] Furthermore, the value of ethnicity can be seen in the exceptions that accommodate diversity, particularly amongst immigrant communities in the West. For example, section 17 of the Road Traffic Act 1988 in Britain exempts Sikhs from wearing crash helmets when riding motorcycles, on account of their turbans;[11] in 1990 the then Solicitor General of Canada, Pierre Cadieux, amended the uniform policy of the Royal Canadian Mounted Police to allow officers to wear turbans whilst on active duty; the Caravan Site Act 1968 in Britain recognises the Gypsy way of life; and, finally, the Adoption and Children Act 2002 in Britain makes provisions for a form of 'special guardianship', which is intended to accommodate non-Western forms of adoption where members of the wider family take children into their permanent care.[12]

The final norm relates to nation-building techniques that aim to encourage cohesion and nation-ness. Franck's narrative charting the evolution of loyalty referents within nation-states, and my analysis of Franck's claim, illustrates that traditional nation-building techniques have a tendency of appealing to commonalities and homogeneity in order to engender solidarity amongst citizens.[13] This link between solidarity and homogeneity has become a powerful imagining

9 See Article 9 ECHR; see also *Kokkinakis v Greece* (1994) 17 EHRR 397, where the ECtHR commented that Article 9 ECHR 'is in its religious dimension one of the most vital elements that go to make up the identity of believers and of their conception of life'. Note that Article 9 ECHR has a non-religious dimension since it also covers other forms of belief.

10 For more details on Aboriginal rights in Canada, see Chapter 4.

11 It is telling that the debates in the UK Parliament when this Bill was proposed centred upon the Anglo-Sikh military tradition; it was felt that it would be incongruent to ask Sikhs to take their turbans off and wear a helmet to ride motorcycles when they were not asked to do the same whilst they fought for Britain in two World Wars (Poulter 1998: 296). This legislation is, therefore, another example of an implied normative principle that is promised by this law, but is not reflected in its foundations.

12 See para 18 of the explanatory notes to the Adoption and Children Act 2002. This piece of legislation is especially interesting since this exception is almost hidden; but for the reference made in the explanatory notes, it is not evident that this legislation is designed to accommodate a non-dominant practice.

13 This argument was made in Chapter 3, where Franck's thesis was covered in greater detail.

within nation-states to the extent that it is now difficult to imagine diversities, pluralities and differences as having the capacity to permit a cohesive nation. Indeed, plurality and the one-ness attributed to a loyal citizenry seem antithetical to each other.

This norm of cohesive commonality is not only seen within public policy that uses the language of integration and common values, but a useful example can be seen within English law.[14] It is evident in those cases where official law enforces what is perceived to be a specifically British way of behaving and promotes a message of 'when in Rome, do as the Romans'. In the unreported case of *R v Adesanya*, a Nigerian mother scarred the face of her child in accordance with Yoruba traditions,[15] and was tried for the offence of actual bodily harm. She was convicted of the offence and the judge remarked that this sort of behaviour was not acceptable in Britain, even though it may be commonplace elsewhere. This mother was given an absolute discharge because the traditions took place in an air of celebration, they were only superficial in nature and, crucially, she was a new immigrant in Britain who could not yet be expected to be aware of British ways,[16] the implication being that, given enough time, immigrants will assimilate to British ways. It would be fair to say that judicial attitudes have evolved since this case; nevertheless, this norm can also be seen in more recent cases in Britain. For example, in *Gereis v Yagoub* a Coptic Orthodox Christian marriage took place in a church that was not licensed in accordance with the Marriage Acts, as required by English law, but was nevertheless upheld as valid because Aglionby J saw the marriage as one that bore all the hallmarks of an ordinary Christian marriage.[17] In the judge's reasoning in this case it is possible to see a willingness to accept a marriage that takes place in accordance with the British, Christian, way of life, whereas alien customs are denied any such validity, unless they fulfil the necessary requirements of English law.[18]

My intention here is not to provide a detailed consideration of these norms, particularly because none of them is especially controversial. Instead, my aim is to create a platform upon which a normative framework that can accommodate the specificities of diversity can be constructed. I have argued that fresh perspectives on diversity are necessary, and that these must have sound normative foundations. At present the normative frameworks underlying official law in this particular field are implied. There is, therefore, a mismatch between the assumed normative groundwork of official law and the issues that these laws actually attempt to resolve. In such circumstances it is unsurprising that the challenges of justice are neither clear nor are they being met. The fresh perspective on diversity that I offer

---

14 For a particularly overt example of this language in public policy see Blair (2006).

15 Unreported.

16 For a note on the case see *R v Adesanya* (1975) 24 ICLQ 136.

17 [1997] 3 FLR 755.

18 For further detail on marriage and diversity under English and American law see Hamilton (1995).

in this book must, therefore, have a clear normative framework that is expressly set out, since an assumed normative shorthand is insufficient and this, I argue, is detrimental.

I propose, in the remainder of this chapter, a triad of norms that position the perspective on diversity offered in this book. This triad of norms follows on from the global normative groundwork that was undertaken in Part I. The ground covered in these chapters was, however, global or universal in nature; my fresh perspective on justice, I believe, applies to any liberal plural nation-state. The normative framework proposed here is intended to make space for the local and specific experiences of diversity. The local dimension of this normative framework will, I believe, allow insights that speak to the social realities of diversity to find expression. Nevertheless, my aim, in setting out these local normative foundations, is also to achieve a conceptual clarity and integrity that appears to be currently lacking in this area.

A Triad of Norms

The triad of norms proposed here are: (1) heterogeneity; (2) expansive justice; and (3) post-colonial and post-9/11 peoples. To a small degree these norms are simply a statement of normative principles that were previously implied. To a much larger extent they are a modification of familiar normative principles with the aim of addressing the limits I identified in Part II of this book, and therefore expanding law's role beyond its current boundaries. The norms here have novel content and, where this is the case, the goal is to make space for the expression of the unique social realities of diversity and ground the expansion of law's role, so that it may meet the challenges of a diversity-conscious justice.

Heterogeneity

I argued earlier that two developments were acting to change the dynamic between nation-building techniques and their capacity to manage diversity.[19] First, I isolated communications across distances, both transnational and national distances, and explained that the accessibility of these distances has become easier.[20] Secondly, I stated that the strength of self-determination in matters of identity has reached hitherto unknown heights. Further exploration of exactly how these two elements have created a new confidence in difference provides the opportunity to illustrate that nation-building projects must learn to combine heterogeneity with ideas of

---

19 See Chapter 3.

20 By the onset of easier communications I mean to include telecommunications as well as web-based communications. Furthermore, by accessibility, I meant to refer to the greater ease of global travel.

national cohesion, rather than focusing upon core common values that all citizens must share.

The first element I have identified refers to phenomena that have been given labels such as transnational solidarity.[21] These developments have altered the way minority identities are able to express themselves. The accessibility of groups along all sorts of axes of diversity, whether it be along the lines of gender, Aboriginality, class or immigrant status, not only allows for the reinvigoration of connections that were previously difficult,[22] but also contributes to a far less separated psychological attitude amongst diverse societies. With this accessibility there is also an element of accountability to other like-minded individuals who can now form transnational groups; those who are considered to be different must now account for their chosen way of life amongst these newly accessible groups, as well as in their country of residence. This connection in turn impacts our impetus to maintain particular identities, as well as increasing the confidence with which those identities are expressed. Furthermore, web-based communications have intensified the confidence with which non-dominant identities are expressed. The anonymity that the internet provides enables users to search for and form web-based communities with like minded individuals without the fear of being ostracised for having identities that differ from those of dominant groups within a national territory. These virtual groupings of persons provide a critical mass that was not possible prior to these developments, and this mass bolsters a level of confidence that makes it increasingly difficult for nation-states to enforce an agenda of homogeneity. Diversity and difference is pushed forward in a manner that cannot be ignored and overridden without storing up issues and problems in the future.

The second factor I identified, namely the increased strength of self-determination of identities, further foregrounds diversity and makes the pursuit of homogeneity an unrealistic goal. We have moved from circumstances where nation-states had a considerable influence upon pivotal aspects of our identity, to a situation where individuals have a much greater say in the processes of their identities (Taylor 1994). Franck claims that 'we have entered a new era … that empowers each of us to ask who we are and then challenges us to make the answering of that question a central enterprise of our lives' (1999: 3). However, as I have already argued, I believe Franck exaggerates his claim for the 'Empowered Self'; this new era

---

21 The idea of transnationality has become a recognisable element of globalisation scholarship, particularly as studies in this field emphasise the increased levels of global interconnectedness as a signature element of globalisation. One prominent example of a text that considers globalisation to be a key dimension when comparing diverse legal systems is Menski (2006). Diverse here is taken to include both internal and external plurality. For more details on globalisation and transnationality, especially in the context of diasporas, see Vertovec (2008) and Vertovec and Cohen (1999).

22 I am referring here to the greater possibility that immigrants now have to maintain links to their countries of origin.

does not mean that identity is a matter of preference and choice; rather, that the focus of identity processes has shifted away from the nation-state, and towards the individual. Nevertheless, the nation-state is not without influence in these matters, nor does this focus upon individuals allow them to pick and choose their identities, as if choosing a red or blue jumper. It does not, as Franck interprets it, mean that individuals are not influenced by external facts, such as the group associations they may have, whatever that group connection may be based upon, whether it be familial, friendship, religious, gender, class or otherwise. Franck collapses the new ways in which individuals are able to determine their own identities with the advent of individual rights and, correspondingly, the demise of group rights.

As well as accessibility across greater distances influencing this self-determination of identities, this phenomenon has also been precipitated by developments in civil societies. Charles Taylor writes of the 'collapse of social hierarchies' that has taken place (1994: 26), and describes a world where identities were based upon honour giving way to democratic societies based upon the inherent dignity of all citizens. It does not follow from these changes that individual rights are prioritised over group rights. Acknowledging new identity processes does not necessarily correlate with the ushering in of an era of individualism and prophesising the demise of the influence of group associations. Franck, therefore, inflates the impact of technological developments upon today's societies.

My claim is that this development in identity processes, together with changes in the accessibility of and communications across distances, has blunted the nation-building technique of fostering a cohesive nation through enforcing homogeneity. One understanding of the nation-state is as a set of individuals with some sort of common thread, whether that be language, religion, culture, ethnicity, and so on. As I have illustrated, this commonality was often fictional, and was something that a nation-state would aspire to achieve. However, owing to the developments in modern technology that I have identified, we live in a world where the dynamic between diversity or heterogeneity and the nation-state has shifted. Diversity has been foregrounded in a way that makes this homogenising agenda not only ineffective, but also potentially harmful. Homogenising processes act to exclude, marginalise and even oppress those that are labelled as deviants from these dominant norms.

If developments in modern technology had not created this critical mass of confidence and self-determination, this technique may well be effective in its social engineering of behaviour. However, countered by this bolstered confidence and self-awareness, these nation-building processes act to alienate and oppress confident individuals, and this has a counter-productive impact on their feelings towards, loyalty and attachment to the nation-state of their residence. Moreover, the ease with which it is possible to form associations across national boundaries is amplified and more eagerly pursued as a consequence of this detachment from a nation-state of residence. It is this disenchantment, together with the growing identification with transnational associations, that is hijacked by terrorist groups

(Ignattieff 2003: 7).[23] My claim is that the changes in the dynamic between diversity and the nation-state that inform my fresh perspective on justice, mean that nation-building projects must take on a modified understanding and acceptance of diversity if they hope to be effective. It has become crucial to background dialogues that focus upon integration, such as legal mechanisms that claim to protect core values, and instead it is vital that the powerful historic imaginings of nations as homogenous are tempered, and the feasibility of cohesion, nation-ness and plurality is foregrounded. For official law, as a powerful tool in the project of nation-building, this signals the need to modify the conceptual tools it uses to approach the diversity related issues that come before it, if it is to pursue justice and ensure that the unique and specific experiences of diversity are not excluded from access to and participation in civil society.

Expansive Justice

The second element in this normative triad resembles Nancy Fraser's (2005: 73) 'participatory parity', which also forms part of my fresh perspective on justice. Fraser gives justice a general meaning of parity of participation, although her elaboration of this conception of justice shows it to be three-dimensional. These three dimensions correspond with the forms of injustice that can impede people from 'participating on a par with others, as full partners in social interaction' (2005: 73). These impediments to justice come in the form of distributive injustice, misrecognition and political injustice. The first two have been widely theorised, but Fraser summarises them as follows (2005: 73): distributive injustices refer to impediments to full participation as a consequence of economic structures that deny the resources necessary to participate; whereas misrecognition involves obstacles to participation on a par with peers as a result of 'institutionalised hierarchies of cultural value that deny' parity or even a platform from which to participate.

Political philosophers working within the redistribution paradigm are primarily concerned with theorising an egalitarian just society along socio-economic lines, and thus tend to be concerned with the egalitarian redistribution of resources and wealth. This paradigm is familiar and well established, with latter day proponents including John Rawls and Ronald Dworkin.[24] In contrast, the recognition paradigm is a more contemporary framework. Although such theories reclaim a (not so contemporary) Hegelian notion of recognition,[25] they are firmly rooted within a contemporary phase of political-philosophy that aims

---

23 I do not propose a solution to recent terrorist activities with this point; instead, I aim merely to shed some light on *one* of the many issues that surround this problem.

24 See, for example, Rawls (1993) and Dworkin (1977).

25 In fact, such theories do not just reclaim Hegelian recognition, they also reconstitute it. In its Hegelian form recognition is the antithesis of liberal individualism, although the same cannot be said of the politics of recognition. For example, Taylor (1994) attributes some of the modern condition which necessitates recognition to liberal individualism. It is,

to understand our very contemporary struggles over identity and difference and mould a just society based upon that understanding.[26] The main proponents of recognition theories are Charles Taylor, Jürgen Habermas, Nancy Fraser, Axel Honneth, James Tully and Iris Marion Young, although Young and Tully do not use the terminology of recognition.[27]

Whilst both of these dimensions of justice are political, in the layman's use of the term, Fraser seeks to isolate something qualitatively different in her final dimension of justice, namely political justice. She uses the term to convey the 'constitutive' aspects of a state; here justice concerns the ambit of the state's jurisdiction and the mechanisms through which it constructs the arenas where both redistribution and recognition disputes are resolved. Focused upon the more procedural aspects of justice, Fraser encapsulates this dimension of justice by terming it 'representation' (2005: 75). This third dimension of justice, which she argues is irreducible to either of the other two dimensions, has come to light, Fraser states, as a result of a consciousness of globalisation and 'post-Cold War geopolitical instabilities' (2005: 71). Globalisation challenges the dominant framework of sovereign territorial states and welfare state economies,[28] which in turn has changed how we argue about justice. Prior to these challenges, what Fraser labels the 'who' of justice was not in question; she contends that when we argued about justice we were in no doubt that it concerned the national citizenry, and actually argued over what it was that those citizens owed to each other (the 'what' of justice). However, with relations, at both citizen and supra-citizen level, spilling over territorial borders, the 'who' of justice is now up for debate, and this gives rise to recognising this political dimension to justice.

The above argument captures, I believe, a complex series of developments in the worlds that we all live in. Furthermore, the political dimension of justice is a convincing and accurate analysis of what these developments mean for theories of justice. However, I have summarised these claims in order to argue that, for the purposes of my claim, we need only take on this expansive understanding of justice, while leaving aside the details of its various dimensions. Fraser's three-dimensional justice is theorised in response to the vastly changed terrain in which

in part, liberal individualism that has precipitated a new attachment to the development of our own authentic identities.

26 Fraser links the rise of theories of recognition with the 'post-socialist condition' (1997: 1). The collapse of socialism gave rise to serious doubts about, and exhaustion with, the utopian ideals which underpinned socialist emancipatory reforms. This coincided with a change in the nature of political claims which, from this point on, began to be formed in terms of the recognition of group difference, moving away from redistribution claims. The final element of the post-socialist condition is rapid and aggressive marketisation giving rise to sharp material inequalities, which in turn have thrown equality based claims off-centre (Fraser 1997: 1–3).

27 See, for example, Fraser (1997, 2003a, 2003b, 2005), Habermas (1993, 1996, 2003), Honneth (1992, 1995, 2003a, 2003b), Tully (1995), Taylor (1994) and Young (1990, 2000).

28 Fraser calls this a 'Keynesian-Westphalian frame' (2005: 69).

justice must now be delivered, and this is the key to the way that justice must be understood in my normative triad. Fraser is concerned with putting forth a (global) theory of justice, which must work in a world where justice is not confined to the boundaries of nation-states. In contrast, I am concerned with the need to make room for the manifestation of plural forms of diversity. To put this another way, my aim is to take the local into account. I am not concerned with the construction of a global theory of justice. Thus, for the purposes of this normative framework, my argument is that it is vital to recognise that justice is expansive because it must be able to respond to the varied changes that are taking place across many societies, and it must continue to respond to changes in these societies since there is no endpoint to this trajectory of evolution.[29]

In this normative framework it is vital that justice becomes a living concept, with room to grow and change in harmony with the ebb and flow of societies, and to be interpreted according to the specific experiences of diverse groups within these societies. Assuming that justice has a fixed meaning merely produces a dialogue where concepts intended to address a particular set of injustices are contorted to fit different circumstances. As the ways in which we order our lives, and the ways that we understand our lives, evolve and vary across the globe, so should our understanding of justice. By giving my conceptualisation of a diversity-conscious justice a general meaning, whilst requiring here that it is an expansive concept, this dynamism and local specificity can be maintained. Moreover, making justice an evolving concept creates an obligation to revisit and reconsider what the challenges of justice entail when crafting new legal responses to diversity. This, therefore, avoids the possibility of limiting the normative frameworks that ground these new legal responses.

Post-colonial and Post-9/11 Peoples

The world is home to a great many diversities, but the focus of this project is those people that in some way or the other are part of non-dominant groups, or are non-dominant individuals, in liberal societies. Typically it is these groups whose voices have to compete with dominant voices to be heard. Often these non-dominant groups are categorised as minorities. However, this label is troubling, especially because my focus in this book is to consider those who are subjected to injustices and excluded from accessing or participating in civil society. Lord Bikhu Parekh, for example, rejects the terms 'minority' and 'majority', arguing that they are merely numerical concepts, and that he feels they remove the sense of community that attaches to the collections of individuals that come within this bracket (1990a:

29 I am confident that there is no endpoint to the changing terrain of the nation-state. Nation-states continue to experience new waves of migration, technological developments continue at a pace that does not appear to be slowing down and identity processes continue to evolve along many non-linear trajectories. An expansive understanding of justice sits well with an understanding of the nation-state amd identities as continually evolving projects.

60). On the basis that these collections of individuals are not formed by chance, and that there is sense of community which binds these groups together and, indeed, singles them out for protection, he prefers to see Britain, which is the focus of his studies, as a 'multi-communal' or 'plural' society.

There has also been some criticism of the concept of ethnicity on the basis that it is a nebulous concept that fails to capture the essence of the groups and individuals it seeks to pinpoint. Vertovec (2007: 1026) argues for a 'multi-dimensional perspective on diversity' that goes beyond ethnicity. He suggests that the axes of diversity are far more complex and wide-ranging than current social science labelling permits. He prefers, instead, to use the shorthand 'super-diversity' to convey this perspective, and challenges social scientists to explore novel ways of understanding diversity, so that we may shed light on patterns of injustice.

Taxonomies only make sense according to the logic that they work within, thus Foucault laughed at the Chinese typology of animals in the *Celestial Emporium of Benevolent Knowledge* which read as follows (quoted in Ali, Kalra and Sayyid 2006: 1):

> (a) belonging to the Emperor, (b) embalmed, (c) tame, (d) suckling pigs, (e) sirens, (f) fabulous, (g) stray dogs, (h) included in the present classification, (i) frenzied, (j) innumerable, (k) drawn with very fine camelhair brush, (l) et cetera, (m) having just broken the water pitcher, (n) that from a long way off look like flies.

This Chinese taxonomy of animals did not work within a logic that Foucault could appreciate. As arbitrary and absurd as these classifications seem to us, and to Foucault, they held meaning for the Chinese that were working within this logic, and thus it was epistemologically sound for them. I introduce this account to emphasise that in endeavouring to arrive at an appropriate label, the primary concern should be the structure within which this label must do its work. Since my primary concern is not the ethnicity or Aboriginality of these groups of people, nor is it, their status as a numerical minority, terms such as 'ethnic minorities' or 'Aboriginal peoples' are not helpful in this regard.[30]

My concern in this project is groups and individuals whose diversities result in them being excluded from participating in and/or accessing civil society. This injustice can occur along many lines; it may be ethnic or Aboriginal status, but it could also be based upon one's linguistic choices, gender, class, religion, belief system, age, sexuality, political beliefs, and so on. The list is not only endless, but these axes of injustices are, in many cases, not very easily separated; when we are excluded from civil society, it is quite likely that this exclusion is based upon a number of axes, rather than just one. These difficulties, with taxonomies

30 I should note that it has, nevertheless, served a useful purpose since it provides a globally understood method loosely to delineate the groups and individuals that form the focus of this project.

and the multi-dimensional, intensely plural, nature of diversity, leave me with no simple way of labelling difference other than terming it 'diversity', for the moment. At present, it is, I believe, far more appropriate to focus on the nature of the injustices that create the challenges that I seek to meet in this book. With that sound normative groundwork to my arguments, I can move on in later chapters to propose a new way of theorising this diversity that fits within my proposals for a new constitutional vista.

Although I am endeavouring to leave the door open as wide as possible to include the complex ways that diversity manifests itself, there is a common thread that can be broadly identified without trespassing into territory which homogenises diverse groups. In fact, this common thread is proposed with the intention that it makes space for diverse societies to negotiate their local specificities on their own terms. We are all, I believe, post-colonial and post-9/11 peoples.

Most, if not all, of the globe can be said to have been affected by colonisation in one way or another. Britain, for example, was not only a coloniser, it could be argued it is now going through a period of reverse colonisation. Following the Second World War Britain experienced labour shortages that were initially addressed by bringing in labour from European countries such as Poland. However, these European volunteer workers were unable to meet the demands for labour and so Britain began to recruit in the West Indies, one of its colonies. This then gave way to migration from other parts of the British Empire, such as South Asia, East Africa and Hong Kong. Primary migration, that is, worker migration, occurred largely in the 1960s and 1970s, although this was then followed by secondary migration in the form of family reunification and family formation (partners and dependent children and transnational marriages). Whilst the diversities that pose these contemporary challenges have their origins in these waves of post-war migration, a significant, and ever-increasing, number of generations are now born in Britain. Therefore, labelling them as immigrants mischaracterises them. I believe it is far more appropriate to label them according to the issues that are presenting themselves, namely diversity and the roots of this diversity, and therefore I prefer 'Afro-Asian diversity' as a collective noun that best describes Britain's diversity. It is clear, however, that Britain's engagement with colonisation did not end as its empire fractured. Afro-Asian diasporic settlement in Britain has been described as a 'postcolonial suffix to the colonial relationship between Britain and its … empire' (Ali, Kalra and Sayyid 2006: 15).

Countries such as Canada, Australia and the United States have also engaged with colonisation, albeit in different ways. These countries have histories of white settler colonisation that we are only just beginning to unravel. Moreover, countries that were part of empires during colonisation and have since achieved independence, also occupy and are negotiating post-colonial spaces. One such recent example can be seen in Kenya's adoption of a new constitution. Kenya's political system has been plagued with corruption, and this new constitution is intended to address this corruption in ways that the constitution it inherited after independence was not able to. Indeed, I would go so far as to argue that debates such as the Asian Values debate, and issues that focus upon East and West, or North and South, are linked to colonisation, and more precisely to the racial ideologies and hierarchies that were integral to colonisation.

There are some painful realities to empire that nation-states are still coming to terms with. The post-Second World War period of history has been dominated by recounting and recalling upheavals within Europe, and the United States, and the disjuncture and dislocation of an era of decolonisation has been pushed aside.[31] Moreover, periods of white settler colonisation, and processes of decolonisation are still so recent that their stories are only just being revealed. This lacuna leads to a misunderstanding of the nature and specificities of diversity that jeopardises the potential of all responses, legal or otherwise, to diversity. One example of this mischaracterisation can be seen in the narrative underlying British race relations legislation, where British Afro-Asians are cast as the problem.

Empires were predicated upon racial hierarchies, and colonisers ruled according to a pigmentocracy (Williamson 1944). However, it is not the injustice of empire that I wish to highlight with this norm; instead, I want to refer to a post-colonial condition that diverse societies are navigating as part of their identity processes. I have purposely avoided using the term 'the politics of recognition' precisely because of this post-colonial condition: Edward Said has warned us of the dangers of this kind of Orientalism, where the hegemonic 'white'/'West' claims the right to theorise the post-colonial experiences of the 'non-white'/'non-West' (Said 1995).[32] This post-colonial condition does not require recognition that colonialism involved the imposition of injustices to its colonial citizens and, therefore, some sort of reparation is due to their ancestors. Instead, it signals a need for institutions, including and beyond official laws, to shed their colonial structures and assumptions, which may in part persist because there has been a collective failure to address the darker side of colonialism. This task is by no means easy; however, I believe that nation-states are making strides towards doing this. Macpherson's recognition, for example, of the persistent institutional racism amongst the police represents an attempt to address entrenched colonial hierarchies within Britain's institutions. The extreme difficulty is that such exorcisms are excruciatingly painful in a world that likes to look back on history as the glory days. As a consequence, there is a tendency to sugar coat these bitter pills, as Macpherson did, and this leads to confusion: as a response to institutional racism, section 71 RRA 1976 fails to address the issues that Macpherson raised of providing services that are appropriate to all of our differences. Nevertheless, I am confident that with time nation-states will confront their colonial legacies.

31 The fact that history seems to be written by the victors also distorts our views of colonisation and decolonisation.

32 See Mudimbe (1988) and Inden (2000) for similar arguments in, respectively, the African and Indian contexts, and Fabian and Bunzl (1983) for a similar argument from an anthropological perspective.

The ability of institutions to navigate their colonial histories is only one-half of this final norm. Diverse communities must also navigate their own personal post-colonial condition. British Afro-Asians, for example, represent the 'racialised ex-colonial "immigrant" who stands betwixt and between citizen and foreigner, a colonial past and a national present, West and "non-West", one of us or one of them' (Ali, Kalra and Sayyid 2006: 30). Their decolonisation has not yet taken place. What, then, can be done to navigate this post-colonial condition? The expansive justice that I set out above, with its emphasis upon full, free and unencumbered participation in civil society as a living concept, goes some way to aid this navigation. However, in labelling diverse societies as post-colonial individuals and groups I aim to emphasise that this is a path that they must be given room to navigate themselves. We live in a world where the self-determination of identity processes is crucial, and post-colonial individuals and groups need to be given sufficient and appropriate spaces to exercise this self-determination in order to define their own personal brand of nation-ness.

The second element of this norm, that we are all post-9/11 peoples, refers to the attacks upon the Trade Towers in the United States. The difficulty with this norm is that the attacks are still so recent that any analysis of this post-9/11 condition that we live in is largely speculation. However, without straying into this speculative territory, it is clear that 9/11 (and perhaps even other terrorist attacks around the world) has changed our worlds, and has impacted the way we view diversity, and the way that diverse communities express themselves. Islam is rapidly becoming synonymous with terrorism in many people's eyes, which means that Muslims and non-Muslims are organising themselves in response to these external factors.[33] The aim of introducing the idea that we are all post-9/11 peoples is merely to recognise the impact that this event has had upon our worlds. My hope is that this cognisance will provide the necessary room for diverse identities to express their local specificities and develop on their own terms.

33 The very fact that references to a dichotomy of Muslims and non-Muslims almost seem trite is indicative of our post-9/11 condition. A further example of our post-9/11 condition is the recent debate and protests surrounding the possibility of a Muslim centre being situated two blocks from Ground Zero. Not only has the proposed centre been dubbed the 'Ground Zero Mosque', it has also led to an American pastor threatening to burn copies of the Koran.

Chapter 7
An Accurate and Just Understanding of Diversity

Having located law's role in meeting the challenges of a diversity-conscious justice by considering official legal responses to diversity, I turn to consider how official law understands diversity. My aim in this chapter is to demonstrate that current understandings of diversity are lacking in light of the realities of contemporary diversity. My claim is not that these perspectives are wholly inaccurate and that they should be cast aside as useless, but that they harbour certain unhelpful tendencies which do not correspond to the reality of diversity and, thus, provide an illusory focus to law's role in diverse societies. This illusory focus distorts law's capacity to meet the challenges of a diversity-sensitive justice, precisely because it presents a picture of diversity that does not accurately portray its reality.

For the purposes of illustrating the unhelpful tendencies of dominant views of diversity I have separated those theories which make diversity their core subject matter into two broad categories. The first category I label 'multiculturalism' as it encapsulates discourses which visualise diversity in terms of ethnicity, culture, religion and/or race. The second category I label the 'politics of identity', as I will consider those theories which understand diversity as an issue of identity and the importance of difference. I sustain my claim that the current conceptual tools available to understand diversity are unsatisfactory by first arguing that ethnicity, culture, religion and race have blurred boundaries, and that in setting these boundaries we engage in a value judgment that is not helpful to the pursuit of justice. Secondly, I demonstrate that in employing these conceptual tools, we exacerbate a tendency to singularise identity in terms of one of these categories. This is problematic because it excludes the political dimension of diversity. Lastly, I consider the concept of identity as a replacement conceptual tool. Whilst I believe that it overcomes the boundary and political exclusion difficulties of ethnicity, culture, religion and race, I argue that it has a tendency to reify diversities, and therefore also fails to reflect the realities of diversity.

Theories of Multiculturalism: Contestable Boundaries and the Exclusion of the Political

Within the category of discourses on multiculturalism, my concern here is their use of the terms ethnicity, religion, race and/or culture to describe diversity. The object is not to provide a review of the work in this field, but to reveal the unhelpful aspects of these terms in describing the challenges of diversity. It is crucial to stress that these unhelpful tendencies do not negate, *in toto*, the utility of discourses which employ these terms, nor do they render the use of these terms obsolete; at the very least they are social constructs which are employed in popular and academic discourses. On the contrary, my claim is that it is possible to understand more accurately what diversity really means in contemporary societies, without having to begin this debate with a clean slate.

Social scientists have made, and continue to make, considerable efforts to define and separate the terms 'ethnicity', 'culture', 'religion' and 'race', yet no clear boundaries result from these labours.[1] These unclear boundaries are more than just a manifestation of the lack of consensus on the definition of each concept owing to their internal plurality. Rather, the very attempt to construct these boundaries and define each concept is antithetical to the 'value pluralism' inherent in each concept.[2] The essence of each of these concepts is that they are fluid and dynamic so that they display internal plurality; yet the difficulty goes deeper than this and each concept has a varied, and varying, value for individuals and groups. They are value pluralistic in at least two ways: (i) they are multivocal since they can speak to and through individuals in a variety of ways; and (ii) their value can temporally and contextually vary.

First, in order to illustrate the lack of clear boundaries between these concepts I consider Eriksen's (2002) anthropological review of 'ethnicity', English law's understanding of ethnicity and Kymlicka's (1989, 1995, 2001) philosophical use of 'culture', as part of his *Theory of Multicultural Citizenship*. I argue that these contestable boundaries are not merely a reflection of a lack of consensus amongst social scientists, but are also a consequence of value pluralism. Secondly, I endeavour to illustrate that the use of the concepts of culture, race, religion and ethnicity to understand diversity neglects the political dimension of the construction of diverse identities.

1 Kroeber and Kluckhohn (1952) identified 162 different definitions of culture as part of their critical review of the concept of culture.

2 The term 'value plural' is borrowed from T. Macklem (2000) who uses it in the context of justifying freedom of religion. He explains (2000: 69) that 'we have different understandings of the nature of value', and that this theoretical question has practical ramifications as to why we would want to secure freedom of religion. Note, however, that whilst value is not monistic, nor is it subjective. Macklem convincingly argues that value is objective in the sense that it is a property of the object, and not a property of the person who finds the object valuable. I use the term 'value pluralism' to indicate two forms of plurality (as elaborated above), whilst also accepting that value is objective in the sense that Macklem describes it.

The Contestable Boundaries of Ethnicity, Culture, Religion and Race

Eriksen's (2002) anthropological account of ethnicity and nationalism provides an excellent departure point in a vast and ever increasing field of academic research; not only does it review the work of leading academics in this field, it also considers ethnicity's relationship to race, culture and religion. First, in defining the criteria of ethnicity Eriksen notes the blurred boundaries that are our concern here (2002: 34): '[f]or a long time it was common to equate "ethnic groups" with "cultural groups"[,] any category of people who has "a shared culture" was considered an ethnic group'. However, anthropologists encountered problems with this conflation of concepts since cultural attributes are often shared across ethnic boundaries. Moerman encountered this problem when he attempted to define what made the Lue in Thailand a distinct ethnic group (1965, quoted in Eriksen 2003: 11–12). Since '[t]hey lived in close interaction with other groups in the area; they had no exclusive livelihood, no exclusive language, no exclusive customs, no exclusive religion' (Eriksen 2002: 12), Moerman concluded that their character as an ethnic group was an emic category of description, thus one is a Lue by categorising oneself as Lue and behaving in ways that confirm Lueness (Moerman 1965: 1219, quoted in Eriksen 2002: 12).[3] Eriksen uses this to conclude that ethnicity is understood better as a relationship of communication, and not as the cultural quality of a group (2002: 34). However, culture is not entirely absent in this understanding of 'ethnicity': although this relationship involves the communication of ethnicity to other ethnic groups, it necessarily entails the communication of *cultural* differences.

Abner Cohen's instrumentalist elaboration of ethnicity also sheds light upon the difficulties of severing the ties between ethnicity and culture. In disagreeing with what he sees as Barth's 'primordialist' position, namely that ethnicity defines 'a person in terms of his basic, most general identity, presumptively determined by his origin and background' (1969: 13, quoted in Eriksen 2002: 53), Cohen adopts the stance that this is too static a view of ethnicity.[4] For him ethnicity is a pure form of political organisation, cultural traits may be invoked but only in so far as they can aid the securing of scarce resources and achieve political objectives (Cohen 1974a, 1974b, quoted in Eriksen 2002: 53–4). In this way Cohen draws a clear and distinct line between culture and ethnicity. Yet this division is problematic. As Eriksen points out (2002: 54), if ethnicity is a wholly political process, then it ought to be possible to create any identities that an individual or group chooses. In Cohen's view it should be possible to avoid all levels of ethnic conflict and struggle simply by changing ethnic groups when the political climate requires.

3 *Emic* is an anthropological term used to refer to the native point of view; in contrast, *etic* refers to the analyst's descriptions.

4 'Primordialist' views of ethnicity see it as an almost predetermined category, whereas 'instrumentalist' positions see ethnic categories as constructs which are instrumental to achieving some other end.

However, history confirms that it has not been possible to persuade Croats to take on a Serb identity, and so on. Culture and history, therefore, have a role to play in ethnicity, and a neat division between them is not possible.

Secondly, in listing the 'standard kinds of ethnic relations' (2002: 14–15), and considering the ethnic groups in Mauritius (2002: 24, 26, 32–3), Eriksen demonstrates the contestable boundaries between religion and ethnicity. 'Proto-nations' or 'ethnonationalist movements' are those groups who 'have political leaders who claim that they are entitled to their own nation-state and should not be 'ruled by others' (2002: 14). As examples of these groups Eriksen lists, inter alia, 'Sikhs, Palestinians and Sri Lankan Tamils' (2002: 14). This type of ethnic relation, therefore, encompasses the religious group of Sikhs, but defines two other groups according to their nationality, when these latter two could equally be defined according to their religious affiliation (Muslims and Hindus). One possible reason for categorising the latter two groups in this manner can be found in the fact that all Muslims and Hindus cannot be included in these groups that are making these particular claims for a nation-state. However, the same applies to Eriksen's category of Sikhs: it is not all Sikhs that are involved in making, or even happy to support, claims for a Sikh state of Khalistan.

Alternatively, it may be possible to explain Eriksen's proto-nation of Sikhs as an anomalous erroneous classification. However, this is not the only incidence of ethnic categorisations which are co-terminous with religious affiliations. In the context of stereotyping, Eriksen refers to his own fieldwork on ethnic groups in Mauritius and identifies the following main ethnic categories (1988, 1998 quoted in 2002: 24): Hindus; Muslims; Creoles; Coloureds; Sino-Mauritians; and Franco-Mauritians. Two of the six categories are defined according to their religious affiliations. Moreover, the Constitution of Mauritius recognises these two religious groups as two of the four communities on the island (Eriksen 2002: 26).[5] Eriksen goes on to explain that in Mauritius (2002: 33), ethnic membership can provide people with their religion. Although there is no explicit consideration of the relationship between ethnicity and religion in the same way that Eriksen analyses ethnicity and culture, it is possible to extrapolate from this that religion cannot easily be separated from ethnicity. Whilst religion and ethnicity are not synonymous categories, it has not been possible to define where one ends and the other begins. For the purposes of my claim here it is sufficient to demonstrate that there is no absolute delineation that has been made between ethnicity and religion.[6]

Thirdly, Eriksen's review also considers the relationship between ethnicity and race. Eriksen explains that race 'has dubious descriptive value' since 'modern genetics tends not to speak of races' (2002: 5). This, he explains, is because

5 The other two communities recognised by the Mauritian Constitution are the Sino-Mauritians and the 'general population', with the latter group encompassing everyone that does not fit into the other three categories.

6 This seems to be an area that is ripe for further research.

(i) there has been interbreeding between populations so that there are no fixed boundaries between races; (ii) hereditary physical traits tend not to follow clear boundaries so that there is great variation within racial groups; and (iii) no scholar today believes that genetic inheritance explains cultural variations (Eriksen 2002: 5). However, it does not follow from this that race is a term that can be disposed of entirely, as it exists as a social construct; it is a concept that is socially constructed and ideas of race continue to be important to individuals and groups. As such, the term continues to have a contemporary relevance. Banton puts forward the view that it is essential to distinguish between ethnicity and race, and explains that race carries with it a negative exclusionary categorisation of people, whereas ethnicity is concerned with the positive inclusionary identification of a group (1967, 1983: 106, quoted in Eriksen 2002: 5–6). However, as Eriksen points out, the atrocities of Yugoslavia and Rwanda evidence a less positive notion of ethnicity. Furthermore, Eriksen states that 'the boundaries between race and ethnicity tend to be blurred, since ethnic groups have a common myth of origin' (2002: 6). Ethnic groups often identify their common descent in constructing boundaries around their group and thus ethnicity can be related to notions of race, although it is not always a decisive factor. Indeed, in the context of boundary transcendence, Eriksen notes that identity change is not always possible, stating that 'Blacks in the United States ... cannot choose to become white' (2002: 40). This observation illustrates the ease with which (socially constructed) categories of race are equated with ethnic categories, and just how difficult it is to identify where one stops and the other begins.

These contestable boundaries are also reflected in English legal understandings of ethnicity. The RRA 1976 prohibited direct and indirect discrimination on 'racial grounds',[7] which was defined to cover 'colour, race, nationality, or ethnic or national origins'.[8] In clarifying the definition of 'ethnic origins', the House of Lords set out a test, which has provided protection for a limited number of religious groups.[9] Lord Fraser stated that ethnic groups were defined more widely than merely 'race', the two essential characteristics of an ethnic group being (1067):

1. a long shared history, which the group is conscious of distinguishing it from other groups; and
2. a cultural tradition of its own, including family and social customs and manners, often but not necessarily associated with religious observance.

Lord Fraser then went on to identify five further relevant, but non-essential, characteristics of an ethnic group (1067):

7 RRA 1976 s 1(1).

8 RRA 1976 s 3(1).

9 In *Mandla v Dowell Lee and Another* [1983] 1 All ER 1062 (HL). The groups excluded from the protective ambit of the RRA 1976 are noted in Chapter 4.

1. either a common geographical origin, or descent from a small number of common ancestors;
2. a common language, not necessarily peculiar to the group;
3. a common literature, peculiar to the group;
4. a common religion different from that of neighbouring groups or from the general community surrounding it;
5. being a minority or being an oppressed or a dominant group within a larger community.[10]

Employing this definition of 'ethnic group', the House was able to provide protection for a Sikh boy refused entry to a school on the basis that wearing his turban violated the school uniform code. For the purposes of the RRA 1976, Sikhs, therefore, are an 'ethnic group'. Lord Denning, however, came to the polar opposite conclusion when the case was before the Court of Appeal, and he understood ethnicity in a very different manner.[11] Basing his conclusions on a dictionary definition of ethnicity,[12] he saw ethnicity to be definable by racial characteristics; thus, those with a common religion, social customs or political aspirations could not fall within this definition. Confusingly, Lord Denning saw the inclusion of 'ethnic origin' in the RRA 1976 as an expression of Parliament's intent to ensure that anti-semitism was prohibited by the legislation. For Lord Denning, Jews are not merely identifiable by their common religious beliefs; they also have a common racial descent, which is exclusive to the Jews. In contrast Sikhs share their Punjabi territorial origins with other religious denominations, such as Hindus; thus, Sikhs do not possess a common racial descent.

In contrasting the House of Lords and Court of Appeal judgments in this case, it is possible to reinforce the conclusion that ethnicity, race, religion and culture have contestable boundaries. Taken in isolation, both Lord Denning's and Lord Fraser's elaboration of the meaning of 'ethnicity' further illustrate the lack of clarity and the contestable boundaries between these concepts; Lord Fraser employs both culture and religion in his definition of an ethnic group, and Lord Denning is unable to separate ethnicity from race.

The case of a British schoolgirl who claimed that her human rights had been violated because she was not allowed to wear a *jilbab*, a long flowing gown, to school could also be used to illustrate the contestable boundaries between religion, culture and ethnicity. However, there are many more dimensions to this case that I could not do justice to by introducing it at this juncture. I shall instead return

10 For Lord Fraser's full judgment on the meaning of 'ethnic origin' see 1065–69.

11 *Mandla v Dowell Lee and Another* [1982] 2 All ER 1108 (CA).

12 Lord Fraser also used a dictionary definition to elucidate his definition of ethnicity, but whilst he used the 1972 Supplement Volume 1 to the Oxford English Dictionary, Lord Denning used the 1934 edition of the same dictionary. The divergent definitions in each edition provide further illustration of the contested and evolutionary nature of the concept of ethnicity.

to consider it in greater detail when putting forward my arguments for a new analytical tool to understand diversity.

My final illustration of the contestable boundaries between these concepts is found within Kymlicka's (1995) explanation of culture in his *Theory of Multicultural Citizenship*. In my earlier account of this aspect of Kymlicka's defence of minority rights I explained that he employs a concept that he terms 'societal cultures'. With this concept, he is not concerned with isolating the character of an historical community at any moment in time, so that any changes to this community would be considered a loss of culture. His focus is culture as a 'context of choice', with such a structure persisting even if its members should decide to modify the character of the culture, should it no longer find those ways worthwhile (1989: 166–77). It is worth repeating that societal culture 'provides its members with meaningful ways of life across the full range of human activities, including *social*, educational, *religious*, recreational, and economic life, encompassing both public and private spheres' (1995: 76, emphasis added). Kymlicka makes it clear that he is of the opinion that immigrant groups do not and cannot be allowed to have 'societal cultures' (1995: 78): '[s]ome immigrants might hope to re-create these practices in their entirety in their new country. But that is effectively impossible without significant government support, which is rarely if ever provided'. It is only societal cultures that have a legitimate claim to survive into the future (1995: 80): '[i]n short, for a culture to survive and develop in the modern world, given the pressures towards the creation of a single common culture in each country, it must be a societal culture'.[13]

Immigrant groups do not possess a societal culture, but it is evident from Kymlicka's distinction between 'national minorities' and 'ethnic groups' that immigrants possess some sort of a culture which does not include institutional structures or practices. From this account it is possible to conclude that Kymlicka's definition of culture includes religious beliefs and, in the case of immigrant groups, has some loose association with ethnicity.[14] On this view culture becomes an inclusive term which encapsulates religion and ethnicity; thus it is evident that Kymlicka is also unable to draw distinct and clear boundaries between the concepts of ethnicity, religion and culture.

These contestable boundaries are not just a reflection of disagreement amongst social scientists, or commentators in the field; they are also a manifestation of value

13 It is not the purpose here to consider the justice of Kymlicka's claim that some but not all minority cultures have grounds to survive into the future. For a critical analysis of this claim see Bhamra (2007).

14 Kymlicka's definition of culture appears somewhat vague and lacking a concrete description and thus comes across as unsatisfactory. This intuition, of the unsatisfactory nature of culture when it is not concretely defined, is, however, due to the second unhelpful tendency of these concepts which is explored later in this chapter.

pluralism.[15] The question of whether diversity presents situations of intractable conflicts of value is a crucial one to this thesis. However, justice cannot be done to this question as part of this claim, and I leave it to be considered later in this book. My claim here is that the contested boundaries between these concepts are due, inter alia, to the fact that there are many 'maximal forms of life'. Raz explains (1986: 396) that a maximal form of life is a 'life that cannot be improved by acquiring different virtues, nor by enhancing the degree to which [one] possesses any virtue, without sacrificing another virtue [one] possesses or the degree to which it is present in [one's] life'. The often cited example to explain this claim is that of a nun and a mother's life: one cannot have all the virtues of a nun and a mother.

Value pluralism means that the way we define the religious, cultural, ethnic and racial aspects of lives are influenced by the virtues that we value. Thus, if I believe that a religious life is a valuable one because it offers a life of meditation, worship of god and pious reflection, then I might argue that a person who does none of these things, but takes part in the occasional ritual which is associated with a particular religion, is not in fact religious but displaying cultural or ethnic traits. For example, those Christians who do not attend church might be considered to be non-practising Christians, or simply wrong if they declare themselves to be Christians. The contestable boundaries between race, religion, ethnicity and culture are, in part at least, a consequence of this value pluralism. However, allowing the plural nature of our values to influence how we categorise issues of diversity provides an illusory focus to our understanding of diversity, particularly when this categorisation corresponds to the relative strength of the legal rights that can be claimed.

The Exclusion of the Political

Employing religion, race, ethnicity and/or culture as tools to understand diversity contributes to a phenomenon that Sen has termed the 'singular identity' (2006). The singular identity is one where individuals become identifiable according to one aspect of their identity, thereby sidelining all the other elements that make up that individual. Various factors, including the increasing salience of religion on a global level, have led to a greater identification of individuals on a religious basis. This singular religious identity has particular relevance in a post-9/11 world. Such singular religious identities deny individuals access to the other varied and important facets of their identity.

Sen emphasises (2006) that our identities are in fact plural and that this reductionist logic is damaging. He notes that we belong to a number of groups including 'citizenship, residence, geographic origin, gender, class, politics,

15 Pluralism is used here in accordance with Isaiah Berlin's definition (1997: 9): pluralism is 'the conception that there are many different ends that men may seek and still be fully rational, fully men, capable of understanding each other and sympathizing and deriving light from each other'.

profession, employment, food habits, sports interests, taste in music, social commitments' (2006: 4–5). However, my concern here is that in shaping singular identities the political dimension to our identities have been ignored, and this has distorted how questions of diversity are related to in legal spheres.

Movements away from the use of 'Black' to describe all victims of racial discrimination, combined with a political climate where the relevance of religion has steadily increased, has led to many people primarily defining themselves along religious lines. Whilst there are strong arguments that can be made against the generic use of the term 'Black', this trend towards a dominant religious categorisation of individuals ignores any political aspects of their identity. Furthermore, religious identities are employed in such a manner that the ways in which these religious identities are used in political senses are excluded. Religion may be increasingly relevant in political spheres, but in legal spheres the manifestation of a religious belief is not co-terminous with the manifestation of a political view or political values.

The ways in which individuals, and groups, define themselves includes an element of responsiveness to political climates of the day. Thus, for example, the increasing numbers of young girls who are choosing to wear the Muslim *hijab* or the Sikh turban, when their elder relatives do not, are not only a reflection of an increasing interest in religion amongst these communities; these trends also reflect responses to political climates – perhaps these communities feel under threat and the overt expression of religious affiliation is a response to this. It is difficult to speculate here what the political undertones of these religious choices are, but my point is that an understanding of identity as religion, and nothing more, excludes the possibility of exploring these political undertones, and this is detrimental to how we understand diversity. In particular, legal claims made on the basis of religious freedom fail adequately to explore this dimension of identity. The case of Shabina Begum illustrates well how this avenue becomes closed off when diversity is understood in singular religious terms, and this case is considered in detail in support of my claim for identity markers as a new way of understanding diversity.

The Politics of Identity: The Determinist Hindrance of Identity

The notion of identity overcomes the problem that the concepts of culture, religion, ethnicity and race present in understanding diversity. Not only does it overcome the difficulty of the contestable boundaries between each individual concept, it respects the value pluralism which is at its root and does not exclude the political. With identity the focus shifts from whether a particular trait is cultural, religious, ethnic or racial in nature, towards the fact that it is part of the self or the group and, therefore, holds value. Nor is the degree of the value the focal point of the concept, so the question of creating a hierarchy of values is separated from the task of understanding diversity.[16] However, identity also has a proclivity which presents an obstacle to its use as a tool to understand diversity. Identity has a tendency towards creating definable, tangible and complete sets of characteristics that come together to describe an individual. I call this the determinist hindrance of identity. In contrast, the reality of the self and the group is of an ongoing, unfinished and unfinishable process; we are far more fragmented, transient and dynamic than the concept of identity allows.

Despite my claim that identity has a determinist hindrance, literature that seeks to elucidate the nature of identity, more often than not, emphasises its fluid and dynamic nature. Young expresses this idea eloquently when she refers to Elizabeth Spelman's metaphor of identity as a string of beads (2000: 102): '[i]s my individual identity somehow an aggregate of my gender identity, race identity, class identity, like a string of beads ...'. This notion of a 'pop-bead' identity miscasts the self (Young 2000: 102): '[a] person's identity is not some sum of her gender, racial, class, and national affinities'. Rather, it is something beyond this aggregate, but the question then remains exactly what is 'identity'? It is precisely the unavoidable nature of this latter question that makes identity problematic as a tool to understand diversity. In spite of almost universal recognition that identity is fluid, and that it is not an aggregate of a person's affinities, it nevertheless makes irresistible moves towards requiring some kind of tangible, finished, whole product. Whilst most commentators recognise that identity is dynamic and changeable, implicit in conjuring up the notion of identity is the suggestion that it should be possible to set down the attributes of the group or individual, and thus fully define their identity.

Young expresses this proclivity when she argues against understanding group difference as a matter of identity. She claims that '[t]hose who reduce group difference to identity implicitly use a logic of substance to conceptualize groups' (2000: 87). The notion of group identity necessitates the assignment of a set of essential characteristics according to which membership is decided, and those that do not possess the mandatory attributes are then excluded. However, this is problematic since 'there always seem to be persons without the required attributes whom experience tends to include in the group or who identify with the group' (Young 2000: 88). Employing the concept of identity, therefore, fixes boundaries and ignores the social realities of internal plurality and the porous nature of the boundaries of identity. The self and the group are far more fragmented than the concept of identity permits, and this then obfuscates an accurate understanding of diversity.

---

16 Note that I am not suggesting that there should be no hierarchy of values and that we should tolerate all kinds of lifestyles without question. Rather, I am arguing that this process of assessing the value of an aspect of identity should not be conflated with the question of whether a trait is cultural, ethnic, religious, and so on. The dialogue about what behaviour and lifestyles should and should not be tolerated requires serious and separate consideration.

Sen's (2006) connection between identity and violence also rests upon this determinist tendency. He argues that in our worlds there is an 'insistence, if only implicitly, on a choiceless singularity of human identity', which diminishes the reality of our plural and multiple identities (2006: 16). He illustrates (2006: 40–58) that Samuel Huntingdon's division of the world into 'civilizations' ('the Western world', 'the Islamic world', 'the Hindu world', 'the Buddhist world' and so on) is simply historically inaccurate. For example (2006: 46–9), to paint India as a 'Hindu civilization', the way Huntingdon does, ignores the fact that India has the third largest population of Muslims in the world; with 145 million Muslims it (only just) ranks behind Indonesia and Pakistan. Moreover, such singular imaginings of the world ignore the plural nature of our identities (Sen 2006: 4–5):

> In our normal lives, we see ourselves as members of a variety of groups – we belong to all of them. A person's citizenship, residence, geographic origin, gender, class, politics, profession, employment, food habits, sports interests, taste in music, social commitments, etc., make us members of a variety of groups.

Sen's thesis, therefore, relies upon this determinist hindrance of identity.

Those concepts that are familiar within discourses on multiculturalism also display this determinist tendency. Kymlicka states that 'for a culture to survive and develop in the modern world, given the pressures towards the creation of a single common culture in each country, it must be a societal culture' (1995: 80). It was noted above that the distinguishing feature of a 'societal culture' is its institutional structures and practices (Kymlicka 1995: 76). This emphasis upon a tangible, completed project provides a neat illustration of this determinist propensity. Kuper (1999: 236), furthermore, expresses this tendency when he notes that one of the problems of theories of multiculturalism is that '[o]nce a cultural identity has been established, the pressure is on to live it'. Appiah's response to Taylor's Politics of Recognition elaborates upon this pressure to live an essentialised identity (1994). He states that 'one reasonable ground for suspicion of much contemporary multicultural talk is that it presupposes conceptions of collective identity that are remarkably unsubtle in their understandings of the processes by which identities, both individual and collective, develop' (1994: 156). These identities that claim recognition project strong norms of behaviour, and it follows that these 'scripts' narrate what it means to be, for example, a Mauritian Hindu, an African-American or a Sami (Appiah 1994: 160). By projecting acceptable norms such scripts do violence to the very processes of identity they seek to isolate, since they essentialise what it means to be African-American or a Mauritian Hindu and present these identities as finished projects (Appiah 1994: 159–63). In this way these theories also rob individuals and groups of the agency involved in the development of identities; crucial to the process of identity is individual and group participation.[17]

17 The agency intrinsic to identity processes is explored in greater detail in Chapter 8.

In summation, the concepts of culture, religion, ethnicity and race have contestable boundaries. In using them as tools to understand diversity considerable effort must be made to justify whether the trait in question is religious or cultural, racial or ethnic, and so on. This focuses attention away from the nature of the challenges that diversity presents and therefore distracts us from the real issues to be dealt with. Furthermore, our view of what can legitimately be included in each category is influenced by our values. Since these values are plural we implicitly make a judgment as to what aspects of diversity are more, or less, acceptable, as each of these categories has varying strengths of legal rights attached to them. This value judgment is made too early, when the task at hand should be to understand the kinds of diversity that exist in today's world. With the rise of singular religious identities, using religion as a description of diversity has had the side-effect of excluding the political dimensions of diverse identities.

Whilst it is possible to use identity as a label to describe diversity, since it avoids value judgments and can include the political dimensions of who we are, it also presents its own obstacle to understanding diversity. Despite strong moves to cast identity as dynamic, it has an irresistible inclination towards imagining finished and defined individuals and groups. This determinist hindrance is not only the antithesis of the dynamic processes that constitute identity, it also denies the agency intrinsic to these processes. For these reasons identity also provides a misfocused understanding of diversity. It is within this context that I propose the concept of 'identity markers' as a mechanism through which a more accurate understanding of diversity can be achieved.

Chapter 8
Identity Markers

In this chapter I propose the concept of 'identity markers' as a tool that overcomes the unhelpful tendencies of current conceptual tools used to understand diversity. Identity markers are intended to contribute to my local normative framework, and this normative framework is intended to provide a fresh perspective on law so that it can meet the challenges of a diversity-conscious form of justice by making space for local specificities. This fresh perspective on justice and law, offered by my global and local normative framework, grounds my proposal for a new vista on constitutional pluralism. Moreover, it is this new vista that provides a platform for new legal responses to diversity.

I sketch out the nature of identity markers by referencing the meaning of identity. This enables me to pinpoint six key characteristics of identity markers. The fluid and evolving nature of identity markers makes it particularly difficult to pinpoint a concrete definition. I address this difficulty in two ways. First, I explain how the six key characteristics of identity markers relate to the social realities of British South Asian diversity. I pinpoint this particular form of British diversity because the socio-legal literature is readily available, although my claims apply to all forms of diverse identities. Secondly, I use a case concerning the prohibition of religious dress at a public school to demonstrate the role of identity markers. I argue that identity markers provide a more accurate and just understanding of diversity, and consequently shed new light on the issues in this case.

Identity Markers: What is Identity?

Of late, appeals to identity as an apt description of diversity have multiplied and possibly now equal those discourses which I earlier termed theories of multiculturalism. Having established that identity has the unhelpful tendency of imagining individuals and groups as completed projects, I propose to take a further step and claim that discourses concerned with plural societies must move beyond identity in order to get to the root of the challenges of justice in diverse societies. I propose to complete this step by employing a concept I have termed 'identity markers'. Identity markers act as an adjunct to identity, to aid in overcoming the latter's determinist tendency; as a consequence, the lion's share of understanding identity markers must be done by setting out the crucial elements of identity. As such, contemporary literature which comes within my category of the politics of identity remains an important resource, particularly in its exploration of the meaning of identity. It is these accounts which inform my identification of six key characteristics of identity.

I begin, first, by reviewing the etymology of identity. This review builds a platform for the next section, where I consider contemporary literature in this field and aim to isolate six key characteristics of identity. In this section I consider Erik Erikson's work, which highlights the first characteristic of identity, that is, a set of processes which are neither finished nor finishable. I then explain the internal aspects of identity – the second characteristic of identity – by referencing Taylor's work in this field. The next key aspect of identity, that it is external, is elaborated by describing Derrida's system of *différence* and Lacan's subject-of-language approach. Identity's fourth key characteristic is that it is not singular, and I illustrate this by surmising Sen's connection between identity and violence. Sen's work on identity also provides occasion to substantiate my claim that the processes of identity take place both inside and outside of the domain of reason – the fifth characteristic of identity. The sixth aspect of identity is that its processes take place at the core of the individual and the group. In order to demonstrate this, I reveal that Young's arguments, that there is no group identity, cannot be sustained. In the third and final section I provide a concrete example of these characteristics of identity in the form of a socio-legal account of the South Asian presence in Britain.

The Etymology of Identity

A sound point to start unravelling the meaning of identity is the etymology of the word. Whilst it seems as if there ought to be clarity as to the etymology of identity, this is very much a contested field (Hughes 1995: 9–11). The word can be traced back to the classical Latin *identitatem*, meaning sameness, the root being *idem*, the same.[1] However, connections can also be made to the medieval Latin words of *identidem*, meaning repeatedly, and *iterare/idemtitare*, meaning to repeat.[2] In classical Greek the term *tautos* was used to signify something like identity, the root being *autos*, meaning the self or itself. Indeed, it is clear that translations of Aristotle's works into Latin show that the term *identitas* or *idemtitas* was used to mean *tautos*. Plotinus thought that identity was central to the concept of the Divine Mind, *nous*, which not only included the One but also the Many (Hughes 1995). This illustrates that the notion of identity has not been exclusively connected to the individual, but that it can also carry broader connotations which link it to the group. Identity can also be linked to classical Sanskrit terms such as, *idam*, *iyam*,

1 This sheds some light on the collective quality of identity, something that will be explored in greater detail later.

2 This elucidates the connections made between identity and continuity throughout time.

idam vid, meaning knowing or conversant with this, *idem tana*, meaning being now or living in this time and *idam-ta*, meaning being this.[3]

Contemporary debates concerned with the concept of identity make reference to the social psychology of the 1950s as the starting point of the modern use of identity and, in particular, the work of Erik Erikson is singled out.[4] Erikson had an interest in the process of individual identity formation and the role of identity crises in that formation.[5] He notes (1968: 16), that over time the connotations of crisis have changed so that it is now understood as a crucial turning point in an individual's development, when her identity must move forward in one way or another, as opposed to suggesting an impending disaster.

Erikson points to the personal writings of the psychologist and philosopher William James and also the writings of Sigmund Freud (1968: 19–21), as examples of early descriptions of identity. William James wrote to his wife about a voice inside which said '*This* is the real me!' at those times when one can deeply feel one's character in the form of a moral attitude (1968: 19). Erikson sees James's description as exemplary of his understanding of identity as 'a *subjective sense* of an *invigorating sameness* and *continuity*' (1968: 19). In 1926 Freud described what attracted him to his Jewish faith in an address to the Society of B'nai B'rith in Vienna, and talked of 'a clear consciousness of inner identity, [and] the safe privacy of a common mental construction' (Erikson 1968: 20).

Using these as a starting point, Erikson sketches out his understanding of identity (1968: 22–3). Following on from Freud's analysis, he notes that individual and group identity may be relational and contextual, and the sense of pride one gains in attaining a strong sense of identity may be a sign of inner liberation from a more dominant group identity. Therefore, identity formation is a process that takes place at the core of an individual, yet also at the core of one's communal culture, and thus this process shapes two identities. In psychological terms, the process takes place on all levels of mental functioning, involving judgments of the way one is perceived by others and reference to how one perceives oneself in comparison to others. The process is necessarily unconscious,[6] except where circumstances (inner and outer) accumulate to create a painful 'identity consciousness'; furthermore, it is an ongoing process, always changing and developing.

Since, for Erikson, individual and group identity cannot be separated, it is not possible to separate personal growth from communal growth. It follows, therefore, that individual crises and crises in historical developments of group identity

3 Sanskrit has an Indo-European linguistic root; thus, this linguistic connection is not as unusual as it may first appear.

4 See, for example, Appiah (2005: 65).

5 'Identity crisis' is a term that Erikson accepts at least partial responsibility for coining (Erikson 1968: 16–17).

6 Psychoanalytical accounts of identity tend to focus on the unconscious nature of identity, whereas philosophical accounts, such as Taylor's (1989), tend to allow greater room for agency and consciousness in the process of identity.

cannot be separated, precisely because the two refine and are relative to each other, and the interplay between them is part of the process of identity formation (1968: 23). Identities can be negative and positive, and negative identities can be recovered; Erikson notes the universal use of literature in the recovery of identity in marginalised and oppressed groups (1968: 25).[7]

The Six Key Aspects of Identity

This excursus into the work of Erikson is relayed here not just because it informs contemporary work on identity,[8] but also because it raises two issues of importance to the following discussion. First, it is clear that whilst Erikson locates questions of identity within the individual, by no means does this negate the salience of the group, and group identity. This is something that I explore in greater detail later. Secondly, and more importantly at this juncture, Erikson's work elaborates the first key characteristic of identity, namely that it encapsulates the processes of being.[9] As processes, identity is a work in progress that is subject to continual change and growth; it is neither finished nor finishable. The unfortunate side-effect of this aspect of identity can be seen in the vagueness with which Erikson writes of the process of identity; it is often not possible to pinpoint the nature of these processes of identity beyond descriptions of existentialist questionings of 'who am I'.[10] In fact, the unsatisfactory nature of this vagueness contributes to the determinist hindrance of identity explained earlier. The need for something more specific perpetuates identity's essentialist tendencies, despite ample recognition of its dynamic nature.

7 Erikson is making reference here to literature which is active in reconstructing broken identities, or dispelling stereotypes. For example, Salman Rushdie believes that his novels make visible the invisibility caused by migration, and he is sometimes credited with providing a glimpse of the 'real' India in his work.

8 By contemporary work on identity, I mean to include work on the 'politics of identity', as well as including work which is often described as coming within the field of culture studies.

9 Although Erikson writes of the process of identity, I prefer to term these processes to reflect the complex interactions that embody the formation of identities.

10 Taylor (1989) stands out as the exception to this characteristic of identity discussions. He writes of the notion of 'modern identity' as encapsulating 'what it is to be a human agent, a person, or a self' (2000: 3). However, his work is one of abstract philosophy and concerns the connection between selfhood and the moral self, which is explored by tracing various aspects of modern identity. Whilst this account is compelling and persuasive, its use for the construction of a notion of identity that seeks to encapsulate the specific social realities of diversity is limited. Nevertheless, value can be found in the emphasis in modern identity on the authentic self coming from within, such that it is less important to see modern identity as a construct which stems from the hierarchical predetermined orderings of any society. This notion is also reflected in Taylor's work on the Politics of Recognition (1994: 25–37), which was discussed in greater detail in Chapters 2 and 3.

The second characteristic of identity is that it is internal in its processes. It is internal in that it reflects processes of human agency, whereby the individual and the group consider who they are and how they choose to define themselves. Taylor explains that this concept of listening to our inner voice is an aspect of modern identity and one connected to morality (1989, 1994), such that there is an identity 'particular to me, and that I discover in myself' (Taylor 1994: 28).[11] With the 'collapse of social hierarchies' so that everyone is born as an equal in a democracy, the importance of internal discoveries of selfhood are magnified (Taylor 1994: 26–7).

The significance of the agency involved in the processes of identity cannot be overemphasised. The magnitude of the importance of this agency can be seen in the link Taylor makes between identity, human dignity and recognition (1994: 27). Modern identity involves a 'massive subjective turn of modern culture, a new form of inwardness, in which we come to think of ourselves as beings with inner depths' (Taylor 1994: 29). This 'inwardness' engages human agency, which then acts as a form of investment in ourselves, thus contributing to our notion of dignity and worth. It follows from this that misrecognition has a greater impact than merely being erroneous; it chips away at our dignity and implies more humiliation than describing it as a false interpretation can possibly suggest.

However, identity is not just self-ascriptive and a product of human reflection and choice; our inward interpretation of our identity cannot draw upon an endless spectrum of choices. The third aspect of identity is its external nature, and contemporary work in this field has recognised at least two ways in which they are externally processed. The first represents the relational ascription of identity that Derrida has encapsulated with his view of identity as an aspect of the system of *différence*. Derrida puts forward the idea that a present being (a form, a state, a power, and so on) exists only in relation to that which it is different to (2001). This is the system of *différence*. Derrida argues that in order to visualise the form of something, it is necessary to know what it is visualised in reference (*différence*) to. For example, to know what a civilised European is, one must have the notion of a barbaric African, or an exotic Oriental in mind.[12]

This system of *différence* has implications for the processes of identity; not only do identity processes draw upon individual and group choices and ascriptions, but they also involve external descriptions of what these individuals and groups are and are not. This means that identities are formed by reference to those points of difference that exist around them. The external environment within which the processes of identity take place have a distinct impact. Thus, being a Christian in

11 Listening to the inner voice represents an act of moral probing, in asking 'who am I' the human agent engages in questions of 'who I ought to be' (Taylor 1994: 29–30).

12 Derrida places far more emphasis upon *différence* as the mechanism through which present beings are understood than I argue for. I argue that the external processes of identity are but one of six key characteristics, any of which can be fore- or back-grounded in particular circumstances.

Britain is very different to being a Christian in China, which is very different to being a Christian in the United States. In fact, the implications of *différence* spill much further than this, since the fluidity of meaning in language is something that also occurs within the external environment. Derrida terms this 'deferral' of language, and it means that the particular description of processes of identity are subject to constant change. Therefore, the meaning of being a Christian in the United States is constantly subject to deferral. The picture of identity as fixed and constant is inaccurate; by its very nature it is plural, fluid and amorphous, so that it does not lend itself well to visualisation in the mind's eye.

The second meaning of the external processes of identity draws upon the 'subject-of-language' approach that Lacan elaborated.[13] The core of this post-structuralist account of identity is that there is no pre-social self, and that identity is constructed in the sites made available in language and society. Indeed, some see Derridian *différence* as an aspect of this approach.[14] However, it seems more accurate to view them as two separate ideas, which both express the external nature of the processes of identity. The crux to this approach is that identity is socially constructed from places outside of the individual and the group. Lacan's early expression of this approach in 1949 uses the 'mirror stage' to explain these external processes. In the early infant stages the baby misrecognises itself in the mirror (Lacan 2006) and this is the pre-social self. It is through external learning that the infant comes to recognise itself and it is in these sites that the processes of identity are located.

Taylor also acknowledges the external element of the processes of identity by writing of the '*dialogical* character' of 'human life' (1994: 32): '[w]e become full human agents, capable of understanding ourselves, and hence of defining our identity, through our acquisition of rich human languages of expression'. We acquire these 'languages of expression' through our social interactions with others. Taylor clearly explains the interdependent and conflicting nature of these internal and external aspects of the processes of identity (1994: 32–3). He states that these languages of expression are not just adopted and then used for 'our own purposes' (Taylor 1994: 32). Of course, individual and group opinions are formed and used, but this formation does not take place in purely solitary processes (1994: 32–3): '[w]e define our identity always in dialogue with, sometimes in struggle against, the things our significant others want to see in us'.

---

13 There are a variety of ideas in the 'subject-of-language' approach that have been developed within the field of culture studies, some of which are conflicting, but there is a common underlying thesis which is of relevance here, and this is the meaning employed here. For an example of one such approach see Althusser who argues that ideology 'interpellates' the individual, and thus the individual is less an agent and more a subject of this interpellation (1971: 170–86). See Hall (1996) for a point of introduction into these debates.

14 See du Gay, Evans and Redman (2000).

Whilst the above aspects pay considerable heed to the plural, fluid and changeable nature of identity, the fourth characteristic, namely that it is not singular, especially highlights this. Sen's (2006) important work on identity makes a link between the reductionist expression of singular identities and contemporary instances of violence. There is a painful truth in Sen's observation that 'violence associated with identity conflicts seems to repeat itself around the world with increasing persistence' (2006: 3). Throughout his work he makes reference, inter alia, to Yugoslavia, Rwanda, the Congo, Sudan, Israel and Palestine, Sri Lanka, Al Qaeda and Abu Ghraib as examples of violent 'identity conflicts'. *One* of the incitements of this form of violence, Sen argues (2006: 16), is '[t]he insistence, if only implicitly, on a choiceless singularity of human identity'. The most prominent contemporary example of this singular identity is the 'increasing reliance on [a] religion-based classification of the people of the world' (2006: 12). This singular conceptualisation of identity is wholly misrepresentative of the social realities of how people see themselves.

Sen explains that people see themselves as made up of many different identities, and they have good reason to view themselves this way (2006: 18–39); identity is plural, individuals belong to a great many categories, and this plurality is also fluid and changeable. He provides a succinct and cogent example by describing himself (2006: 19):

> I can be, at the same time, an Asian, an Indian citizen, a Bengali with Bangladeshi ancestry, an American or British resident, an economist, a dabbler in philosophy, an author, a Sanskritist, a strong believer in secularism and democracy, a man, a feminist, a heterosexual, a defender of gay and lesbian rights, with a nonreligious lifestyle, from a Hindu background, a non-Brahmin, a nonbeliever in an afterlife (and also, in case the question is asked, a nonbeliever in a 'before-life' as well). This is just a small sample of the diverse categories to each of which I may simultaneously belong – there are of course a great many other membership categories too which, depending on circumstances, can move and engage me.

In this paragraph Sen persuasively demonstrates that identity is not only plural, but value plural, and fluid and dynamic in its processes. The fourth characteristic of identity can thus be expressed by explaining that identity is not singular in its processes.[15]

Sen's work raises an important point that merits clarification. If it can be accepted that a key characteristic of identity is that it is not singular in its

15 Sen, of course, goes further than merely 'making sense of identity' (2006: 18–39), and not only dismantles Huntingdon's 'Clash of Civilizations' thesis by deconstructing the strength of its premise that the world can be divided into a federation of civilisations, but also by explaining the ways in which the world has fallen into accepting and propagating singular identities, he makes considerable strides towards revealing escape routes which could provide access to a more just, and less violent, world.

processes, has the 'determinist hindrance' that was earlier identified, and which drives identity markers, not been overcome? Regrettably, this is not the case; Sen's identification of the non-singular processes of identity is neither novel nor unique. Much contemporary literature, in fact, recognises the dynamic, plural and multiple nature of identity.[16] Sen's cogent illustration of the 'insistence … on a choiceless singularity of human identity' merely further confirms the irresistible essentialist tendencies of 'identity' (2006: 16). Sen is mainly concerned with the flammable world that this singular identity creates, yet he also notes precisely what is argued here, that this understanding of identity 'diminishes us all' (2006: 16).

The fifth aspect of the processes of identity, namely that they take place within *and* outside of the domain of reason, can also be explained by making reference to Sen (2006). Sen argues that in order to resist singular identities, 'the role of reasoned choice needs emphasis' (2006: 8), and he implores that reason must be given priority (2006: 161–5). He makes this plea by referring to the Mughal emperor, Akbar, who, whilst a Muslim throughout his life, insisted that reason must come before faith. Akbar stated in the 1590s (Athar Ali 1997: 220, quoted in Sen 2006: 161): '[t]he pursuit of reason and rejection of traditionalism are so brilliantly patent as to be above the need of argument. If traditionalism were proper, the prophets would merely have followed their own elders (and not come with new messages)'. Sen also (2006: 36–9) persuasively questions the idea that identities are something that we discover, in an almost predetermined fashion. Whilst he does not advocate a limitless choice of identities, by summarising Rabindranath Tagore's novel, *Gora*, he illustrates the fragility and fallacy of the bonds we have to our roots (2006: 38–9). The protagonist of Tagore's novel, Gora, is a staunch advocate of conservative Hindu traditions. However, at the end of the novel Gora's mother tells him that he was adopted as an orphan and that his parents were actually Irish. Thus, Gora becomes one of the 'foreign-borns' that his own conservative traditions exclude. Sen, thus, demonstrates that the processes of identity are not just a matter of discovery.

Sen is, I believe, correct to illustrate that the processes of identity are more than just a voyage of discovery. However, prioritisation of reason is, I submit, an aspect of Sen's ideal theory of justice, and forms part of his argument of how our diminishing singular identities can be overcome. Whilst Sen accepts that prioritising reason does not translate into an open-ended choice of identities, by making this move he excludes those who choose not to privilege reason; some are moved more by intuitions, imaginations, emotions and feelings than reasons and logic. Although it is clear that Sen's claim is that we *ought* to prioritise reason in order to overcome singular identities and the insidious violence linked to these singular identities, it is equally clear that we do not all share in his choice to prioritise reason. Individuals and groups regularly refer to their heritage to explain the processes of their identities. The phrase 'my parents were artists, so it is only

---

16 For a summary of this approach to identity across a variety of disciplines see Taylor and Spencer (2004: 1–11).

natural that I followed the same path' does not seem out of place, and demonstrates well the oft-made appeal to other-wordly domains, outside that of reason, that are connected to the processes of identity, even if these connections are fragile, as *Gora* illustrates.

The sixth, and final, aspect of identity is that it takes place at the core of the individual *and* the group.[17] Although Erikson's work buttresses this conclusion, this is a contested viewpoint which requires more thorough contemplation, and Young's (2000) argument against the notion of group identity provides this opportunity. Her arguments also present occasion to demonstrate my claim that, in spite of its determinist hindrance, abandoning identity altogether in order to understand diversity will do more harm than good.

Young claims (2000: 81–107) that there is no such thing as group identity as part of her argument that it is inappropriate to reduce a politics of difference to the issue of identity, and that group differences must be separated from identity. Viewing group difference as a question of identity employs what Young terms a 'substantialist logic', whereas she proposes that a 'relational logic' provides a better focus (2000: 82, 87). The nature of this 'substantialist logic' was explained earlier, but in essence Young claims that in order to visualise a group's identity, it is necessary to assign it with a list of essential features. Any list of essential features is, however, problematic since 'there always seem to be persons without the required attributes whom experience tends to include in the group or who identify with the group' (2000: 88). Young explains that this substantialist logic fixes group boundaries when experience informs us that these boundaries are fluid. Furthermore, she points out that there are many individuals who deny that group membership is significant to their identity (2000: 88): '[s]ome women, for example, deny reflective awareness of womanly identity as constitutive of their identity, and they deny any particular identification with other women'. Finally, Young notes (2000: 88–9) that a common group identity denies the internal plurality and varying interests that groups display, and more importantly it ignores the intersectionality of group membership.

By casting a group as a united set of individuals with common interests, identity violates the social reality of our relations with a myriad of groups which intersect; an individual can be a woman, as well as associating with the middle class, the Hindus, the Australian, the Indian, the retired, and so on. Instead of viewing groups as having a substantive unified identity, Young (2000: 99) suggests that they are better seen as the product of differentiated relations. Groups position individuals, but they do not constitute their identities. Identity, for Young, is a wholly individual endeavour which is formed with reference to, inter alia, one's group positions.

17 These six aspects of the processes of identity are not, of course, an exhaustive list of the nature of identity. They merely represent six pivotal characteristics which provide a broad sketch of the meaning of identity, and aim at elucidating the concept of 'identity markers'.

Young's threefold criticism of group identity as essentialist, incongruent with social realities and blind to internal plurality is well-founded. However, my claim is that this does not translate into an abandonment of the notion of group identity, for two reasons. First, she fails to explain why these critiques cannot equally be levelled at the concept of individual identity. Secondly, and crucially, she also fails to explain the move from these flaws in the concept of group identity to the conclusion that groups do not possess an identity. Therefore, whilst Young's criticism is accurate, it does not justify the claim that groups do not have an identity. My claim here is that the unhelpful determinist tendencies of identity are better resolved by employing my new conceptual tool of identity markers.

First, Young's criticism of group identity mirrors the unhelpful tendencies outlined in my earlier account of the determinist hindrance of identity. By making reference to Elizabeth Spelman's pop-bead metaphor, Young herself explains that a 'person's identity is not some sum of her gender, racial, class, and national affinities' (2000: 102). As I argued earlier, it is in fact identity, and not just group identity, which is unable to resist this temptation of viewing individuals and groups as tangible wholes that display a definable list of attributes. By identifying an individual as a woman, she is not just categorised as part of a group of individuals that display an essentialised list of womanly characteristics, she is also conceptualised as an individual, existing independently of this group, who displays these attributes.

At the root of this impossibility of separating out individual and group identity is their intimate connection. Erikson (1968: 22–3) clearly expresses that the processes of identity take place at the core of the individual *and* at the core of one's communal culture. Thus, to identify individual and group identity is to isolate the inseparable twin aspects of the same processes. Young's example of the woman that denies identification with other women is actually an example of how one's communal growth contributes to the processes of identity. It does not justify the conclusion that group identity is a fallacy; rather, it demonstrates that the processes of identity can take place in cooperation with, or opposition to, shared group understandings, but that they nevertheless draw upon this communal aspect of identity.

Furthermore, Young's argument that this essentialised list of attributes denies groups their internal plurality also applies to individuals. Individuals have multiple and conflicting identities that vary over time and space, and from individual to individual. Young's woman that denies identification with other women may still view being a woman as part of her identity, whilst the person next to her may envisage her identity as a woman in a radically different way. However, they both still possess identities as women. Young's criticism of group identity can, therefore, equally be levelled at individual identity, primarily because the two represent inseparable twin aspects of the processes of identity.

Secondly, Young never explains how she moves from the premise of these essentialist tendencies of the notion of identity, to the conclusion that groups cannot possess an identity. Without explanation of the progress from premise to conclusion, this appears to be an untenable position, not least because groups not only possess characteristics and traits that contribute to their processes of identity, but that they also perceive of themselves as possessing a group identity. Indeed, it is often this sense of group identity which is crucial to the solidarity and loyalty of social groupings. Whilst this lack of explanation could be seen as a lacuna in Young's argument, I would argue that close inspection reveals that Young does not, in fact, assert that groups do not have identity, and that there is no such gap in the progress of her argument. She merely makes the claim that 'we should affirm that groups do not have identities *as such*' (2000: 82, emphasis added), in order to permit a better focus upon how her relational logic allows for a more accurate understanding of group difference. At its core, her argument runs on similar tracks to the one that I am making here: she isolates three unconstructive tendencies of group identity and suggests that viewing group difference as a product of the structure, and more specifically the structural inequalities, of our social lives is more accurate, and would therefore better inform theories of justice.

Young's (2000: 92–9) focus on structural inequalities provides a sophisticated and accurate account of how social relations can act as oppressive forces, which then go on to shape relations between groups and our allegiances. In particular, she makes reference to Marilyn Frye's metaphor that oppression operates like a birdcage (Frye 1983, quoted in Young 2000: 92–3); it is only possible to understand the impact of oppressive social relations when they are viewed as coming together like the wires of a birdcage that then have the cumulative effect of ensnaring the bird. Viewed one wire at a time, it is not possible to see how one wire can stop the bird flying. It is these differences, 'as structured by a set of relationships and interactions[,] that act together to produce specific possibilities and preclude others, and which operate in a reinforcing circle' (Young 2000: 93). However, my contention here is that this structural inequalities perspective of diversity loses all of the advantageous aspects of identity. Identity may harbour an unhelpful tendency, but it nevertheless captures some crucial aspects of the nature of diversity, such that it cannot be cast aside altogether in the way that Young proposes. Tied up with the concept of identity are notions of dignity, self-worth, the moral self and the voice of nature within us.[18] It follows from this that identity can encapsulate the (plural) values that people attach to their diverse traits and characteristics. By casting aside identity all of this is lost. My proposal, therefore, is that by using the concept of identity markers, as an accessory to identity, it is possible to surmount these essentialist tendencies without losing all of the useful and vital elements that identity provides when employed as a conceptual tool to understand diversity.

This consideration of Iris Marion Young's structural inequalities view of diversity provides two important conclusions. First, groups can and do possess identities. Secondly, complete abandonment of the notion of identity when understanding diversity is more harmful than useful, because of the vital elements

18 See Taylor (1994: 25–37) for an account of the importance of identity and the nature of the role it occupies in people's lives.

that are encompassed within the concept. These final conclusions complete the six key characteristics of the processes of identity.

There are two further crucial points to emphasise at this juncture. First, in drawing some boundaries around what the processes of identity entail, it does not follow that the concept of identity has been reified or essentialised; indeed, identity is not so much a thing, as much as it is processes that occur both in the self and the group. Secondly, it is crucial to recognise that there are no clear boundaries between identity and identity markers. Like identity, identity markers display these six characteristics: they are (i) part of processes which are neither finished nor finishable; (ii) constituted internally and reflect human agency; (iii) external in nature and are social constructs; (iv) not singular in nature; (v) constructs of domains inside and outside of reason and logic; and (vi) formed and found amongst both individuals and groups.

Social Realities and Identity: Examples of the Six Aspects of Identity

A useful example of the six aspects of the processes of identity outlined above can be found in socio-legal accounts of South Asian settlers in Britain. In these accounts of the qualitative character of the South Asian presence in Britain, a more tangible and pragmatic description of the process of identity can be found than the theoretical account above. I use here Ballard's (1994) anthropological work on South Asians in Britain and Menski's legal work on 'ethnic minorities' in Britain (1988b, 1993, 1998), which draws upon anthropological and sociological studies, to inform this tangible example of the six characteristics of identity processes.

Earlier I introduced Roger Ballard's account of the creation of *Desh Pardesh* amongst British South Asians and Professor Werner Menski's observation of the creation of legal hybrids within Britain's ethnic communities. Ballard identified that South Asians in Britain continue to draw inspiration from their cultural, religious and linguistic heritage, but that the process of creating *Desh Pardesh* involved reinterpreting and rebuilding 'their lives *on their own terms*' (1994: 5, emphasis added). It was noted that the creation of *Desh Pardesh* did not correspond with the official expectations of assimilation by Afro-Caribbean and South Asian diasporas into mainstream British society. Additionally, the idea that *Desh Pardesh* is the product of strategies that aim to cope with the changed requirements in Britain was also found in Ballard's work (1994).

I went on to relate *Desh Pardesh* to Pearl and Menski's (1998: 51–83) observation of the creation of legal hybrids amongst British South Asians. In particular, I considered Menski's example of the double marriage amongst British South Asians. Moreover, I used this as a platform to move to Menski's explanation of the creation of hybrid laws within these communities, laws which govern day-to-day life.[19] Indeed, the existence of hybrid laws has been observed beyond

19 See, for example, Menski (1988b, 1991, 1993, 2001) and Pearl and Menski (1998).

Britain's Muslim community. Zaman (2008), for example, charts the evolution of hybrid Islamic laws, which she terms *Amrikan Shari'a*, that live in the shadow of the official American legal system. She describes these hybrid laws as processes whereby Islamic law is reconstructed to take the American legal context into account.[20] Finally, I introduced Ballard's concept of skilled cultural navigators, a term he uses to describe those individuals who develop an accomplished capacity to switch cultural codes (1994: 30–31). However, given my objections to the use of 'culture' to conceptualise diversity, it seems appropriate to adapt this term and reinterpret it so that it becomes 'skilled *identity* navigators'.

Ballard's explanation of the reconstruction and renegotiation of aspects of day-to-day life by South Asians in Britain, and Menski's observations of this reconstruction within a legal context, clearly draw out the six aspects of the processes of identity that I have isolated. Intrinsic to the nature of identity is that it is neither reified nor absolute; it is a set of processes that are neither finished nor finishable, and this explanation of the continual adaptation and reinterpretation of life illustrates this. Ballard's study also demonstrates the internal aspects of the processes of identity: the reinterpretation and reconstruction of day-to-day life takes place 'on their own terms' (1994: 5, 34). Vital to the processes of identity is the agency that it involves: were the processes to take place on another person or group's terms, this agency would be violated and the sense of self or group inherent in identity would be lost, doing damage to individual or group dignity in the process.

Menski's explanation of the double weddings that take place amongst British South Asians provides a neat illustration of the external aspects of the processes of identity. Furthermore, Ballard's description of the creation of *Desh Pardesh* as an adaptive strategy born of the need to cope with a new environment, equally demonstrates the impact of external climates upon the direction of the processes of identity. The multiple, conflicting and value plural character of identity processes is precisely what precipitates the 'skilled identity navigator' who is able to negotiate the plural arenas of her identities.

The final two aspects of identity processes, that they exist within and outside of the domains of reason, and that they take place at the core of the individual and the group, are more camouflaged. However, if the double wedding scenario is contemplated, they begin to take shape. If reason were privileged in the processes of identity, one would expect to see far fewer double weddings: it is questionable whether, when reasoned out, quite so many people would feel the need to have a religious ceremony, which holds no legal value under English law, as well as

20 Zaman (2008) notes that in the United States at least, these developments are almost completely unstudied. I suspect that this is the case in many other jurisdictions, making the socio-legal literature that I can draw on to support my arguments largely limited to Britain's South Asian population. This, however, seems to be slowly changing, and one recent notable study, Fournier (2010), involves a comparative analysis of *mahr* in the official legal systems of Canada, the United States, France and Germany.

incorporating the civil ceremony, required for the marriage to be valid according to English law. The observation of the phenomenon of the double wedding, with the English legal requirements taking a backseat role, confirms that processes of identity can take place in the more vague domains of intuition and unreasoned attachment, and draw upon heritage and tradition far more than they would if they exclusively took place in the more calculated domain of reason. Furthermore, the very nature of a wedding ceremony vindicates the inseparability of the individual and group processes of identity. The individual and intimate commitment of the bride and groom necessarily involves the familial and kinship group, whose presence and participation in the wedding is also vital.

Desh Pardesh, therefore, provides an elegant and fitting example of the six key characteristics of the processes of identity. Nevertheless, it does not illuminate and clarify the role of identity markers in surmounting the irresistible proclivity towards determinist classifications that identity displays.

The Role of Identity Markers

I propose 'identity markers' as a supplemental concept to 'identity', with the purpose of overcoming the latter's irresistible moves towards essentialised and singular identities. In order to grasp fully the role of identity markers, it is crucial to appreciate that they do not act as a substitute for identity, nor are they an attempt to deconstruct and reconstruct identity. Identity markers act as an accessory to identity, a method of surmounting its determinist tendency, thereby making room for the six key characteristics of identity which are otherwise obscured by its determinist tendency. Furthermore, they move away from the singular affiliation that the concepts of race, religion, culture and ethnicity promote, and do not engage in a process of ranking values.[21]

In fulfilling the purpose of surmounting these essentialist and reductionist tendencies, identity markers permit a more useful and accurate understanding of diversity in contemporary societies, in particular because they allow a greater correspondence to social realities. Identity markers, therefore, are vital to the local normative framework employed in this project, since in accurately portraying the nature of diversity in contemporary societies they have two vital, and interrelated, roles. First, they speak to my diversity-conscious conception of justice and the expansive character of justice explained as part of my triad of norms. By circumventing the discussion of boundaries and the value judgment that comes with the use of ethnicity, culture, religion and race to understand diversity, identity markers permit the necessary focus upon justice. The very idea of a form of justice that values and therefore encourages the self-actualisation of authentic and diverse identities is lost and obscured in the premature process of defining boundaries. Furthermore, where a value judgment is made as part of the conceptualisation of

21 In essence, my aim is to overcome the limitation that I identified in Chapters 4 and 5.

diversity, the ideal of free and fair access to and participation in civil society is negated. Secondly, in overcoming the determinist hindrance of identity, identity markers make room for the local specificities that I have argued must be accounted for. Identity markers permit a greater degree of fluidity and dynamism in the conceptualisation of diversity, and, in turn, this allows the notion of what it means to inhabit a particular skin to evolve according to local variances, and in so doing it respects my triad of norms. As part of the global and local normative framework argued for in this project, identity markers ground the new vista on constitutional pluralism that I offer, and thereby contribute to a platform upon which new legal responses to diversity can be crafted. However, prior to setting out my new vista on constitutional pluralism, it is necessary to be as clear as possible in my definition of identity markers and their role.

Like identity, identity markers are part of fluid and dynamic ongoing processes; they are internal and reflect the exercise of human agency; they are subject to external environments and influences, and are socially constructed; they are multiple, intersecting, conflicting and value plural; they are constructs of domains of reason, intuition and emotion; and they relate to the processes of selfhood and group. We must not, however, conceptualise identity markers as points marking out identity, since this falls into the essentialist trap and views identity as a whole. Rather, they should be understood as the beads of fragmented, often conflicting and always unfinished identity processes.[22]

Identity markers reflect those points in time and space when the beads of identity are at their most tangible. They are particularly apt to describe the challenges of justice in diverse societies since identity markers are visible at the heart of the sites of conflict and debate in this field. In fact, the most instructive explanation of the role of identity markers can be achieved through analysis of the case of *R (on the application of Begum) v Headteacher and Governors of Denbigh High School*.[23] In this case, Shabina Begum sought judicial review of her school's decision not to allow her to wear a *jilbab*,[24] on the grounds that the decision breached her right to manifest her religion or belief enshrined in Article 9 of the ECHR.[25] Ms Begum attended a secondary community school with a diverse mix of pupils, and a school uniform policy that endeavoured to reflect this diversity. As such the uniform

---

22 Sen makes note of this aspect of identity, most recently terming them 'contrasting' and 'non-contrasting' identities, and earlier calling them 'competing' and 'non-competing' identities (2001a: 322–5, 2001b: 12–13, 2006: 28–9).

23 [2005] 2 All ER 396 (CA); [2006] 2 All ER 487 (HL).

24 The *jilbab* is a long loose-fitting one-piece garment which goes down to the ankles and is intended to hide the shape of the wearer's body. It is often worn together with a *hijab*.

25 The respondent also claimed that she had been excluded from school on account of her choice to wear the *jilbab* and that this infringed her right not to be denied an education under Article 2 of the First Protocol to the ECHR. However, this aspect of the claim is not relevant to the arguments made here.

included provisions for a *shalwar kameeze* and head-scarves of specified design, which were thought to satisfy the Islamic requirements of modest dress. Although Ms Begum had worn the *shalwar kameeze* for two years without encountering any difficulties, she arrived at school with her brother wearing the *jilbab* arguing that this was her interpretation of the modesty necessary to satisfy the requirements of Islam. The relevant school authorities informed her that this was not part of the school uniform and that she would not be admitted to school wearing the *jilbab*, but that she was free to attend school wearing the prescribed uniform.

Not willing to wear anything but the *jilbab* Ms Begum took matters to court. The Administrative Court in England & Wales dismissed her claims; however, the Court of Appeal reversed this decision and found in her favour. This judgment was then reversed when Denbigh High School appealed to the House of Lords. Three of the Lords found that Shabina Begum's Article 9(1) ECHR rights had not been infringed, and two of the Lords found that whilst her Article 9(1) ECHR rights had been interfered with, this interference was justified under Article 9(2) ECHR. However, what is relevant to my illustration of identity markers is not the outcome of the case, but the way in which both the Court of Appeal and House of Lords handled the Article 9 claim. My claim is that Ms Begum's *jilbab* is an example of an identity marker. Furthermore, the incoherent manner in which the courts dealt with this matter evidences the limits of viewing diversity in the isolated terms of religion, or ethnicity, race and culture. In order to demonstrate this I will first identify the confused and incongruent aspects of the reasoning of the Court of Appeal and the House of Lords. I will then explain and justify my claim that the *jilbab* is an identity marker, something more than merely an expression of a religious belief, by making reference to the six key characteristics of identity markers and the political dimension of identity. Finally, I will demonstrate how viewing the *jilbab* as an identity marker in this case provides routes to officials that would allow them better to deal with the challenges of justice in diverse societies.

The *Begum* case was argued on the basis that wearing the *jilbab* was the expression of a religious belief (and as such it was protected by Article 9 ECHR). None of the courts that heard the case, the Administrative Court, the Court of Appeal and the House of Lords, questioned that this was a claim centred upon religious belief. Indeed, Lord Bingham of Cornhill stressed that the House viewed Ms Begum's choice to wear the *jilbab* as a sincere interpretation of her faith, and thus it required respect. Moreover, the fact that she had changed her views and gone from wearing the *shalwar kameeze* to the *jilbab*, and that her interpretation was only shared by a small minority of people, did not in any way impact upon the sincerity of her religious belief (para 21). Yet, the way in which the Court of Appeal and House of Lords reasoned out their judgments reveals a lack of clarity and some inconsistent reasoning. My argument is that this is due to the court's inability to express the real concerns that lie at the heart of this case, and that this inability is a consequence of the limitations created by viewing this case as being concerned with the manifestation of a religious belief.

In response to Ms Begum's claim the Headteacher and Governors of Denbigh High School argued that the school uniform was a crucial aspect of promoting social cohesion, a sense of communal identity and a positive ethos (para 59, CA; para 6, HL). It is made clear in both judgments that the school had made significant efforts to consult various religious groups in that locality to ensure that the uniform reflected the diversity of religious beliefs of the school's pupils. Not only was it possible to wear a *shalwar kameeze*, but the school also allowed Muslim pupils to wear a *hijab*. Within such a context it becomes hard to justify why the addition of a garment, which it is accepted represents a genuine interpretation of the requirements of Islam (albeit a minority view), would threaten the school's community and cohesion.

Both the Court of Appeal and the House of Lords make reference to the fact that the school's Headteacher is herself Muslim and state that this means she has a good understanding of Islamic dress requirements. Even if it is accepted that religions are internally plural, and she could not possibly have knowledge of all the interpretations of the Islamic faith, at the very least it is suggested that her position as a female Muslim makes her more sensitive to Ms Begum's claim. This, in turn, acts to legitimise her refusal to allow the *jilbab* as part of the school's uniform, since it places her beyond accusations of Islamaphobia or even discrimination. This seems somewhat inaccurate given the internal plurality and conflict within all groups, whether such groups are based upon common religious beliefs or not.

Arguments on behalf of the school included the claim that other female Muslim pupils would feel under pressure to adopt the *jilbab*, and that the introduction of the *jilbab* would create a hierarchy of believers based upon the strictness of the views of those believers. One of the aims of the school's uniform policy was to protect the rights and freedoms of those pupils who would come under pressure to don the *jilbab*. These arguments can be contrasted with the assertion that Ms Begum was free to attend other schools where the *jilbab* was permitted. It can be accepted that it is for each individual school to balance the rights and freedoms of its pupils when deciding upon an appropriate uniform. However, the House of Lords' choice not to interfere in the school's decision that it needed to protect its pupils from 'an extremist version of the Muslim religion' (para 65, HL), taken together with its strong words of praise for the school and its Headteacher who had turned a poorly performing school into a school with excellent results, and a beacon of multiculturalism, makes the first steps of the creation of what constitutes an acceptable British Muslim, and those non-British Muslims that do not fit into this category. The message appears to be that moderate Islamic views and the *hijab* can make a well-adjusted and successful British citizen, and that this garment will place no pressure on other believers, nor will it contribute to a hierarchy of believers; the *jilbab*, however, does not fit into this category. Not only does this dichotomy of the acceptable and non-acceptable Muslim venture onto troubling terrain, this message fails to sit well with the assertion and acceptance of the *jilbab* as merely a manifestation of a sincere religious belief. Furthermore, it seems inconsistent with the House of Lords' insistence that it is not in any way questioning the sincerity of Ms Begum's interpretation of her faith.

In both the Court of Appeal and House of Lords judgments it is clear that diversity is not viewed as an issue of identity. The courts fall into the trap of assuming that the boundaries between religion, race, ethnicity and culture are fixed and identifiable. Furthermore, in assuming the labels religion and ethnicity to describe the diversity of the pupils within the school they ignore the political aspect attendant to diverse identities. There are two particular aspects of the judgment which illustrate this point. First, the courts mention the way that the school was careful to consult a number of Muslim organisations within its locality before deciding on the specific design of the school uniform. It is implied by this that the school has therefore made the necessary efforts to ensure that the tenets of Islam have been respected. It is arguable that the extensive consultation that the school undertook is more than reasonable. Given the vast internal plurality of interpretation within any religion it would be unreasonable to expect any school to reflect each and every interpretation. However, the emphasis placed upon this as an example of the school's efforts to accommodate the diverse backgrounds of its pupils clearly illustrates the way in which diversity is understood. Seventy-nine per cent of the school's pupils are described as 'Muslim' and its 'very diverse intake' encompasses '21 different ethnic groups and 10 religious groupings' (para 3, HL). The diversity within the school, then, is understood in terms of ethnicity and religion. Moreover, Ms Begum and her brother also view the matter on these terms. This is evident when it is mentioned that Ms Begum's brother views the *shalwar kameeze* as a cultural rather than a religious garment (para 14, CA). This strict delineation of categories, and its consequences, is precisely the problem that identity and identity markers seek to remedy.

Secondly, a political dimension to the case seems occasionally to be drawn out by both courts. The school's argument that it needs to protect its pupils from extremist views, and that it wants to guard against the creation of religious inferiors evidences this point (para 51, CA), as does the mention of the threatening manner in which Ms Begum's brother and another young man approached the school when she first attended wearing the *jilbab* (para 15, CA; para 10, HL). It is worth noting that the media have reported that Ms Begum's brother has connections with a radical group named Hizb ut-Tahrir and speculated that Ms Begum had come under the influence of her brother. Indeed both courts mention that Ms Begum lost her father at an early age, and that she had recently lost her mother, who spoke no English. A picture which invokes political activities emerges with the mention of these facts. That they are not relevant to the legal question as framed is clear from Brooke LJ's sensitive attempt to steer clear of the label 'fundamentalist' in describing those who believe it is necessary to wear the *jilbab* (para 31, CA). Nevertheless, the political dimension of this choice to wear the *jilbab* still appears throughout the case. Here is a clear example of how the labels religion, ethnicity, culture and race are inadequate in describing the diversity in question.

My claim is that Ms Begum's *jilbab* is an example of an identity marker, and the facts of the case confirm that the six key elements of identity markers are present. Identity markers reflect a fluid and dynamic ongoing process; Ms Begum's choice to wear the *jilbab*, having happily worn a *shalwar kameeze* for two years, is an example of the way in which individuals revise and rethink their identities, and that these are ongoing processes that never come to completion. Yet in pleading her case it was felt necessary to point out that she came to this decision as she took an increasing interest in her religion (para 14, CA). Her choice to wear the *jilbab* merely reflects the natural and ongoing processes of identity. The human agency and internal element of identity markers can be seen in Ms Begum's choice to express herself through changing the way she dressed. However, there is also an external and socially constructed aspect to this identity marker: it is entirely possible that her family's views had an influence upon her choice, and the socially constructed political ramifications of such a garment are bound to have had some role to play in her decision. That identity markers are multiple and conflicting can also be seen in this case; Ms Begum's identity is more than just her *jilbab*, she probably had valid reasons for not wishing to attend any other school which went beyond just wanting to make a point about her *jilbab*. Perhaps she had a close circle of friends and these friendships were also crucial reference points for the creation of her identity markers. Fifthly, the mention of Ms Begum's parents, their status and her brother's influence evidences that identity markers are not only situated within domains of reason; they also exist in the domains of emotions and intuitions. Finally, that Ms Begum's *jilbab* involves not merely her own decision but the influence of radical groups and family members illustrates that identity markers relate to processes of selfhood *and* the group.

Viewed as an identity marker, rather than a manifestation of a religious belief, Ms Begum's claim to have the right to wear the *jilbab* takes on a different hue. It becomes unimportant whether the school has consulted various different religious sources, or whether the right decision-making process has been followed, as the Court of Appeal held, because this is no longer just a religious matter. No school could reasonably be expected to cater for all the diverse identity markers that its pupils create. It is irrelevant that the Headteacher has the same or similar religious background to Ms Begum. More importantly, the true arguments which deal with the political dimensions of the *jilbab* not only make more sense, but become relevant. The core issue in this case is exposed by viewing the *jilbab* as an identity marker: the school is entrusted with the care of these young children and the question is whether it is appropriate and safe, given the political climate that we live in, for the school to allow its pupils to be exposed to extremist and radical Islamic views. Once this becomes the core issue of the case the school's argument that including the *jilbab* in its school uniform threatens cohesion within the school makes far more sense. Gone also are the questions of whether a sincere interpretation of a religious belief ought to be accommodated, and so the courts avoid indirectly endorsing or rejecting certain religious beliefs and creating a vision of the acceptable British Muslim. More importantly, the courts would be at liberty fully to explore the most troubling aspects of this case, namely the influence of the brother upon Ms Begum and the potential exposure of the school to extremist groups. Viewed as an Article 9 ECHR matter, none of these considerations can be legitimately considered. However, if the *jilbab* is viewed as an identity marker, serious dialogue of these pressing issues can be entered into by the courts.

Chapter 9
Identity Markers and Legal Pluralism

Identity markers provide an account of diversity that gives law the potential to fulfil its role in meeting the challenges of my diversity-conscious conception of justice. However, they are intended as an analytical tool, rather than the basis for legal claims. In order to emphasise this, in this chapter I illustrate the relations between identity markers and law. First, this requires an account of the plural nature of law, and I use Chiba's model of legal pluralism as my reference point. This account of Chiba's model also provides an opportunity to demonstrate that the idea of the plurality of law is not antithetical to dominant jurisprudential theories. By contrasting traditional explanations of British constitutional law against Chiba's model of law, I show that the gap between them is not as wide as one might assume. I specifically target British constitutional law in large part because its unwritten nature makes it ideal to illustrate the plural nature of law, but also because there is an assumption, even amongst lawyers, that jurisdictions without written constitutional documents must have no constitution. As well as facilitating an analysis of constitutional law as the embodiment of plural conceptions of law, Chiba's three layers of law permit an illustration of identity markers beyond the confines of case law and legislation. Revealing the relations between identity markers and law opens the door for me to explain the conceptualisation of law that forms an integral part of my fresh perspectives on law. In the final section of this chapter, I summarise Menski's global working definition of law. Furthermore, I present this as the model of law that corresponds with realities of diversity and, therefore, provides the opportunity for law to begin to meet the challenges of a diversity-conscious justice.

Chiba's Tripartite Model of Law

A constructive starting point to introducing the idea of the plurality of law is the challenge that legal pluralism makes to dominant conceptualisations of law. Anderson usefully separates this challenge into three strands (Anderson 2005: 39): there are challenges 'first, to the centralist notion that law only emanates from the state; secondly, to monist ideas of the systematic coherence and singularity of law; and thirdly, to the positivist view that we can trace a legal order as something "out there" apart from the agents who created it'. For the purposes of this project this 'debunking' quality of legal pluralism is crucial (J. Griffiths 1986: 5). A key component of the constitutional pluralist vision that I argue for is its ability to open up areas and ideas that traditionally do not fall within the sphere of constitutional law. It is equally as crucial to note that the form of legal pluralism that supports my construction of constitutional pluralism is not anti-statist. The aim is neither to deny the relevance of the nation-state, nor is it to replace the nation-state with a post-modern site of power; rather, it is to suggest that we need to think *beyond* the nation-state if we hope to clear the obstacles that hinder the path towards justice.

I propose to use Anderson's three challenges, outlined above, together with Masaji Chiba's tripartite model of law, to explain my pluralist vision of constitutions and constitutional law, and reveal the relations between identity markers and law.[1] Chiba is a Japanese scholar whose work on legal pluralism focuses upon reassessing the orthodox jurisprudential account of the 'development of a non-Western legal system as a history of received Western law' (Chiba 1986: v). Chiba writes that his is a non-Western point of view, and from this vantage point the orthodox account of received Western law does not seem reasonable.[2] To explain these complex interactions of laws from a non-Western point of view, he constructs a tripartite model of law, with the specific aim of placing law within its social and cultural context. Chiba writes that 'law is so inseparably rooted in society as to be approachable by sociological methods. Furthermore, it has also become accepted that law must be recognized as an aspect of the total culture of a people' (1986: 1).[3] Arguably, Chiba's non-Western model has relevance for this project, because it is so intimately tied to post-colonial peoples and therefore concerned with understanding law in the context of non-Westerners, or more precisely those with a non-Western heritage.

The three levels of Chiba's tripartite structure of law are official law, unofficial law and legal postulates (Chiba 1986: 5–6):

> *Official law* is the legal system sanctioned by the legitimate authority of a country. *State law* is ordinarily understood as a typical official law or even the only official law. Truly, it is directly sanctioned by the legitimate authority of the government of a state to have overall jurisdiction over the country. But as a matter of nature it is only one among many official laws of a country, however dominant it may appear over the others. For instance, as in most contemporary countries with established religions, religious laws may be partially included in or accommodated by state law, but partially functioning out of the jurisdiction of the latter, thus forming its own system different from state law.

1 See Menski (2006: 119–28) for a detailed account of Chiba's tripartite model of law. I am borrowing the description 'tripartite model of law' from Menski; it is not one that Chiba himself uses.

2 Although he writes from a non-Western perspective, Chiba's work has a Japanese influence: see Menski (2006: 33) citing Igarashi (1990), Oda (1992) and Dean (2002).

3 I would argue that instead of writing of the culture of a people, or a nation, it would be more meaningful to write in terms of the identity or identities of a people or nation.

It is crucial to emphasise that Chiba takes a plural approach to constructing the concept of official law. There is no absolute consonance between state laws and official law; instead, religious laws, customs and other practices that are not usually regarded as law within a dominant framework, can come within the purview of official law, so long as they are 'sanctioned by the legitimate authority of a country'. In this context, Chiba provides a sophisticated structure of law, where unofficial law is not just a tier of law that describes elements outside of state law. Instead, Chiba describes it thus (1986: 6):

> *Unofficial law* is the legal system not officially sanctioned by any legitimate authority, but sanctioned in practice by the general consensus of a certain circle of people, whether within or beyond the bounds of a country. That general consensus may be either consciously recognized and expressed in formal rules, or unconsciously observed in particular patterns of behaviour. However, not all such unofficial practices supported by general consensus are to be included in unofficial law. Unofficial law is here limited to those unofficial practices which have a distinct influence upon the effectiveness of official law; in other words those which distinctively supplement, oppose, modify, or undermine any of the official laws, including state law.

A full picture of Chiba's conceptual scheme requires an understanding of his final tier of law, legal postulates, which act as founding elements to unofficial and official laws. He explains that a legal postulate is (1986: 6–7):

> [A] value principle or value system specifically connected with a particular official or unofficial law, which acts to found, justify and orient the latter. It may consist of established legal ideas such as natural law, justice, equity, and so on in [dominant] jurisprudence; sacred truths and precepts emanating from various gods in religious law; social and cultural postulates affording the structural and functional basis for a society embodied in clan unity, exogamy, bilineal descent, seniority, individual freedom, national philosophy, and so on; political ideologies, often closely connected with economic policies, as in capitalism or socialism; and so on. The legal postulates of a country, whether official or unofficial, are as a whole required to keep a certain degree of consonance with one another. But complete consonance cannot be expected. First, because as each legal postulate is in support of a particular system of official or unofficial law, the potential of conflict with other systems, as pointed out above, is high. Second, because the legal postulate may tend to upset the *status quo* of its supported official or unofficial law in order to improve or even replace the latter.

British Constitutional Law as Legal Pluralism in Action

The idea that constitutional law emanates from the state is unexceptional, and certainly summarises the current view of the British Constitution. However, in the British context, the sources of constitutional law take on a broader definition than the usual positivist conceptualisation of law as state law; the uncodified nature of the British Constitution makes historical struggles over power constitutive of its content. Stating that *sources*, for there is no one ultimate *source*, of the British Constitution can be found outside of the dominant notion of state law evokes Chiba's definition of official law. Nevertheless, understanding the contemporary British Constitution in terms of key historical moments is a technique that has not only been employed by eminent experts on British constitutional law, such as Professor Vernon Bogdanor,[4] but constitutional history has long since been accepted as a vital facet of public law scholarship. In this regard one can readily recall F.W. Maitland's *The Constitutional History of England* and, of course, A.V. Dicey's seminal text, *Introduction to the Study of the Law of the Constitution*, both of which have substantial historical content. Indeed, Bogdanor notes that 'in Dicey's day ... there was a thriving tradition of constitutional history' with leading scholars in the field being historical jurists; in this regard he references 'Maine, Pollock, Vinogradoff, Bryce, Maitland, Hancock and Richey' (Bogdanor 1987: 459). Official constitutional law, therefore, can be understood to include those elements that may not have been produced by a state organ, but have been legitimated by a state organ. This traditional view of the British Constitution not only corroborates Chiba's belief that 'legal pluralism is a universal phenomenon' (Menski 2006: 119), but also hints at the saliency of Chiba's model in Western countries.

In emphasising the normative content of the British Constitution, as is the case with the prescriptive approach taken here, it is easy to become detached from the importance of its historical elements. To ensure that the importance of constitutional history is underlined, let me provide one striking example of an historical narrative that tells us something important, perhaps even radical, about the nature of the British Constitution. It is not possible at the first reading of the European Communities Act 1972 (ECA 1972) to grasp what it truly means for the British Constitution. From an initial reading of the ECA 1972, it would certainly be possible to understand that this statute was passed to implement Britain's membership of the European Community (as it was at that time; it is now the European Union). The ECA 1972 contains various measures and mechanisms that ensure European legislation has effect in English law. However, section 2(4) of the ECA 1972 tells us something about the relations between English law and EU law.[5] Simple reading of this section would allow one to conclude that English

4 See Bogdanor (2004).

5 I have deliberately not included the exact wording of this section as the cross-references made to other sections of the ECA 1972 would render it almost meaningless

law is subordinate to EU law. Yet, this is only a partial account of these relations, which is deficient precisely because it lacks any historical context.

Dicey saw the two pillars of the British Constitution to be parliamentary sovereignty and the rule of law, the former being of concern here. The doctrine of parliamentary sovereignty states that there are no legal limits upon Parliament's legislative power, except that Parliament cannot fetter its own powers in the future. With this historical context, the tension between parliamentary sovereignty and section 2(4) ECA 1972 becomes clearer: if Parliament cannot fetter its own powers in the future, section 2(4) must be ineffective since it aims to prohibit Parliament from passing any legislation that overrides EU law. The gravity of this constitutional issue is clearly visible in the careful wording of the judgments in the case law surrounding this question,[6] as well as in the diametrically opposed conclusions of commentators following these cases.[7] In this particular context, it does not matter what the correct interpretation of this relationship is, or even if there is one correct interpretation; rather, it is crucial that it would be impossible to understand this constitutional question without an historical narrative. This one episode of constitutional history, and there are many others,[8] illustrates the importance of constitutional history to our understanding of the British Constitution.

Chiba's definition of official law acts as a strong reminder of the importance of factors aside from state law that are sources of constitutional law, although, of course, these non-state sources must be ultimately sanctioned by the legitimate authority within the state to be considered as official law. Moreover, the consonance

---

without reproducing a substantial portion of this piece of legislation. It is suffice to note that s 2(4) ECA 1972, on its face, appears to stop Parliament from passing any laws that conflict with European legislation.

6 See *Macarthys Ltd v Smith* [1979] 3 All ER 325; *Factortame Ltd v Secretary of State for Transport* [1990] 2 AC 85; *Factortame Ltd v Secretary of State for Transport (No 2)* [1991] 1 AC 603; *Equal Opportunities Commission v Secretary of State for Employment* [1994] 1 WLR 409; and also the 'metric martyrs' cases, which as decisions of the lower courts in England and Wales are not as authoritative as the *Factortame* and *EOC* cases, but nevertheless involve consideration of the relation between EU law and domestic law: *Thoburn v Sunderland County Council, Hunt v London Borough of Hackney, Harman and Dove v Cornwall County Council and Collins v London Borough of Sutton* (2003) QB 151.

7 For example, Hartley (1998: 254–5) concludes that following *Macarthys* and *Factortame*, sovereignty remains with Parliament since Eueopean law prevails only because Parliament gives it such supremacy; whereas William Wade interprets the position as a technical legal revolution because an ultimate legal principle has been modified (Wade 1996). See also Professor Bogdanor who agrees with Wade (2007: 483): 'The supremacy of European law over national law must surely imply a limitation of the sovereignty of Parliament'.

8 One of the difficulties of historical accounts of the British Constitution is that there is rarely agreement upon which the key episodes are, and even how best to account for these episodes; should they be pure historical narratives, or should they be arranged in terms of the relationships of power they belong to?

of Chiba's official law with dominant conceptualisations of the sources of the uncodified British Constitution makes one wonder how many theories of law rely too heavily on the accessibility of tangible sources of law, such as legislation, case law and constitutional texts, without critically analysing what truly constitutes the essence of law. This segues neatly into a second source of constitutional law, politics, which is arguably a part of dominant jurisprudence, but is also a non-state source. Again, this may well be a consequence of the uncodified nature of the British Constitution, which forces constitutional lawyers concerned with this jurisdiction to look beyond the immediately accessible.

The idea that the British Constitution and politics are inextricably linked is not novel: de Smith, in his inaugural lecture in 1960, stated that 'in England the constitutional lawyer and the political scientist are forever undivided' (quoted in Bogdanor 1987: 454). Recent historical events in Britain are a good illustration of the way in which its constitutional law is very much a product of the political sphere. For example, in 1950 the United Kingdom joined the Council of Europe, which ultimately led to the ECHR coming into effect and its implementation in the Human Rights Act 1998. Whilst the decision-making process to join the Council of Europe took place within British political circles, it has had clear ramifications for its Constitution, leading, as it did, to the adoption of a set of fundamental human rights, the like of which this Constitution has not seen before. In 1973 the United Kingdom joined the European Community, which, as mentioned above, has altered the ways in which constitutional lawyers conceptualise the British Constitution. 1998 saw the introduction of devolved government in Scotland, Wales and Northern Ireland, all of which followed political negotiations and bargaining. Devolution has changed the power structures of the British Constitution; Bogdanor (1999: 290) has gone so far as to describe the United Kingdom as 'quasi-federal' as a consequence of devolution. It is evident from these few examples that politics and the British Constitution go hand in hand.

Up to this point I have not ventured off dominant British constitutional terrain, and in that regard have not explained the relations between identity markers and law. Yet, it was important to show that British constitutional law, in its traditional conceptualisation, is already plural in nature. I wish to ground my case for fresh perspectives, however, on the central role that identity processes play in our lives, and consequently as a part of an expansive form of justice.

Identity Markers and Law

It is my contention that identity markers can be found within each of the three levels of Chiba's model of law. My reference to identity markers here recalls the earlier discussions, where I considered the nature of identity processes and their relation to culture, race, ethnicity, religion and nationality, and also the consideration of the importance of identity markers for a diversity-conscious conception of justice. In this context, I want to dwell less on the ground that has already been covered and more on how identity processes are a constituent element of law. To explain law in this manner it is necessary to take a pluralistic view, and I rely upon Chiba's tripartite model to show the various levels at which identity markers are relevant.

It is, I believe, possible to make an uncontroversial case for identity markers as part of Chiba's official law. There are numerous laws which quite evidently take matters relating to identity into account. These are most tangibly identifiable in legislation that relates to religious accommodation. For example, India maintains a personal law system whereby its Civil Code contains separate laws that pertain to Hindus, Muslims, Christians, Parsis and Jews, as well as a secular set of family laws.[9] Less obvious is the case law which adjudicates the expression of certain identity markers as lawful, and the legislation which does not permit for specific exemptions but accommodates identity markers on a more general level; these, I argue, also come within the concept of official law. Examples of the former are the *Mandla* and *Begum* cases; and an example of the latter can be found in the provincial Human Rights Codes in Canada. Each province in Canada has its own Human Rights Code that protects individuals from discrimination by legal entities in their daily lives. This means, for example, that universities must accommodate religious observances, private housing cannot be rented out on a discriminatory basis and employers cannot discriminate on any of the enumerated grounds.

Even less evident are those laws which on their face do not appear to concern themselves with identity, yet are intimately linked with who we are, who we want to be and who we ought to be. A good departure point to illustrate this can be found in the history of England's trading laws, precisely because religion and law are so inextricably linked in this jurisdiction. Historically, trading on a Sunday in England was prohibited;[10] this prohibition was embodied in the Shops Act 1950, although even prior to legislation this practice was widely observed in England. This latter observation is particularly important because it highlights that law cannot only be understood as legislation and case law – the essence of law cannot simply be that law is created by national governance structures. Moreover, this example also illustrates one of the intricacies of Chiba's tripartite model of law. Whilst there may not have been any legislation prohibiting Sunday trading, it remains a practice that was sanctioned by the legitimate authority in Britain, thus bringing it within Chiba's definition of official law. Indeed, there is evidence that in Anglo-Saxon

---

9 This system persists despite Article 44 of the Indian Constitution, which directs the state to 'endeavour to secure for the citizens a uniform civil code throughout the territory of India'. Note, however, that whilst this personal law system may appear to be intensely plural in character, Menski has observed (2006: 274) that there has been a gradual 'equitable harmonization across the board', so that one's personal laws hardly make any difference at all.

10 I am purposefully writing about England and not Britain since trading in Scotland was already deregulated; recent legislation has provided workers in Scotland with the right to refuse to work on a Sunday (Sunday Working (Scotland) Act 2003) and this, presumably, is also grounded upon the notion of the Sunday Sabbath as a day of rest.

times trading on a Sunday was treated like any other misdemeanour.[11] In contrast, an unofficial law need only be sanctioned in its practice by a wide consensus.

Although the exact origins of Sunday as the Christian Sabbath are uncertain, over time it has come to be widely (globally) accepted as the day of rest for the Christian faith, and the prohibition of trading on a Sunday in England was a reflection and accommodation of this element of Christian identities. This is particularly evident in the fact that the Shops Act 1950 permitted Jewish traders, who were closed on a Saturday (the Jewish Sabbath), to trade on a Sunday. Arguably, the Sunday Trading Act 1994, which made Sunday trading lawful for all (with limits upon the duration of opening hours),[12] reflected the evolution of this aspect of England's Christian identities. To put this another way, the move away from Sunday as a holy day of rest was not only a way to make space for other religious identity markers, such as the Jewish Sabbath, but also a reflection of the changing nature of Christian identity markers in England; given that nearly 70 per cent of the population of England and Wales identified themselves as White Christians it is difficult to argue that Christianity in England (and Wales) is irrelevant or dead;[13] however, the identity markers through which Christianity is expressed have certainly changed over time. The prohibition of Sunday trading was an official law which expressed an identity marker, and the subsequent amendments to this prohibition chart identity processes and express the identity markers that reflect those processes.

Perhaps, however, a better example of the expression of identity markers in laws beyond legislation and case law is the related area of weekends. In non-Islamic nation-states such as India, Australia, the United States, Germany and Canada, the working week runs from Monday to Friday, and the bulk of employees engaged in regular weekly work are not required to work on the weekends. In contrast, in Islamic nation-states the weekend is Thursday and Friday, because

11 Britain, with its organic evolution of laws, and in particular its early equitable jurisdiction and writ system, has a striking salience with Chiba's definition of official law, as it embodies law which goes beyond our contemporary, and convenient, equation of law with case law and legislation.

12 The six hour limit on the Sunday trading hours helped assuage trade union opposition to the Sunday Trading Bill, together with stipulations that Sunday working had to be strictly voluntary and that premium pay would be offered. As well as opposition from trade unions, in particular the Union of Shop, Distributive and Allied Workers, the Bill received considerable opposition on religious grounds from groups such as the Lord's Day Observance Society and the Christian Keep Sunday Special. See BBC News Online (1994).

13 These statistics are taken from the 2001 census, which, for the first time, asked individuals to identify their religion, although this question was answered on a voluntary basis. For a snapshot of the data on religion and ethnicity see http://www.statistics.gov.uk/cci/nugget.asp?id=395 (last accessed 21 September 2010).

this accommodates Friday as the main day of prayer for Muslims.[14] Saturday and Sunday as the weekend is not stipulated for by any legislation or case law in these countries, but it forms part of the official *law*, because in its nature it is something more than just a regular occurrence.

Recall that in Chiba's model of law, unofficial law can be found in the practices that achieve a general consensus, but that only those practices that have some sort of effect upon official laws can be considered as laws. One very prominent example of identity markers in unofficial laws can be found in marriage rites amongst British South Asians that was referenced earlier. Menski (1991, 1993) has documented the double marriages that take place amongst Hindus, Sikhs and Muslims: there will be, for example, a Muslim, Sikh or Hindu marriage as well as a civil marriage which complies with the requirements of English law. The religious marriage is sometimes adapted (reconstructed) to accommodate the elements required by English law, since English law does not recognise religious marriages aside from those conducted in accordance with the rites of the Church of England,[15] Judaism and the Society of Friends (Quakers).[16] My point is that the marriages that take place according to religious rites, which in the early days after the Second World War had no meaning in English law, are examples of identity markers in unofficial law. They provide a particularly convincing example because marriage rituals are more amenable in our imaginings to the label of law, and therefore less at odds with the idea that law exists beyond state sanctioned law. Marriage is widely appreciated as a life-cycle ritual which holds a particular significance (Hamilton 1995: 37), and although that significance varies across time and space, it holds a special meaning for the participants. It follows that the rites which are chosen, or when marriage rites are rejected, involves a deliberate and often thoughtful decision process, because these choices involve the consciences of those involved. This implicit context makes it easier to appreciate that these rites, or lack thereof, have a law-like quality for those that have chosen them.

Importantly, this example of religious marriage rites also illustrates the interaction between official and unofficial laws that Chiba writes of in his definition of unofficial law. By the time of the Marriage Act 1949 it was possible to register places of worship so that, with the inclusion of certain words,[17] and the presence

14 The United Arab Emirates are the one exception to this, where the weekend has moved to Friday and Saturday, in order to further involvement in the global economy, international relations and, perhaps, growing non-Muslim communities. See Janardhan (2006).

15 Marriage Act 1949 ss 78(2) and 80(3).

16 Marriage Act 1949 s 26(1)(d) for the Society of Friends, and s 47 for Judaism.

17 These words reflect English law's conceptualisation of marriage and are, in fact, taken from the case of *Hyde v Hyde and Woodmansee* (1865–1869) LR 1 P & D 130, where in Christiandom a marriage was understood as 'the voluntary union for life of one man and one woman, to the exclusion of all others'. They are not required by law per se, in its positive incarnation, but are used as a matter of common practice. Arguably this situation

of an authorised official to administer the prescribed format, the civil marriage, which was required by English law for a valid marriage, could take place in the same building and at practically the same time as the religious marriage rites.

Care must be taken not to confuse this with recognition by English law of these religious marriages. Instead, this statute was a functional solution to the problem posed by marriages that took place within Christian denominations that were outside of the Anglican Church of England – 'non-denominational churches' – and therefore not recognised as valid marriages by English law. Although it was designed with other purposes in mind, this statute seemed also to provide a device that could be utilised by other religions and so could have purpose beyond denominational divides. However, few British South Asians seemed to make use of the device in the 1970s and it was felt that a major factor in this slow uptake was the structure of the regulations for the registration of places of worship.[18] The regulations required that in order for a building to be eligible for registration it had to be used 'solely for the purpose of worship',[19] which proved to be problematic within British South Asian communities. In the early days of migration these communities were often not in a position to purchase properties for worship, whether purpose built or converted, and so worship would take place at the residence of a member of the community. In this situation, registration was clearly not possible. Yet, the lack of registration persisted into the 1980s, by which time there were numerous places of worship outside of personal residences. The lack of registration was, therefore, due to a much deeper mismatch between the regulations and the nature of worship in these communities. Whilst places of worship in Christian traditions are often solely for the purpose of worship, for Muslims, Hindus and Sikhs (the largest religions amongst Britain's South Asian population) places of worship are also places where the community gathers and other social events take place; many purpose built Sikh Gurdwaras have sports facilities in their grounds, and many Muslim Mosques have teaching facilities within them. Furthermore, the dictates of these religions do not require that marriage ceremonies take place within a place of worship, instead the marriage rites pertain to other matters, such as the presence of a Pandit and fire in Hinduism, or the presence of the *Guru Granth Sahib* (the

reflects the plural nature of law, and their usage can be considered to be official law, in accordance with Chiba's (1998: 5–6) definition.

18 See Pearl (1983). Whilst this structural barrier provides an explanation for the lack of registered places of worship, there were, arguably, other factors at play also, including a simple lack of awareness of the requirements of English law. Given that these religious marriages were recognised under the British Raj in India, why would one assume that anything would be different in England? Menski (1988b: 64–5) writes of a three stage 'process of adaptation of the Asian communities to English law and its requirements', which begins with a lack of awareness of particular English legal requirements resulting in the continuance of previous practices.

19 Places of Worship Registration Act 1855.

Sikh Holy Book) within Sikhism. As a result, many of these marriages took place, and continue to take place, in hotels and other such buildings.

In recounting these matters it is possible to see that these unofficial laws of marriage rites have had an effect upon official laws. The Marriage (Registration of Buildings) Act 1990 amended section 41(1) of the Marriage Act 1949 by deleting the eligibility requirement that a building must be solely for the purpose of worship and, instead, inserted section 41(7) into the 1949 Act, which now reads: '[a] building may be registered for the solemnization of marriages under this section whether it is a separate building or forms part of another building'. Moreover, the number of marriages taking place in hotels, stately homes and other such buildings led to the Marriage Act 1994, which provides for marriages to take place in any premises approved by local authorities, without requiring them to be places of worship. Needless to say, this latter development was no doubt influenced by non-religious developments in Britain, for example, the increasing number of couples who are deciding that religious marriages do not accord with their belief systems and nor does a registry office offer them a ceremony that reflects their beliefs and identity, whereas a stately home or hotel can offer them a more appropriate space in which they can create a ceremony that better reflects their identities. As well as evidencing the ways in which unofficial laws impact on official laws, this example provides further confirmation of the role that identity markers play in unofficial laws.

A second, less immediately obvious, example of the intrinsic relation between identity markers and unofficial laws can be found in the consideration of Britain's Rastafarian communities. Central to the Rastafarians' belief system is the uncut hair which they keep as dreadlocks; this is one of their identity markers. Many Rastafari men choose to wear a particular style of hat known as a *tam*; although there is no prescribed style, *tams* tend to be in the colours of the Ethiopian national flag (red, gold, green and black) or the Jamaican national flag (gold, green and black). Moreover, this identity marker is an unofficial law, since Rastafarians feel bound by this part of their faith, and this unofficial law has ramifications for official laws.

Two examples involving this aspect of the Rastafarian faith allow me to illustrate that unofficial laws can affect official laws and, furthermore, that they affect official laws in ways that go beyond legislation and case law. In *Crown Suppliers (Property Service Agency) v Dawkins* a Rastafari man who refused to cut off his dreadlocks was not offered a job that he was interviewed for and he claimed that this was racial discrimination and brought action under the RRA 1976.[20] The Court of Appeal held that his claim did not come within the ambit of the RRA 1976 because, applying the criteria set out in *Mandla*, Rastafarians could not be considered an 'ethnic group'; the court felt that 60 years was not long enough to satisfy the 'long shared history' criterion set out in this test.

Whilst this is ample evidence of an unofficial law pushing up against official laws, a further neat example can be seen in the Equal Treatment Bench Book,

20 [1993] ICR 517.

produced by the Judicial Studies Board (2008). The Bench Book is used to assist in diversity training for English law judges and, amongst many other things, it provides judges with guidance as to what is and what is not suitable in the affirmation of oaths in court, in accordance with Britain's diverse identities. At paragraph 3.2.3, it is noted that Rastafarians should not be asked to remove their head coverings whilst in court by virtue of the importance that this hat, and their dreadlocks, have in their faith.[21] The disparity in treatment that this creates is worth noting: English judges ought to respect a Rastafarian's beliefs as part of the equal treatment of those before them in court, but employers are entitled to discriminate against Rastafarians because they can only be considered as an ethnic group that is separate from Jamaicans since the 1930s, and this is not long enough to merit protection under the RRA 1976.[22] This incongruence speaks of the way that identity markers are viewed by official laws: they are not viewed as binding the conscience of adherents, and hence are not considered to be laws in any sense; moreover, the very root of adherence is misunderstood, as the question becomes whether these identity processes can be categorised as an ethnicity, race, religion, and so on, rather than recognising the value and importance of identity processes in our lives, as I argued earlier. In addition to this, these two examples are indicative of the relations between identity markers and unofficial law, and of the less conventional ways that unofficial laws, in this case dreadlocks and *tams*, impact official laws.

Very little needs to be said about legal postulates, not because they are unimportant – on the contrary they are the very building blocks and foundations upon which laws, both official and unofficial, are built – but because Chiba's definition of legal postulates is self-explanatory. Legal postulates act to give laws depth and meaning and, as Chiba explains, they are values and principles such as equity and justice, they are political ideologies, sacred truths, and cultural and social postulates. With specific regard to the global normative framework I constructed, there are a number of readily identifiable legal postulates. I have set out in this study the form of diversity-conscious justice that grounds this project. Mindful of the fact that my purpose was not to construct and make arguments for a comprehensive theory of justice, I mapped out a form of justice that emphasises the importance of the liberal ideals of self-actualisation and fullness in a world where the central project of our lives revolves around the questions of 'who am I?', 'what is my authentic self?', 'how can I live my life in a way that realises my authentic self?'. This existential life project has, I explained, led to a situation where the roles of both autonomy and the community have been magnified, and I argued that

21 It is troubling to note that at Judicial Studies Board (2008: 3–67), the ratio of *Dawkins* is cited as 'a Rastafarian cannot be refused employment because of his refusal to cut his hair (dreadlocks)'. One is left wondering how many other errors may be found in a document that was amended as recently as March 2008.

22 One would assume and hope that this inconsistency would no longer persist under the EA 2010.

justice must reflect these social realities. I also identified free and fair access to and participation in civil society, whether this is conceived in terms of Fraserian participatory parity or Habermasian radical democracy, as an essential component of this fresh perspective on justice. This form of justice justifies and orients my account of a plural conceptualisation of law which focuses upon identity markers, and my claim for new constitutional pluralist discourses. Thus it acts as a legal postulate. However, there are also other legal postulates which orient the laws considered in this project, and they too must be mentioned.

I have also argued for a triad of norms that were intended to guide and orient this project, and form part of my fresh perspective on law. I justified this need for guiding norms by illustrating that much of law, in particular rights and laws that form the basis of legal claims, function and are given meaning by an underlying series of unspoken but vividly present norms. Moreover, I explained that laws within this bracket act as a kind of normative shorthand, because they implicitly invoke their corollary norms when they are utilised. I argued for a review and reassessment of these norms to reflect the significant changes to diversity in our contemporary societies. I went on to propose a triad of norms to supplement and modify the existing norms, as a response to the limits I identified within law's current responses to diversity. It will be recalled that I identified the importance of making space for heterogeneity and, more specifically, heterogeneous identities, an expansive conceptualisation of justice that is able to change in response to the evolving needs of those that seek its protection, and an understanding of diversity that specifically considers the legacies of colonialism and 9/11, and therefore considers us all as post-colonial and post-9/11 peoples. This triad forms part of the normative foundations of the new vista on constitutional pluralism that I am calling for in this project, as well as acting to orient the identity markers that are expressed as official and unofficial law, and in this regard each of the norms can be understood as legal postulates. However, at this juncture a cautionary note is necessary; I do not interpret Chiba's legal postulates and law's normative shorthand as being identical. A reasonable reading of Chiba's definition of legal postulates makes it clear that he intends to encompass far more than just law's normative shorthand and, in fact, lists other things such as social and cultural practices and sacred truths. Nevertheless, it does appear as if official law's normative shorthand will always fit within Chiba's definition of legal postulates.[23]

A small comment needs to be made to clarify the relation, or lack thereof, between identity markers and identity postulates. In elaborating upon his schema of legal pluralism, Chiba introduces the concept of 'identity postulates' (1998: 241). Identity postulates must be understood within the context of the three dichotomous forms of law that Chiba posits (1998: 240–41): official law and unofficial law;

---

23 I make this assertion rather hesitantly as further, detailed consideration is necessary to be certain of this conclusion. However, such consideration is not required to sustain my arguments here, neither does it fall within the ambit of the purposes of this project; thus, it is not a feasible point to pursue in this particular context.

indigenous law and transplanted law (laws received from or imposed by foreign cultures); legal rules ('clearly formulated legal standards') and legal postulates. These three dichotomies are faced by each 'socio-legal entity', and the 'identity postulate of a legal culture ... guides a socio-legal entity to choose the particular combinations of three dichotomies of different laws and the conglomeration of them into a workable coexisting structure like legal pluralism' (1998: 241).

From this very brief synopsis of identity postulates, it is immediately apparent that there is no overlap between identity postulates and my analytical concept of identity markers. Identity markers are intended to (i) better express the value of difference within the terms of a diversity-conscious conception of justice; (ii) move away from the derailing task of justifying the nature of practices and attributes as cultural, ethnic, racial, religious and national, and therefore prematurely engage in a process of ranking and valuing aspects of our identities, whilst still retaining a vital connection with this general sphere; (iii) provide an analytical tool to help elucidate the unexplored and unconsidered constitutional dimension of diversity and law; and (iv) help law, in its pluralistic sense, fulfil its role in meeting the challenges of a diversity-conscious justice. In contrast, identity postulates are the landmarks that socio-legal entities use to guide them through the chaos of choices available amongst the plurality of laws in any legal system.

I have tried here to sustain my claim that law, in its varied plural forms, has an important relationship with identity processes, and also expresses identity markers. It is important to clarify that I do not claim that all identity markers are laws, or indeed that all laws contain identity markers. Moreover, my concern is not to debate theories of law, in their general sense, or even 'prove' a particular theory of law. Since the literature on legal pluralism is no longer in its infant stages, it obviates the need to construct my own theory of law, or even any need to start from scratch and survey the varied and rich literature that makes up the school of legal pluralistic thought. Additionally, having moved on from infancy, legal pluralism has left behind much of the combative nature that went hand in hand with a discipline battling to be recognised (J. Griffiths 1986: 1). Instead, the arguments here represent part of a local normative framework intended to ground a fresh perspective on diversity, which is better equipped to meet the challenges of justice in diverse societies and, more specifically, can accommodate local variations in that diversity. Having shown that there is an intrinsic relation between law and identity markers, the second stage is to explain the perspective on law taken in this normative framework.

Menski's Kites: A Model of Legal Pluralism and Interlegality

The idea of legal pluralism has been present throughout this project, but pinpointing the specific aspects of legal pluralism that are relevant to my proposal for a fresh perspective on diversity has not thus far been crucial. However, the final dimension of this local normative framework is an explanation of the notion of law that threads through it. Chiba's tripartite model of laws introduced the idea of law beyond state law, and his idea of legal pluralism evidenced the plurality within dominant notions of law, as well as permitting the illustration of the relations between identity markers and law. The model of law that grounds my fresh perspective draws inspiration from Chiba's tripartite model of law, as well as from a great variety of other legal philosophical accounts. Chiba's model of legal pluralism does not, therefore, in any way conflict with Menski's model of law. In fact, Menski's model is, to some degree at least, an extension of the idea of multiple sources of law, which sits at the heart of Chiba's tripartite model.

There are three reasons why this particular approach to legal pluralism grounds these discourses. First, Menski undertakes a broad survey of the spectrum of jurisprudential accounts that endeavour to pinpoint the essence of law, and in doing so goes beyond merely considering varieties of legal pluralism. He also considers historical legal philosophy (this includes Greek, Roman and medieval accounts of law) (Menski 2006: 131–46), positivism (98–102, 150–60), the development of natural law theories (131–4, 141–50, 168–73), anti-positivism and the Dworkinian field of jurisprudence (102, 159–60, 178), as well as socio-legal perspectives (161–8). His working definition of law is, therefore, the product of a cumulative consideration of the whole gamut of legal philosophy, and consequently provides a unique inclusive and panoramic quality that is a cornerstone of my fresh perspective on diversity.

Secondly, Menski's legal pluralism is 'globality-conscious' in the sense that it seeks to take into account the varied, and sometimes conflicting, consequences of globalisation when theorising the meaning of law. The global context that this provides to his definition of law permits invaluable sensitivity to many of the variables that I have indicated are vital to any legal response to diverse identities. For example, the idea of a global and local normative framework only makes sense when one understands the need to temper the universal ambitions assumed to be intrinsic to globalisation, with the prevalence of local specificities. A definition of law which is sensitive to the ramifications of globalisation aligns well with the reasons behind constructing a local normative framework.

The third reason for employing Menski's definition of law is, in fact, a culmination of the preceding two reasons. Its global context and panoramic quality lead to a definition that is, at its heart, inclusive in its perspective. The nature of jurisprudence, Menski warns, is that it involves 'ideological battles' (2006: 174). Those involved in jurisprudential endeavours approach the subject influenced by their own ideals and notions of justice. Although these factors are 'frequently implicit rather than openly avowed' (Freeman 2001: 1, quoted in Menski 2006: 175), this can be problematic for jurists and for the study of jurisprudence, since it can give rise to an often counterproductive dialogue that becomes sidetracked by securing one's own allegiances through striking down the theories of others. An inclusive perspective that draws inspiration from the whole spectrum of jurisprudence does not get sidetracked in this manner. Without this second agenda, sufficient space is made to focus instead upon the challenges of justice in intensely diverse societies, which must remain the focal point of my fresh perspective on diversity.

In crafting his model of legal pluralism Menski first shows that law has a plurality of sources (2006: 173–90). He does this by illustrating how the claims to universality and global applicability by dominant legal theories are fraught with difficulty: positivism is 'too narrowly focused on rules', as evidenced by the 1958 Hart/Dworkin debate; natural law is criticised for being a form of religious positivism; and socio-legal approaches are judged as too vague (2006: 173). Although he explicitly notes that these difficulties raise the important question of whether it is possible to construct 'any general understanding of the meaning of "law"' (2006: 174), this, he concludes, should not prompt any admission of defeat, but instead leads to the conclusion that a 'search for any neat, agreed definition of law' is too idealistic (2006: 174). In light of this, '[a]ny realistic jurisprudential approach', Menski explains, 'is therefore forced to take account of plurality at various levels and of the dynamic interaction between different elements of law' (2006: 174); and this is what he seeks to do with his kites.

Menski starts with the familiar positivist idea that law is 'a body of rules', and explains that by taking into account other schools of jurisprudential thought this might also be described as 'a collection of rules', 'a system of norms' or 'a set of rules, norms or conventions' (2006: 180). Although there are many more ways this might be expressed to take into account the myriad theories of law, this exercise illustrates the plurality intrinsic to any realistic account of law, and it is this plurality that forms the bedrock of Menski's triangles, which he later evolves into kites (Menski 2009). He explains that even if a narrower view was taken and the focus was upon a smaller body of rules, this would not act to 'de-pluralise' it (2006: 180), since this smaller body will nevertheless be plural in nature. It is evident from the preceding chapters that there is a distinctly plural flavour to identity markers, and this in turn means that the laws that we are concerned with are also plural. Indeed, it is because Menski's model allows us to see the interactions between identity markers and laws, beyond merely positivistic, natural law or socio-legal conceptualisations of law, that it provides the structure which grounds my fresh perspective.

Menski moves on from the idea that laws are a variation upon the idea of a body or system of rules to consider how these rules come into being and what effect they might have. The first postulation alludes to the sources of law and, with reference to Allott,[24] Menski concludes that '[u]nderstanding "law" as a systematic, planned,

24 Allott asks (1980: 6, quoted in Menski 2006: 181): 'Is a legal system natural or contrived, pre-existent or imposed? Like many of the essentialist questions one has to pose in this study, the answer, unsatisfactorily, is "both". A legal system is composed of many elements or items, some of which appear in the real world, like policemen, judges, prisons, lawyers, law-books; while some appear to exist only in the meta-world, a mental world floating in the air over the real world: such abstractions as rules, principles, standards, institutions, norms. *Law* has abstract elements as well as tangible elements. As a complete

well-developed body of rules made for a particular purpose seems sensible, but it does not match reality' (2006: 181). Instead, social realities dictate that law must be understood as being created through a great variety of processes, with the state being only one amongst many sources of law. To test our intuitions with regard to law made by non-state processes, Menski posits the idea of rules laid down by God, or norms applying to a religious community, and politely states that '[r]eaders will have to decide for themselves whether they can accept that such bodies of rules may fall under the definition of "law"', although he makes it clear that this *must* be part of a 'plurality-conscious' conceptualisation of law (2006: 183). This acceptance of plural sources of law is crucial to appreciating the value of the fresh perspectives that I propose: it is in the ability to give non-state aligned identity markers, as well as state aligned identity markers, constitutional status that a productive discourse can be conducted. The idea of plural non-state sources of law is more inclusive than merely religious laws, and Menski provides religious laws as only one example of law beyond state law. To cement the idea of an inclusive and plural conceptualisation of law, Moore's (1978) concept of semi-autonomous legal fields is employed, and Menski explains that customs, social norms and other systems born of these semi-autonomous legal fields can be considered as laws. In this regard, he also cites Chiba's definition of official laws, in order to illustrate that these norms and customs can 'be co-opted by a state as law' (2006: 184). Again, he suggests it is for the reader to decide whether they accept these plural non-state laws as laws, but questions whether rejecting these non-state practices from the domain of law makes 'them less effective in social reality' (2006: 184). In posing this question Menski goes to the heart of the justification for a legally pluralist model of law, and in turn for the local normative framework that I argue for; justice cannot afford to overlook social realities, for if it does, it becomes divorced from the very subjects it seeks to protect and thereby separates itself from the purposes that give it such robust meaning.[25] Whilst it is possible to accept that justice is an ideal concept whose full potential will only ever be just within our sights, a chasm such as this divests justice of the utopian quality that makes it such a potent concept for our legal systems.

Menski's triangular models take shape upon the basis of a number of propositions (2006: 184–5):

- law is a phenomenon that is universal but manifests itself in many different ways;
- law constantly needs to be worked out or negotiated in a culture-specific social context, and is thus inherently dynamic and flexible;

system it continues to function (as already remarked) even if no one is thinking about it, even if no one sets out consciously to design and operate it as a system. In this sense it is natural'.

25 This line of reasoning provides further justification for the expansive form of justice that forms part of this local normative framework.

- law not only takes different forms but also has different sources;
- these sources, in essence different manifestations of the state, society and religion/ethics, compete and interact in various ways;
- any given body of such rules will also contain components of the other two elements, which adds another (generally invisible) layer of plurality; …
- lawyers as professionals and theorists have tended to emphasise the centrality of state law and have thereby underplayed the role of non-state sources of the law including ethics, and particularly society and the element of culture, seriously underestimating the potential for the co-existence of various rule systems;
- whether something is legal or not may well ultimately be determined by lawyers, but they have used the alleged centrality of law to promote a worldview in which 'law' is dominant. One might call this 'legal determinism', a form of positivism, which turns out as legal centralism;
- this may not be a view consistent with people's experiences anywhere in the world;
- such legal centralism therefore needs to be challenged and a wider, global perspective on law needs to be taken.

The idea of different sources of law is first represented in triangular form, with the three angles of the triangle embodying the three broad sources of law, namely the state, society and religion/ethics/morality. These three sources largely correspond to the three major schools of jurisprudential thought: the state and positivism; society and socio-legal jurisprudence; and religion/ethics/morality and natural law theories. These three major schools are included in Menski's triangular representation of law (Figure 9.1), which is intended to provide a legal pluralist perspective (2006: 186):

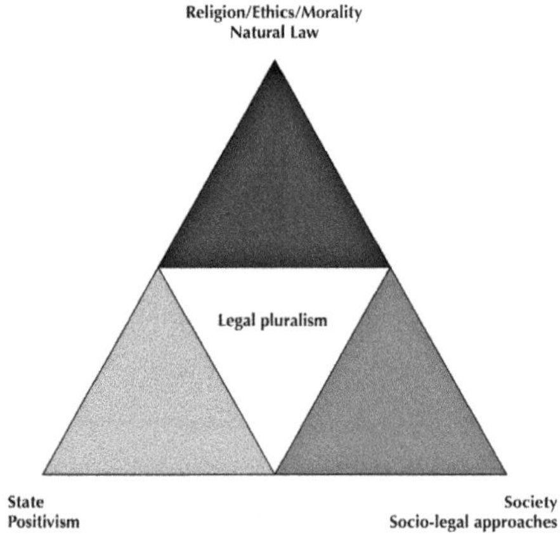

Figure 9.1 Menski's triangular model of law

Legal pluralism is the fourth school of jurisprudential thought, and it occupies the central space within this triangle of laws, which is, at first, represented by an upside down triangle that cuts the space inside the larger triangle into four equal triangles. However, this is changed to a circle because 'the ambit of legal pluralism ... should be shown as large as possible' (Figure 9.2) (2006: 187):

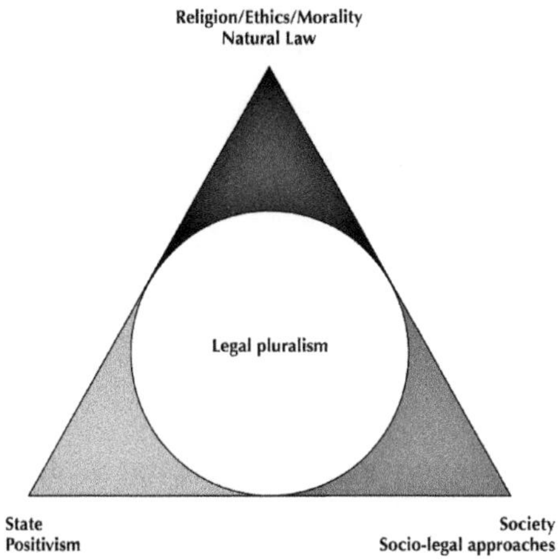

Figure 9.2 Menski's triangular model of law with legal pluralism shown as a circle

Although Menski posits the centre point of this triangle as an ideal conceptualisation of justice, he is quick to add that this ideal of justice must be continually negotiated and reassessed. This is reminiscent of the norm of expansive justice, with its ability to respond to the changing nature of our world, and the changing nature of the ways that our world is understood. However, when Menski concedes that in sizing up this model against reality it becomes clear that a better representation would be an 'enormous plurality of triangles in both time and space' and that the most feasible visual representation of this is a large circle around the triangle of law, 'representing the whole of humanity, better still, the whole cosmos' (2006: 188), I believe this provides a more appropriate expression of justice and, indeed, expansive justice. Although the ideal conceptualisation of justice may sit at the centre of this triangle, justice, in its achievable forms, can be found within and outside of the triangle. The forms of justice that focus solely upon the state, society, religion, or that do not exist within the circle of legal pluralism or at its centre, remain vital and are in no way replaced within a pluralistic framework. Moreover, I discussed earlier how justice is not a concept which is exclusively achieved through law, even in its expanded plural sense; thus, it exists outside of the triangle of law but within the larger cosmos circle. Menski provides the following diagram to expresses this cosmos inclusive model of law (Figure 9.3) (2006: 188):

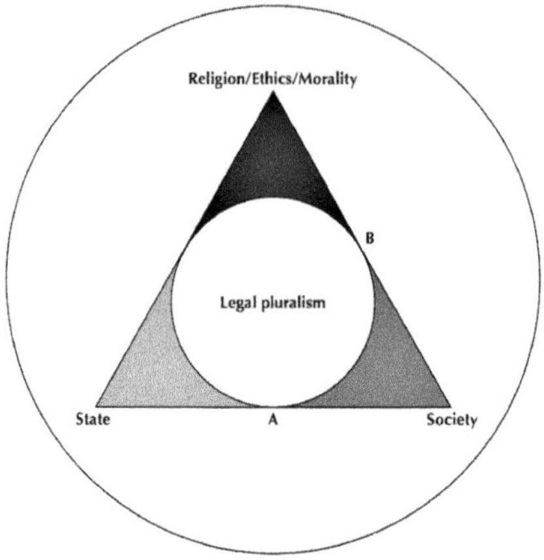

Figure 9.3 Menski's cosmos inclusive triangular model of law

At points A and B, Menski includes foreign transplants and ethnic implants in his model of law; however, these are not pivotal to my fresh perspective on diversity. In order visually to represent the dynamism of interactions between these areas Menski amends the model as follows (Figure 9.4) (2006: 189):

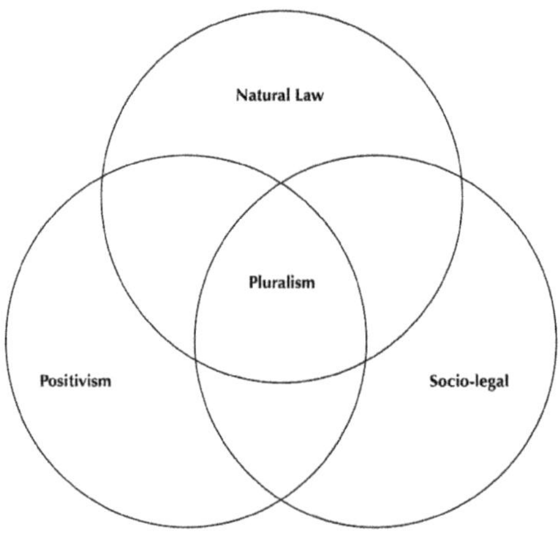

Figure 9.4 Menski's dynamic model of law

This represents an 'emerging awareness that there may be different kinds of natural law, positivism and socio-legal norms' (2006: 190) and recognises Chiba's emphasis upon interactions, fluidity and the lack of definable boundaries in his three dichotomies (Chiba 1989: 180, quoted in Menski 2006: 189). Dominant forms of jurisprudence have focused upon small sections of this model, thus failing to consider the larger picture of laws and its chaotic, messy, but significant, interactions.

Menski further refines his model of laws in the light of consideration of the legal systems of Asia and Africa. He confirms that 'there is no society without law', perhaps thereby showing that there is no law without society, and endeavours to produce a model which elaborates upon the internal plurality of law (2006: 610). This is achieved by assigning each of the triangles of law a number (society – 1; the state – 2; ethics – 3; and so on) and pinpointing areas where noteworthy interactions take place with further additions to these primary numbers. First, he assigns the number 11 to reflect the idea that society and law exist only because of each other; 12 expresses the idea that in some cases societal laws are influenced by state laws, whilst 13 encapsulates societal laws that are influenced or legitimated by ethics. This schema is then applied to the further three triangles. Note, however, that we are warned that this sequence of numbers 'implies no intention of ranking or relative superiority' so we should be careful not to deduce anything from them (2006: 610). Moreover, I include this figure to provide a comprehensive synopsis of Menski's model of legal pluralism and interlegality, rather than as a diagram that is necessary to explain the core of Menski's legal pluralism. In fact, it is the previous diagram's representation of laws that better does this job. Menski translates this schema into a diagram as follows (Figure 9.5) (2006: 612):

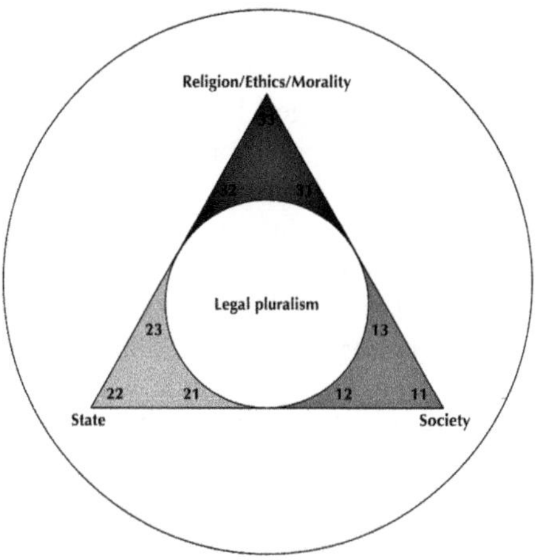

Figure 9.5 Menski's triangular model of law showing interlegality

Menski's circular representation of laws falls short of highlighting the intense level of plurality of law, largely because this kind of messy interlegality is impossible to represent graphically. However, it is, in part, this concern which fuels his later modifications of this triangular representation of plurality and interlegality, so that it becomes a tetrahedron of plurality. In order to demonstrate that globalisation, in all its manifestations, can no longer be seen as an extra-legal force, a fourth corner is added to this picture of plurality (Figure 9.6) (Menski 2008):

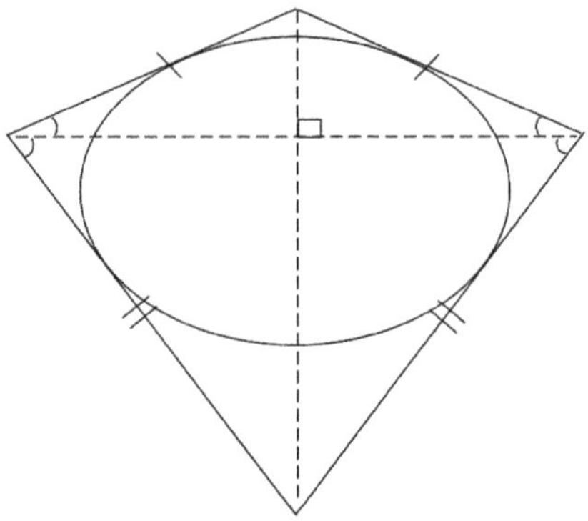

Figure 9.6 Menski's flying kite of law

This fourth corner represents a fourth source of law which can be understood as international law, post-modern legal theory or a set of global values. For the purposes of this project, a key element of this tetrahedron of law is Menski's (2009) use of the metaphor of flying kites to elucidate the challenges of justice in diverse societies. He explains that lawyers today, in all their forms, as individuals, nation-states, international entities, are engaged in a delicate kite-flying exercise. The kite-flyer must manage competing expectations that come from all four corners of the kite and 'harmonise different visions and concepts of law' (Menski 2009). The picture of plurality that this aims to conjure is not one where cutting other people's kites is the end-game, although some, I am sure, view things this way; rather, the aim is to fly as many kites, in harmony, as possible. The appeal of this metaphor is, I believe, in its ability to represent the multiplicity of plurality as something that has the potential for harmony, as opposed to merely visualising the messy and complex interactions of these plural laws and legal systems. This idea of billions of colourful kites flying in the sky is the type of paradigm shift that we need to be able to imagine in order to implement the norm of heterogeneity that I argued is vital to my local normative framework.

Menski (2009) makes clear that these kites are not exclusively about theory, because they must link 'to our lived experience and what the great Austrian jurist Ehrlich (1936) called "living law"'. This, I believe, is vital to any theory of law if it is to be relevant to our real world experiences. Moreover, the expansion of this model, from triangles to kites, reflects the idea that so much that relates to justice and diversity goes beyond law. This fits well with my conceptual tool of identity markers, which are heavily connected with law, but are not exclusively tied to law.

In order to emphasise that identity markers go beyond law, I wish to draw upon a woman's experience of coming out as homosexual. Margolis (2010) explains that whilst she was sure of her sexuality at the age of 10, she did not come out in a meaningful way until much later in her life. Of particular interest is the way she is currently experiencing her sexuality, which I propose is an identity marker. She explains that whilst her parents and loved ones were wholly accepting of her coming out, it did not signal her entry into a group which has the same, or similar, identity markers; 'being gay' she states, 'is still hard' (Margolis 2010). She goes on to say (Margolis 2010):

> As a lesbian, meeting a partner can be fraught. Finding a compatible woman is one thing; discerning whether or not she's gay is another. Unless, of course, you turn to the gay scene. But I don't want to define myself by my sexuality. I think my penchants for Curb Your Enthusiasm, Mexican folk art and camembert are more significant markers of my personality than whom I choose to go to bed with ... Like any group or culture formed as a result of persecution, the gay scene is isolated, and often bitter. Gay and straight can be a real us-and-them situation. This is so frustrating if all you want to be is yourself.

This experience of sexuality highlights that identity markers can be found within law (in its plural sense), as I believe is the case with sexuality. However, they can also go beyond law, as is the case with the author's love of camembert. What Margolis makes abundantly clear is that the most important thing for her is that she has the agency to discover her authentic sense of self.

Margolis's experience succinctly expresses many of the norms I argue for in this book. Her journey is one where she is seeking to express and understand her authentic self: the first pillar of justice. Her frustration lies in how this journey is, in some ways, excluding her from accessing and participating in parts of civil society: the second pillar of justice. She writes of her experience in such a way that asks the reader to temper any universal, stereotypical idea of what it means to be gay, so that there is room for her to express her identity markers in her own way and on her own terms: my local normative framework.

Conclusions

This local normative framework aims to temper any universal ambitions that may be latent in the very idea of a normative framework, and make space for 'super-diversity' (Vertovec 2007) and local variations, as well as providing a sound and clear narrative that can underpin the new vista on constitutionalism that I propose.

By expanding law's potential beyond the limits I identified in earlier chapters, this framework also provides a fresh perspective on law, in all its plural, kite-flying glory. This model of law is provided so that the legal responses that follow are able to fulfil their role in meeting the challenges of my diversity-sensitive idea of justice. The first element of this framework responds to our unsettled moment of time. Technological developments have precipitated a new confidence and bravado in difference and plurality. This confidence has shifted the dynamic between identity processes and nation-building projects. However, I have argued that it is possible to respond to this shift by restating and reworking the norms that position law's role in meeting the challenges of justice. In addition to pursuing equality and valuing culture, religion and ethnicity as primary goods, law must (i) learn to combine heterogeneity and plurality with nation-ness; (ii) employ an expansive and inclusive definition of justice; and (iii) be sensitive to the post-colonial and post-9/11 specificities of its diverse citizens. These norms respect my diversity-conscious conception of justice, and in so doing aid law in overcoming the limitations I identified in my analysis of contemporary responses to diversity.

In establishing the second element of this local normative framework I demonstrated that the current analytical tools employed to understand diversity are lacking. I proposed identity markers as a solution to these deficiencies, but not as a replacement for those current tools. In my analysis of the *Begum* case I demonstrated how identity markers allow the real issues surrounding diversity to surface. However, to show that identity markers are not intended as a replacement for ethnicity, culture, religion and race, and that they are therefore not the basis for new forms of legal claims and rights, I illustrated how, in some cases, identity markers are laws. My aim was to portray identity markers as an analytical tool that permits law to meet the challenges of justice in diverse societies.

Finally, I drew upon Menski's model of legal pluralism to explain my fresh perspective on law. As the last piece of this local normative framework, the compatibility of Menski's intensely plural explanation of law with the social realities of diversity means that it underscores law's ability to meet the challenges of justice in diverse societies. In this plural conception of law, we are offered a more promising explanation of the conflicts and tensions that arise as a consequence of intensely plural societies. This normative framework, both global and local, provides the sound normative foundations that ground my new vista on constitutional pluralism, and that I argued were lacking in contemporary legal responses to diversity.

PART IV
A New Vista on Constitutional Pluralism

Chapter 10
Constitutional Pluralism

Whilst discussing the formation of South Africa as a nation in the 1900s, Thompson asserted that (1960: 482–3, quoted in Dugard 1978: 26–7):

> In following the British example, [the founders of the Constitution and the Union of South Africa Act 1910] had ignored the fact that in so far as the flexible British character of the British Constitution met the needs of the British people, that was because they had become a comparatively homogenous people …; whereas the essence of the problem confronting South Africa was that her peoples were extremely heterogeneous.

Thompson felt that by following the British constitutional model South Africans, specifically the framers of the Constitution and Union of South Africa Act 1910, had ignored fundamental differences between South Africa and Britain. The British Constitution, he felt, was designed to suit Britain, which had a 'comparatively homogenous' population who had a strong respect for constitutional conventions, political compromise and personal liberty, and this respect formed an effective barrier against arbitrary government. South Africa, on the other hand, had a heterogeneous population whose colour consciousness was strong enough to override any feelings its people may have had for conventions, compromise or the liberties of others, thereby leaving them open to the injustices of arbitrary government. Since the flexible British form of constitution provides no legal safeguards against arbitrary government, Thompson concluded that it was ill-suited to South Africa and, at best, did nothing to prevent apartheid.

Thompson made a connection, within the context of South Africa, between constitutions and difference, and this connection forms the backdrop to the new vista on constitutional pluralism that concludes this book. The importance of this connection lies in its suggestion that the functioning of a constitution impacts the nature of the societies that we live in, and vice versa. In this chapter I move forward from this idea, and argue that the new legal responses to diversity that I have made a case for, ought to be the product of constitutional pluralist discourses. I therefore provide a new vista on constitutional pluralism that is grounded by my fresh perspectives on justice and law.

My claim for this new vista is made in four stages. First, I elaborate upon what I mean when I describe my new vista as constitutional pluralist discourses. This involves an explanation of the idea of constitutionalism and consideration of how these discourses contribute to new forms of constitutionalism. Secondly, in order to provide sufficient background to the idea of constitutional pluralist discourses, I set out my vision of the British Constitution from within traditional constitutional theories. The aim here is to support my claims that constitutional pluralist discourses must go beyond traditional constitutional theories, and the unwritten character of the British Constitution provides the ideal terrain from which this can be illustrated. Thirdly, I put forth my justifications for proposing constitutional and pluralist discourses, as opposed to legally pluralist discourses. To underscore these justifications, I briefly consider the flaws of a constitutional monistic discourse as a platform for new legal responses to diversity. Finally, I elaborate upon the character of the constitutional pluralist discourses I propose by assessing them against Walker's (2002: 334–6) criteria for constitutional renewal. This analysis allows me to illustrate the significance of my normative framework, with its fresh perspectives on justice and law, for these constitutional pluralist discourses.

Constitutional Pluralist Discourses?

Creating a platform for new legal responses to diversity does not, I believe, begin with answers; it requires asking new questions, because the old ones lead to stalemates, and stale answers. Unless we become clearer about the questions that arise as a consequence of diverse identities, we cannot hope to arrive at answers that move beyond current legal approaches to the challenges of justice in diverse societies. A proposal for new constitutional frameworks that take diversity into account would fail to take this vital step. It is in this spirit that I propose constitutional pluralist discourses, rather than a constitutional framework or blueprint, as my platform for new legal responses to diversity.

These discourses cannot take one form, or be concerned with one forum; instead, they must take a variety of forms. However, if they are to pursue the spirit of clarifying new questions, they cannot take place within the courts. Court systems are only amenable if one uses the current frameworks that respond to diversity. As a consequence, any discourse that takes place within this format will make no progress beyond the limitations I identified in earlier chapters. Instead, these discourses ought to take place within arenas that are not restricted by adherence to any such frameworks and are free to pursue the task of asking new questions. Examples of appropriate forums are academic scholarship, both legal and non-legal, and think-tanks that do not have a government mandate. Government mandated bodies are too partisan to be able to stray so far from state-sponsored agendas and politics and, therefore, do not provide fertile ground for the freedom of legal imagination necessary for new legal responses. These government mandated bodies are not, however, prohibited from listening to such discourses, and perhaps even participating once they are more securely established.

These discourses must involve their stakeholders, namely a nation-state's diverse citizens, for without them the discourses lack legitimacy. Allowing the voice of stakeholders to be heard has two elements. First, stakeholders must be allowed to participate directly in discourses. This can be achieved by ensuring that discourses take place within civil society,[1] and are not limited to private arenas. Secondly, the voice of stakeholders can be incorporated into discourses by ensuring that understanding the experience of diversity is a key element. In scholarship, for example, this would mean taking an interdisciplinary approach and incorporating sociological, anthropological, psychological and philosophical accounts of the experience of difference. In this regard, my own normative framework seeks to make space so that this reflexive process of taking social realities into account can take place.

I propose that my normative framework grounds these constitutional pluralist discourses. Nevertheless, the very purpose of a discourse would be negated if this framework was not open to discussion. I propose discourses precisely because they provide an opportunity to incorporate the greatest number of voices and opinions, and make it more likely that an agreeable consensus is achieved. Whilst I argue for a particular normative framework, and believe there are good reasons for this framework, it cannot be legitimately adopted unless it is subjected to the scrutiny of a diverse set of perspectives. As such, the normative framework that I argue for here acts as a starting point in these discourses, and must be open to debate and amendment as part of these constitutional pluralist discourses.

The idea of constitutional pluralist discourses, together with the arguments that sustain them, contribute to new forms of constitutionalism. However, constitutionalism is a term that can be used in many ways,[2] making it important to be clear about its specific use here, thereby avoiding any confusion. My use refers to the discourses through which constitutions are engaged with and discussed.[3] Walker describes this form of constitutionalism as 'the normative discourse through which constitutions are justified, defended, criticised, denounced or otherwise engaged with' (2002: 318). The idea that this new vista works towards original forms of constitutionalism acknowledges the importance of a thick definition of the term, for too thin an understanding merely acts to legitimise and perpetuate the constitutional *status quo*. MacCormick (1993: 131) captures this sentiment well when he asserts that too thin a definition of constitutionalism merely extols 'the virtue of exercising political power and of conducting political debate in terms which fully respect and honour the [existing] constitution'. In a similar vein, Griffin (1990: 202) defined constitutionalism as 'the idea that just as it is desirable to restrain and empower the individual through the rule of law, so it is desirable to restrain and empower the state'. Constitutionalism, as used here, involves the

1 I mean to refer here to a broad notion of civil society, as defined in Chapter 2.

2 For five divergent meanings see Craig (2001: 127–8). See also McIlwain (1947), Vile (1967), Pennock and Chapman (1979), Elster and Slagstad (1988), Walker (1996), Alexander (1998) and Walker (2002).

3 See, in particular, Craig's first meaning of constitutionalism (2001: 127) and Walker (1996: 268–9, 2002: 318).

creation of new discourses which have a firm focus upon justice, and this fits neatly with the global normative framework that these discourses are founded upon.

This is a *new* form of constitutionalism, not because the idea of challenging current forms of constitutionalism makes it novel,[4] nor because the coupling of diversity and constitutionalism is novel.[5] Rather, it is new in the particularised perspective and legally pluralist approach it makes to diversity and constitutionalism. Where Tully was concerned with diversity in its abstract sense and approached constitutionalism from a political philosophical perspective,[6] I am concerned with accommodating the local specificities and social realities of diversity, and approach constitutionalism from a distinctly socio-legal perspective. This is not to say that the proposals for new constitutionalism made here in any way stand against those made by Tully. Instead, this project uses the spaces that Tully creates with his work as inspiration. Tully makes a compelling case for an 'inter-cultural dialogue in which the culturally diverse citizens of contemporary societies negotiate agreements on their forms of association over time in accordance with the three conventions of mutual recognition, consent and cultural continuity' (1995: 30). The cornerstone of Tully's dialogical constitutionalism is not only these three conventions, but also the positive role that irreducible disagreements have within this framework: '[t]he answer given by the black canoe [in Bill Reid's sculpture *The Spirit of Haida Gwaii*]' Tully explains (1995: 212), 'is that, although the passengers vie and negotiate for recognition and power, they always do so in accord with the three conventions'. It follows from this 'that citizens are free to call into question unjust forms of recognition, to enter into fair dialogues over their re-negotiation and so to work out their forms of association themselves over time' (Tully 2008). The constitutional discourses proposed here fall clearly within the fair dialogue of renegotiation that Tully argues for. Thus, the new vista offered here is a progression onwards from Tully's thesis.

---

4 See Walker (2002: 319–33) for an outline of five challenges to constitutionalism. See also Anderson (2005), who argues for a legally pluralist understanding of constitutionalism in place of rights constitutionalism, on the grounds that globalisation has created non-state constitutional entities that need to be accountable within a framework of constitutionalism.

5 The work of James Tully stands out because of its explicit consideration of constitutionalism in light of diversity. See, for example, Tully (1995). However, arguably, other academics are making implicit arguments about constitutionalism in their work on diversity. I have in mind here Taylor (1994) and Young (1990, 2000), in particular.

6 Note, however, that Tully's work is influenced by Canadian forms of diversity, and in particular the diversity that First Nations, Inuit and Métis peoples bring to that nation-state.

The Enigma of the British Constitution

The British Constitution is viewed as something of an enigma. In fact, it is often assumed that there is no constitution in Britain at all.[7] It is for this reason that it provides ideal terrain to elucidate what I mean when I refer to something as constitutional. I could simply explain that my concern is the way that nation-states arrange themselves. However, by going further and considering the nature of the British Constitution, I am able to reveal that constitutional arrangements, in the manner in which I am referring to them, are far more complex and plural than the picture that such a straightforward description paints, and go much deeper than just a set of written documents. I have chosen the British Constitution, as opposed to other unwritten constitutions,[8] because of its long history and the wealth of literature on this topic that is available.

The idea that Britain does not have a constitution is too facile an explanation of its constitutional arrangements. It is far more accurate to assert that there is no single document that codifies the British Constitution. The nebulous nature of the constitution can, especially in circumstances such as this, prove to be an advantage: the constitution's uncodified character has given rise to accounts which encapsulate its nature, thus providing rich material that can be usefully referenced. However, elaborating upon the nature of the fresh perspective offered here would not benefit from a full and frank account of the constitution. Instead, I propose only to set out those elements of the British Constitution that are sufficient to provide a vision of this constitution in order to situate and inform the proposals I make here. Although this vista on constitutional pluralism does not require a comprehensive account, it is difficult to propose constitutional discourses with no notion of what 'constitutional' might encapsulate. The emphasis, then, is upon informing the new vista that I propose.

A.V. Dicey's *Introduction to the Study of the Law of the Constitution* has a long history as the starting point for students of the British Constitution, and it

7 For an excellent introduction to the British Constitution see Bogdanor (1996, 2004). Note, also, one of the many oddities of English law is that England and Wales form a separate legal jurisdiction to that of Scotland and Northern Ireland, yet the Constitution covers all three of these jurisdictions. Even with the devolution that has taken place under the prime ministership of Tony Blair and the creation of the Scottish and Welsh Assemblies, it remains expedient to refer to the British or UK Constitution, because Parliament retains power to dissolve these devolved assemblies, and the parliamentary process of governing takes place across the UK. Nevertheless, it is also possible to make a case for describing the UK as a quasi-federation as a result of devolution: see Bogdanor (1999: 290). It is also possible to argue that because the doctrine of parliamentary sovereignty means Parliament can overrule fundamental rights, the British Constitution is, to some extent, a 'façade' constitution: see Barendt (1997: 141–3).

8 Other nation-states with unwritten constitutions include New Zealand and Isreal.

provides a convenient point of departure here.[9] Dicey argued that there are two equal pillars to the constitution, namely parliamentary sovereignty and the rule of law. The doctrine of parliamentary sovereignty expresses the idea that there is nothing higher than Parliament, and that there are no legal limits upon Parliament's legislative power, except that it cannot fetter its own future powers. Furthermore, Dicey identified three principles which combine to embody the rule of law: (i) the absolute supremacy of regular law, as opposed to arbitrary power; (ii) the equality of all before the law, where law means the law of the land as administered by the ordinary courts; and (iii) the law of the constitution as a consequence of rights defined and enforced by the courts. It is noteworthy that this conceptual framework 'still dominates thinking about the British Constitution' (Bogdanor 1987: 455–6), since most constitutional commentary does not contend that this structure be abandoned but, instead, argues for revisions and recapitulations that remain within this broad framework. The status that Dicey's twin pillar formulation of the British Constitution retains means that it provides an apt summary of Britain's constitution for the purpose of my new vista.

The uncodified nature of the constitution has also resulted in an emphasis upon the importance of history and politics when understanding the British Constitution.[10] This is vital to my own understanding of the breadth of the idea of 'constitutional' discourses. Elizabeth Wicks took an historical approach to the British Constitution in *The Evolution of a Constitution*. She approached the study of the British Constitution by isolating eight key moments in its history which she argued contribute to its current form. The eight moments that she focused upon were: (i) The Glorious Revolution of 1688 which led to the principles of sovereignty and liberty; (ii) the Union of England and Scotland in 1707, producing a unitary state and limited parliament; (iii) the establishment of the office of the Prime Minister in 1721; (iv) the Great Reform Act of 1832, which heralded the beginning of representative democracy; (v) the establishment of the supremacy of the Commons over the Lords in 1911; (vi) the enactment of the ECHR in 1953, which created an external influence upon the British Constitution; (vii) accession to the European Community and the ECA 1972, which has resulted in the supremacy of EU law; and (viii) the act of parliamentary devolution to Scotland, Wales and Northern Ireland in 1998, creating a quasi-federation.[11] These historical moments are listed here to provide a flavour of the key moments that have influenced the British Constitution, although they are by no means an uncontested list. My intention is to highlight the importance of historical and political contexts when thinking in terms of a nation-state's constitution.

9 See Dicey and Wade (1959). Dicey's *Introduction to the Study of the Law of the Constitution* was first written in 1885 and Professor Bogdanor (1987: 455), a leading British constitutional expert, has described it as 'Britain's substitute for a codified constitution'.

10 See Wicks (2006), Bogdanor (2004) and Maitland (1926).

11 Wicks does not agree that devolution created a quasi-federation; this is an assessment that can be credited to Bogdanor (1999: 290).

The import of historical events in shaping the British Constitution has led some commentators to conclude that it is nothing more than what 'happens', and that this surmises its relations with history. However, this ignores the fact that history does not just 'happen'. Those who act in ways that create a constitution do not do so in a vacuum; they act from within a substantial matrix, one that is perceived differently across different actors, spaces and times. The historical acts that tell us something about any particular constitution are already informed by an idea of what is constitutional and unconstitutional. This idea represents the constitutional culture or psyche, embedded deep within the motivations behind these acts; this notion of a constitutional psyche can easily be overlooked when there are documents which codify any nation-state's constitutional arrangements, yet it remains just as important.

This constitutional psyche is elusive in nature, an elusion that is exacerbated by the lack of tangible texts that can be used to support any sense of what is constitutional and what may be unconstitutional. Nevertheless, it has a definite presence. Its elusive nature brings me to a further point, namely the importance of constitutional dialogues. The illusion of the British Constitution means it is difficult to argue authoritatively for, or even just pinpoint, specific conceptions of constitutional values and principles. This difficulty privileges all forms of official constitutional dialogue, whether adjudication by courts or other recognised forums, or academic commentary and theory. This creates a cyclical situation where history and what happens is vital to understanding constitutional theory, and constitutional theory is vital to understand what is happening. However, the British Constitution is not only explained by referring to history: politics also plays an important role in this constitution.

John Griffith (1979) wrote of the relation between constitutions and politics. He wrote of constitutions as the legal expression of political developments, arguing, inter alia, that qualified human rights, such as Article 9 ECHR,[12] sound 'like the statement of a political conflict, purporting to be a resolution of it' (Griffith 1979: 16). There is much truth in this interpretation, which particularly resonates for an uncodified and evolutionary constitution such as Britain's, but is relevant to all constitutions. Yet, it is only a partial truth; politics and political conflict do not occur without context and their relations with constitutions are more complex than this reference to Griffith's conceptualisation of constitutions allows.[13] It is better, I believe, to envisage a symbiotic relationship between politics and constitutions, much like the relation between constitutions and history. Admittedly, it is a curious symbiosis that seems vague, because this constitutional culture or psyche is not drawn from a constitutional text. Even when there is a lack of codification, which

12 Article 9 of the ECHR enshrines freedom of thought, conscience and religion.

13 I do not believe that Griffith paints a simple picture of the relation between constitutions and politics; rather, that reference to one aspect of his arguments cannot convey the complexity of this relationship.

leads to a lack of documents upon which political dialogues can be hung, there is a definite sense of 'the Constitution' that informs such debates.

In the same way that a flavour of key historical constitutional moments helps to clear away some of the mystery of the British Constitution, an idea of some of the political content of this constitution goes some small way to clarify things. In this regard, Vernon Bogdanor (2004) recently edited a collection of papers that took a political approach to the British Constitution.[14] The subject matter of the papers in this collection provides a neat illustration of the character of the political content of the British Constitution, and can be summarised as follows: the monarchy; cabinet government; the House of Commons; the House of Lords; the civil service; ministerial responsibility; government and the judiciary; administrative law; civil liberties; the electoral system; local government (and more specifically, its decline); the police; statehood; the Commonwealth and the end of the British Empire; and Britain's relationship with mainland Europe. Again, this list is not intended to be comprehensive, or even uncontested, but gives a modest idea of the sorts of issues included in thinking about the political content of a constitution, and therefore helps in creating a vision of what comes within the concept of 'constitutional'.

The final part of this vision refines the picture that has already been built by setting out the general approach to the British Constitution, taken from within traditional theories, that I favour. I label the approach that I take to the British Constitution as prescriptive, in contradistinction to a descriptive approach. The descriptive approach, as its label suggests, views British constitutional law as a picture of existing practices and allocations of power. These power arrangements and practices may be the product of historical, economic, social and political pressures, but on this view, the British Constitution does not enshrine a set of fundamental values, or reflect a theory of governance, although this does not preclude a Diceyian twin pillar approach. Whilst descriptive constitutional lawyers may disagree as to the substantive content of these twin pillars, they agree that they form the fundamental framework through which the British Constitution can be understood. In support of the descriptive approach to British constitutional law, commentators often reference constitutional conventions, which are, in essence, an *ex post facto* legitimation of political practices that have continued for a sufficient period of time so as to be considered entrenched. An example of a constitutional convention is ministerial responsibility – a cabinet minister bears responsibility for the actions of his or her ministry or department.

In contrast, prescriptive constitutional lawyers do not agree with the view that the British Constitution does not contain normative elements. They argue, instead, that the British Constitution is something more than a description of the structures of governance, and that all values are not up for grabs, as descriptive approaches would suggest. In particular, they argue that the British Constitution is prescriptive

14 My description of this text as recent is relative, and is based upon the fact that British constitutional lawyers continue to work within a framework first constructed by Dicey in 1885.

in character because it confers an authority and legitimacy upon the processes of governance. If this were not the case, then it would be hard to consider Britain as a state that is governed in accordance with any moral values and principles; in fact, it would mean that there was a strong argument that British governance is arbitrary.[15] The position within the spectrum of prescriptive views that I take does not entail rejection of the vital role that history and politics play in elucidating the British Constitution. It is especially important to emphasise this point, as a great portion of conceptualising the idea of a constitutional dialogue comes from taking an historical and political approach. Indeed, much of the normative content that forms the cornerstone of prescriptive approaches to constitutional law is inferred from a constitution's historical development.

This vision of a prescriptive constitutional framework provides the backdrop for my new vista, which takes the form of constitutional pluralist discourses. For those with no experience of an uncodified constitution, the Diceyian formulation, together with this account of the role of historical and political contexts, provide a basic synopsis of my vision of traditional notions of what comes within the idea of constitutional discourses. For those familiar with the British Constitution, the explanation of my prescriptive approach refines this basic framework and clarifies the background to the following arguments.

Justifying a Constitutional and Pluralist Discourse

I have argued, in my fresh perspectives on law, that law and diversity are linked through identity markers and identity processes, and that this relation is best understood through a plural conceptualisation of law. I wish to argue that the link between identity markers and law must be understood as a constitutional discourse and, furthermore, as a pluralist discourse. Using Poulter's (1998) arguments for a human rights framework, I demonstrated that the lack of any constitutional discourses that focus upon the challenges of justice in the light of diversity is a gap in this legal field. I argue here that new legal responses to diversity ought to be discussed within a constitutional pluralist framework, and it is through this lens that the challenges of a diversity-conscious justice become clearer. To make this claim, I hope to show that law's relations with diversity and identity markers must be constitutional and pluralist in nature. I do this, first, by justifying the constitutional character of this new vista and, secondly, by illustrating that it must also be plural in nature. I reinforce my claim that these must be plural constitutional discourses by demonstrating the inadequacies of a monistic constitutional discourse on diversity.

15 See Feldman (2005: 335), who explains that the 'difference between bands of robbers and states is that states are, or should be, organised through their constitutions in such a way as to limit the robber-band's capacity to use its powers in arbitrary, anti-social and unaccountable ways'.

Constitutional Discourses

The first justifying claim for viewing this new vista as constitutional is based on the generative effect of such discourses. Walker explains (2002: 344–5):

> [A] (more or less) successful process of imaginative transformation towards or sustenance of constitutional status itself has the potential to change the texture of the relevant claims, institutions and principles in significant ways. For the claim to constitutional status is always also an assertion of a *right* to self-government in the case of a polity or putative polity, or at least of a general entitlement to be endowed with the symbolic authority associated with constitutional status in the case of another non-polity-based political process. And so, in turn, such claims also necessarily involve an acknowledgement of the *demands* of responsible self-government or of the expectations raised by any claim to constitutional status … Those who wish, from whatever motive or combination of motives, to make a plausible claim to constitutional status, must at least *be seen to* take these values seriously, which in turn imposes real constraints and has real consequences for what they propose and enact. To put this point in perhaps unduly cynical terms, just as hypocrisy can have civilising effects, the invocation of constitutionalism, because of the expectations thus aroused and the constituencies and arguments thus mobilized, tends to structure the ensuing debate … in ways which escape the intentions of the original protagonists.

Casting this as constitutional discourses capitalises upon the generative effect that Walker describes here. The idea (and hope) is that constitutional discourses move beyond the current prevailing paradigms of, for example, human rights and anti-discrimination legislation and provide an appropriate platform for the new legal responses that I argue for. As Walker explains, the symbolic authority of the constitutional character of a discourse acts to change the nature of the arguments and proposals made by all participants, the expectations of the participants and, crucially, the critical analyses and academic commentary in this area. It is not so much that widening the framework to include constitutional discourses will transform the picture so that all the right answers become clear, rather, it will make inroads into transforming the narratives employed so that some of the questions become clearer, and in so doing some of the obstacles that currently stand in the way of a diversity-conscious justice will be removed. For example, the racist undertones of the narrative underlying Britain's race relations legislation is inexcusable under a constitutional light that requires commitment to normative principles, such as a conceptualisation of justice that is sensitive to diversity.

A further justification for *constitutional* discourses, which is related to the generative effect argument above, is that justice, in the sense of Fraserian participatory parity or Habermasian radical democracy, requires constitutional discourses. A constitutional dimension introduces an extra layer to any discourse on diversity, making the issue of membership of civil society in active and participatory ways part of the dialogue. This occurs in a manner that I describe as both foregrounded and backgrounded. It becomes a background issue in the sense that an awareness that claims for the free expression of identity markers impinge upon one's place in civil society, and this has the consequential effect of self-imposed personal checks to ensure an advantageous or agreeable position is maintained. It is foregrounded because, as constitutional discourses, one's position and participation in civil society becomes an issue that is explicitly on the agenda for all participants. If justice, in its general sense, is understood as free and fair participation in and access to civil society, as I argue, it calls out for one's place in civil society to be explicitly discussed and considered.

The final justification for constitutional discourses follows from this idea of justice as a matter of participation in and access to civil society. I argue that identity markers are the product of sites that make sovereign claims upon us and, therefore, these discourses must be considered as constitutional. A traditional Diceyian conceptualisation of the British Constitution gives Parliament exclusive claims to sovereignty, although, of late, constitutional theorists have begun to grapple with the notion that as a consequence of globalisation other sites outside of the nation-state make claims upon us. The most evolved dialogue concerns the proper way to understand the EU, with its claims to sovereignty over English law. There is a growing body of literature, that is gaining momentum, which considers the claims to sovereignty of supranational organisations and orders such as the ECHR, WTO, the World Bank and NAFTA. These non-state sites garner attention not only because their claims impinge in a very real and tangible way upon the nation-state, but also because these organisations and orders are state-like in character. The account of identity processes, of religion, race, ethnicity, culture and nationality, speaks of sites of sovereignty which are neither states nor state-like, but nevertheless make compelling demands of and claims upon us. This idea is more easily grasped in relation to religion, ethnicity and nationality. The sovereign nature of religion is easily grasped since religions often claim to provide their followers with the ultimate truth or truths, and proffer promises of salvation. Moreover, the contemporary explosion of ethnic conflicts, pursued with the seemingly essential component of genocidal vigour, bears witness to the strength of the claims that ethnicity and nation can make upon us. Race and culture, however, require a little more consideration in order to demonstrate their character as sovereign sites.

Race is a difficult concept to deconstruct, especially because it is not possible to write about distinct genetic racial categories, as very few 'pure' races, in the genetic sense, exist. It is a concept that exists as a social construct, one that is readily referred to and believed in by individuals and exists because of that belief (Banton 1998: 196–235). However, I am proposing here, in order to make this particular point, to wrap it up with culture, or at least one idea of culture, and use heritage as an example of the sovereign claims that can be made by race and culture. Before turning to some examples, it is worth recalling that culture cannot be understood solely in terms of the past, and as with race much of what is termed 'our own culture' is a fictional construct born of renegotiations of the spaces and times we live in. Nevertheless, heritage remains an important, if not always accessible, inspiration in the renegotiation and reconstruction of our 'own' culture and race, and provides examples which illustrate the sovereign nature of culture and race.

The increased interest in genealogy has led to a rise in television series which explore the ancestors of celebrities. One such BBC programme, 'Who Do You Think You Are?',[16] involved Jeremy Paxman, a British news and current affairs journalist best known for his hard hitting political interviews and relentless and unforgiving style of questioning (Paxman 2007). His detachment from the project of investigating his heritage is explicit at the outset, as he declares that his ancestors are not a burning issue for him and his involvement results from the fact that this is a chance to have social history programmes on the television instead of what he views as the nonsense that is usually scheduled. However, when he discovers that his paternal great grandparents lived in poverty and hardship and died of tuberculosis and exhaustion, orphaning his 12 year old grandfather, he openly cries. Through tears he explains that thousands must have died in similar circumstances, but they are just numbers, and although he would not have physically recognised his great grandparents, there is something possessive in him that makes their deaths, in such difficult circumstances, emotionally meaningful. This, I contend, is a vivid illustration of the authority of the claims that race and culture can make upon us. A further and particularly lucid example of the potential strength of such claims can be seen in the American PBS series 'African American Lives 2', which has a similar aim to the BBC series, but exclusively focuses, as the title suggests, upon well-known African Americans (Gates 2008). In this particular instance Chris Rock, an African American comedian infamous for his continued and unrepentant use of the 'N' word in his stand-up routines, discovers that his great great grandfather fought in the American Civil War, immediately following his freedom from 21 years of slavery. This brings Rock to tears, but it is his erudite commentary upon this discovery which serves to highlight the impact of heritage upon our sense of self. Had he known about his great great grandfather when he was younger, he explains, it would have removed the inevitability he felt that his destiny was to clear up after white people for the rest of his life.

These two examples do more than illustrate the impact that knowledge of our ancestors can have upon our lives. They show the ways in which we possess our identity markers, which we draw from race and culture, and how they orient our sense of self. This seemingly inexplicable connection has a voracious strength that gives the claims made upon us as part of identity processes a sovereign character. In the examples given these identity markers were undiscovered and unknown until the particular projects took place, but they nevertheless serve as an illustration of identity markers as sovereign sites. These examples underline

16 The popularity of this programme has made it into one of the few British programmes that has been syndicated in the United States.

the strength of the claims that identity markers can make upon us. Our identity markers, therefore, may, although this is not always the case, be constitutional sites that make sovereign claims upon us, and our new discourses must take place in a framework that recognises this. The arguments I make that sustain the claim that we need *constitutional* discourses do not, however, deal with the question of why this discourse must also be *plural*.

Plural Discourses

Having shown good and substantial reasons for understanding this vista as involving constitutional discourses, it remains to be shown why they also need to be plural. In this regard I want to follow directly on from the preceding discussion of identity markers as constitutional sites, as this is directly related to the sense in which these constitutional discourses must be plural.

Dominant constitutional theory places authority and sovereignty within a state, whether that authority lies with Parliament or stems from a constitutional text. However, the increasing numbers of non-state organisations that make sovereign claims have led to new developments in constitutional theory. For example, given the claims to sovereignty that the EU makes over the domestic laws of its member states, the proposals for a European Constitution and the enactment of the European Union Charter of Fundamental Rights, much legal literature has been devoted to consideration of the EU's place in our legal order.[17] Equally as significant and rich is the literature that focuses upon other non-state organisations such as the World Bank, WTO, NAFTA, ECHR and so on.[18] From a distinctly British perspective this literature considers how these claims to sovereignty can be squared with the Diceyian formula of parliamentary sovereignty. In addition to these scholarly inquiries, there is literature, which, instead of focusing upon specific institutions, considers constitutionalism in the light of globalisation, or diversity.[19] This literature considers in more abstract and general terms what these new sovereign sites mean for our conceptualisation of constitutions and the work they are meant to undertake. Whilst this literature does not have pluralism as its exclusive focus, there is a strong trend towards its inclusion, in both the form of legal pluralism and constitutional pluralism, and this tendency lends credence to the arguments that I make here. Nevertheless, I wish to take a slightly different trajectory here and suggest that the plural character of these discourses lies in the imperative to recognise identity markers as sites of constitutional significance. In order to recognise these sites of constitutional significance, a *plurality* of constitutional sites beyond the nation-state must be accepted. This claim differs subtly from the literature I have referenced here since I am proposing a constitutional claim for entities that as well as being non-state entities, as is the case for the EU, WTO, and

17 See, for example, Walker (1996) and Craig (2001).

18 See, for example, Anderson (2005).

19 See Tully (1995), Walker (2002) and Santos (2002).

so on, are also non-state-like, which is not the case for the entities considered by most other scholarship in this area.

The EU, the World Bank, WTO, and so on, are non-state entities, but they bear resemblances to state entities in their structures and, if they do not conform to state structures, they are, at the very least, subjected to criticism within that conceptual currency. Legislative processes within the EU, which make sovereignty claims over the domestic legal systems of the member states, have long since been subjected to criticism on the grounds that they are not sufficiently democratic; indeed, so well known are these criticisms that the shorthand term 'democratic deficit' is used to refer to this set of claims.[20] In contrast, identity markers cannot be understood using a state-framework in this manner.

Thus my claim that these constitutional discourses must be plural has two connected bases. First, they cannot be monistic because not only must they recognise constitutional sites beyond the state, they must also be capable of appreciating a plurality of constitutional sites. Secondly, they must be plural because they need to draw upon the conceptual currency and language of legal pluralism. By conceptual currency I mean to include not only the language of critique and analysis available from within legal pluralism, but also its capacity to debunk dominant forms of thought (J. Griffiths 1986: 5). Recall that Anderson helpfully categorised legal pluralism's challenges to dominant legal theory (2005: 39): legal pluralism, he explained, makes challenges 'first, to the centralist notion that law only emanates from the state; secondly, to monist ideas of the systematic coherence and singularity of law; and thirdly, to the positivist view that we can trace a legal order as something 'out there' apart from the agents who created it'. It is in these challenges that space can be made to accommodate the validity of constitutional sites beyond the state and state-like. Furthermore, it is for these reasons that constitutional *pluralistic* discourses are vital. However, in considering the framework that a monistic constitutional discourse may provide for law and identity markers, the claim for a pluralistic character to these constitutional discourses can be further clarified and justified, and it is this treatment that forms the basis of the final part of this third stage of the arguments in this chapter.

A Monistic Constitutional Discourse: The Functional Approach

One further way of justifying the claim that new legal responses to diversity must be the product of pluralistic discourses is to show that a monistic constitutional discourse would fail to change the lens through which diversity is considered. In order to do this I propose to consider Professor Feldman's functional approach to the British Constitution, as an exemplar of dominant progressive, yet monistic, constitutionalism, and illustrate the key weakness to such approaches. In so doing,

20 On the democratic deficit see Hartley (1998: 29–39) and Craig and du Búrca (2002: 75–86).

I aim to justify further the claim that a pluralistic approach is vital to this new vista on constitutionalism.

Feldman identifies four different functions to constitutions (Feldman 2005: 335–6): (i) the institutionalisation function; (ii) the accountability or corsetry function; (iii) the legitimating or decency-preserving function; and (iv) the flexibility or knicker-elastic function. The institutionalisation function refers to the role that constitutions play in setting up institutions for governance, and outlining their responsibilities, duties and the limits to their functions. Feldman notes that this does not necessarily include a definition of their roles and may just be an indication of the powers of an institution. The second function encompasses the idea of enforcing the limits of institutional roles; constitutions must have 'teeth' and be able to patrol the boundaries of action, ensuring that institutions do not act outside of their assigned competencies. This can be achieved in a variety of ways, but examples include judicial review and electoral accountability.

Feldman's third function alludes to the ways in which constitutions provide legitimacy to acts that would otherwise be arbitrary acts of power. This, Feldman suggests, is where moral content enters the constitutional arena, since making appeals along moral lines is one effective method of legitimating acts that would otherwise appear to be arbitrary. 'These [moral] elements', Feldman explains, 'turn an act of naked aggression into an arrest or lawful imprisonment, the refusal of support to the indigent into an act of state prudence, and the conspiracy of a cabal into an exercise of responsible government by a cabinet accountable to a more or less representative legislature' (2005: 355).[21] Within this function, the constitutional culture or psyche of a nation-state is most apparent: in appealing to morality 'of both the elites and the masses' within a nation-state (2005: 335), reference is made, implicitly and explicitly, to foundational norms, whether they are contained within well known constitutional theories such as social contract theories or are more nebulous in their source. Feldman calls this the 'decency-preserving' function in analogy with the fable of The Emperor's New Clothes. It is also important to note that within Feldman's definition of this third function the continued relevance of the Diceyian framework is evident. The idea that naked acts of aggression become lawful when supported by claims to morality expresses Dicey's first principle of the rule of law, namely the supremacy of ordinary law, as opposed to arbitrary power. The fourth and final function provides a level of flexibility to constitutions since 'the clothes (including the corset) must be sufficiently comfortable and adaptable to avoid the need for a completely new wardrobe each time the body politic changes its shape' (2005: 336). This function is not limitless and the constitution cannot stretch infinitely, because this would hamper the first and second functions. I interpret this function to mean that constitutions must be capable of responding appropriately to changes in the nature of civil society.

21 It is within this function that the normative content of constitutions is most easily identified.

It is well worth mentioning that Feldman's functional approach to constitutions is prescriptive, and not descriptive, since the legitimating and flexibility functions suggest that constitutions have normative content. Moreover, it is these two functions that appear to be promising within the context of meeting the challenges of justice in diverse societies; in their promise of morality and flexibility we are led to believe that constitutions have the capacity to evolve in response to the many diversities and pluralities found within any nation-state. This is, I contend, an empty promise grounded in a misconception of the ramifications of diversity. The functional approach relies upon a monistic conceptualisation of law, which can therefore only conceive of a relation between identity markers and law at the level that Chiba terms official law. The discourse that it engenders, then, only partially considers identity processes and identity markers since it fails to recognise the (sovereign) value of identity markers outside the confines of official law. It cannot comprehend the ways in which religion, race, ethnicity, culture, and other aspects of our identities, can act like our own personal official laws and affect the ways that we choose to order our lives. Moreover, it does not allow us to see how our identity markers make sovereign claims upon us, which jostle up against and interact with the sovereign claims that official laws make. It is this weakness of monistic approaches that makes them inadequate for the task in hand. In contrast, Menski's model of law would permit a view of identity markers as sites of constitutional claims.

Constitutional pluralistic discourses respond to our unsettled moment of time, with its new confidence in difference and plurality. Their constitutional character allows exploration of the new dynamic between identity and nation-building techniques. Furthermore, their pluralistic nature brings into view new forms of constitutional sites that, until now, have been overlooked. These new discourses challenge dominant constitutional thinking, and in so doing create spaces where it might be possible to begin crafting legal responses to the developments that create our unsettled moment in history. Their purpose, therefore, is not to answer the questions raised by the presence of diverse identities, but to start making room so that it is possible to become clearer about what issues diverse identities raise. It is in fulfilling this purpose that the challenges of a diversity-sensitive conception of justice become apparent.

Walker's Criteria for Constitutional Renewal

Professor Neil Walker has written extensively on constitutional theory[22] and, in his consideration of contemporary criticisms of constitutionalism, he sets up the challenges to modern constitutionalism that need to be addressed by

22 Professor Walker's work makes particular reference to European Union structures of governance because they are a natural laboratory for the consideration of scenarios beyond the nation-state. See, for example, Walker (1996).

any fresh constitutional perspectives.[23] One element of his exploration of fresh constitutional perspectives is a set of criteria that he argues are necessary elements of any forms of constitutional renewal (2002: 334–6).[24] These criteria for renewal provide a benchmark against which the viability of my proposal for constitutional pluralist discourses can be assessed. Furthermore, the process of measuring up my proposals for a new vista of constitutional pluralism against these criteria permits further explanation of the idea of this new form of constitutionalism. In particular, these further justifications lead to elaboration of the relations between these discourses and my normative framework. Walker (2002: 334) suggests 'six general and cumulative criteria ... which in turn can be organised into three sets of pairs – spatial, temporal and normative'. I propose to summarise each of the criteria and then go on to consider the idea of constitutional pluralist discourses in accordance with Walker's broad taxonomy of criteria for constitutional renewal.

Spatial Criteria

Walker (2002: 334) describes the spatial criteria as the 'least controversial' of all the criteria for constitutional renewal, explaining that any form of constitutionalism must accept the continued relevance of the state, particularly as a 'significant host to constitutional discourse'. Whilst the main thrust of contemporary constitutionalism seeks to respond to developments beyond the boundaries of the nation-state,[25] commonly referred to as the post-Westphalian order,[26] this must not

23 See Walker (2002: 319–33), where he identifies five major critiques of modern constitutionalism. He summarises these as follows: (i) constitutionalism exists within a state-centred framework and is therefore unable to respond to contemporary forms of power which go beyond the state; (ii) of late there has been significant attention upon constitutionalism which has led to an overestimation of its potential and capacity, Walker terms this 'constitutional fetishism'; (iii) constitutionalism has a normative bias towards certain values and therefore fails to engage fairly with all values; (iv) constitutionalism is used as an ideological resource, without any engagement with or commitment to the normative standards it embodies; and (v) constitutionalism has become a 'debased conceptual currency', arguably as a consequence of the cumulative effect of the previous four critiques.

24 It should be repeated, to avoid confusion, that Walker employs the same definition of constitutionalism as is used in this project. See Walker (2002: 318).

25 See, for example, Anderson (2005), Fraser (2005) and Young (2006). The latter two articles do not explicitly deal with constitutionalism, but in reconstructing social justice in the wake of the effects of globalisation they indirectly contribute new forms of constitutionalism.

26 The Treaty of Westphalia 1648 is widely attributed as the starting point of national sovereignty (by which I mean territorial integrity and the exclusion of external actors from domestic affairs) and therefore as establishing the key characteristics of the modern nation-state system. The idea that we live in post-Westphalian times is especially germane given that the Treaty of Westphalia established peace in the wake of attempts to impose

include rendering the state irrelevant and unimportant in the resulting structures since it retains an important, if modified, role in these emerging post-Westphalian orders. This state-inclusive criterion does not preclude the importance of new forms of constitutionalism being 'open to the discovery of meaningful constitutional discourse and processes in non-state sites and processes' (Walker 2002: 334). Indeed, this is the focus of the second spatial criterion which complements the first by requiring a willingness to see sites of power beyond the state. Walker remarks (2002: 334):

> Even for those who are most sceptical or pessimistic about the viability of constitutionalism beyond the state, their position is based either upon an incapacity to imagine the form in which such post-state constitutionalism might be effectively articulated and institutionalised or upon an unwillingness to concede that the time is yet ripe for such an enterprise, rather than upon a refusal *in principle* to contemplate that a constitutional steering mechanism, or its functional equivalent, might be appropriate for significant circuits of transnational power.[27]

The cumulative effect of these two spatial criteria is to maintain emphasis upon the role of the state, whilst also carving out enough space to recognise non-state sites of authority and power. One way of illustrating that these discourses will do both of these things is in the way that law is conceptualised. However, I want to reserve this particular point for a more involved consideration later in this chapter. At this stage, it is sufficient to landmark that this issue relates to these spatial criteria. There are, nevertheless, a number of other issues which need to be referred to in the context of the spatial criteria. First, recall that a general idea of a diversity-

---

supranational authority upon European states, and we now live in a Europe that is coming to terms with its evolving supranational authority in the form of the European Union. Some commentators also focus upon movement away from the Keynesian models of economics, which concentrate upon the nation-state's role in supporting economic growth and stability. See, for example, Fraser (2005) and Anderson (2005). My own exclusion of the economic elements that also frame our world does not signify its irrelevance. Rather, it reflects the necessary limitations of this particular project.

27 As an example of such a position Walker (2002: 334) refers to Grimm's (1995) defence, in the European context, of constitutionalism as a domain for states and *Brunner v The European Union Treaty* [1994] 1 CMLR 57, where in defending state-constitutionalism the ECJ does not absolutely preclude the idea of constitutionalism beyond the state, although it insists that the conditions that would precipitate such a situation are remote and unlikely. It should be noted that the European-centred debates upon constitutionalism are highly political in nature, and much consideration must be given to the continued sensitivity of the idea that Europe has encroached upon the state-sovereignty of its Member States reflecting the level of entrenchment of the Westphalian model in political imaginings. This is not to say that debates in this field that are not focused upon Europe are divested of such sensitivities.

conscious form of justice was set out. This justice had two main pillars, one of which is free and fair access and participation in civil society (in the Habermasian *and* Fraserian senses of the ideal) and the other being the importance of the self-actualisation of authentic identities, although the value of this enterprise is tied up with *both* autonomy and community. Justice, and in particular this diversity-conscious form of justice, is a key element in motivating these discourses, since it grounds the arguments that lead to the conclusion that new legal responses to diversity are needed. Additionally this diversity-conscious justice acts to shape the nature of the proposed constitutional pluralist discourses, in the sense that the two ideals of justice reflect the two dichotomies of the spatial criteria for renewal. First, its focus upon civil society ensures room for state structures and, secondly, its focus upon the value of identities, individualism and community makes room for sites of authority beyond the state in these constitutional pluralist discourses.

I highlighted the limitations of current legal responses to diversity in earlier chapters and sustained the claim that law needs to expand its role if it is to meet the challenges of justice in diverse societies. I showed that law must move from sound normative foundations; that it must be dynamic enough to make room for the social realities of diversity; that law must not constrain identity processes and instead allow them to take place on our own terms; and that the universal ambitions of law must be tempered by making space for the local specificities of diversity. In my consideration of current legal responses, I argued that whilst they provide a vital source of legal responses to diversity they only represent part of the picture. As such, I illustrated that new legal responses to diversity are needed, particularly in light of the requirements of my fresh perspectives on justice. However, I concluded that these new legal responses must be supplementary to the current ones upon the basis of two cumulative reasons. First, in considering contemporary responses to diversity, it was apparent that they have enjoyed significant successes, despite their shortcomings, and this alone was sufficient to justify their continued relevance. Additionally, my proposed vista, in the form of constitutional pluralist discourses, is suggested as *one other* way of considering diversity in legal fields. These discourses are not suggested on the grounds that they have the capacity to respond to the whole spectrum of injustices raised by diverse identities. I noted that the focus of this study was limited to law's role in meeting the challenges of my diversity-conscious justice. This was because the breadth of the challenges of this form of justice span much further than law, and have social and political dimensions. Indeed, I explored one such dimension in my consideration of nation-states and pluralism. Constitutional pluralist discourses and any new legal responses that result from these discourses are, therefore, limited in their capacity as motors for social change.[28]

Moreover, the idea of discourses is not in itself composed of rights or any other grounds to legal claims, although such discourses may, of course, lead to the consideration of new legal claims. Rather, the discourses are intended to assist

28 This limitation relates to the broader theme of the limits of law (Allott 1980).

in paving a better, more panoramic, path towards justice. These discourses are neither a replacement for existing legal responses, although they seek to learn from the flaws within existing frameworks, nor are they a comprehensive answer to the many and complex questions raised by the particular conceptualisation of justice put forward here. In this way, the discourses I propose respect both of the spatial criteria: as supplementary responses to diversity they seek to recognise the continued relevance of state structures, as expressed through contemporary legal responses to diversity, but at their heart, they also endeavour to clear space for new ways of approaching diversity, and in so doing recognise sites of constitutional authority beyond the state.

My final illustration that these discourses fulfil the spatial criteria relates to the idea of nation-building projects. In my fresh perspective on justice I showed that the project of nation-building is not confined to new nations and that, in fact, it is an ongoing project in which all nations, regardless of their relative maturity, engage in, whether in an explicit or implicit manner. Historically, notions of stable, secure and therefore strong nationhood have been associated with the concepts of oneness and unity. In turn, this has led to an emphasis upon common elements, whether these commonalities are values, morals or identities. Nationhood and nationality have, therefore, been crafted into concepts that we assume can only be stretched as far as common elements allow. Furthermore, they often use fictional reference points of original or indigenous ethnicities and values to make up their core, around which additional complementary common elements can be included. However, if one accepts that all nations are engaged in a process of nation-building, this project is not served well by the boundaries that have been erected around notions of nationhood and nationality, especially in light of contemporary nations as homes to highly diverse identities. Consequently, to meet the challenges of a diversity-sensitive justice, it is not only crucial that the ongoing and protean nature of nation-building is accepted, but this nation-building project must also acknowledge that contemporary trends require a more heterogeneous, and pluralistic, approach than the one taken thus far. It is in this context that this new constitutionalism is proposed. These discourses should be viewed as a nation-building tool, as a (legal) mechanism through which ideas of nationality, and its relations to diversity, can be explored and expanded. This, of course, is very different to direct discourses on the nature of citizenship, such as the one entered into by Lord Goldsmith as part of his report on British citizenship.[29] These latter discourses focus upon the responsibilities of legal spheres in the wake of diverse identities, and of necessity consider national identities in that context, rather than entertaining a direct focus upon the meaning of citizenship in contemporary societies.

This nation-building character raises significant issues and questions. In recognising the importance of nation-building projects, and incorporating it within these discourses, this becomes a constitutionalism that accommodates the

29 See http://www.justice.gov.uk/reviews/citizenship.htm (last accessed 21 September 2010).

continued relevance of state structures. Furthermore, the idea that this nation-building project must modify its messages, responds to a changing dynamic caused, in part at least, by the existence of sites of constitutional power beyond the state. Moreover, the ongoing nature of nation-building projects has become increasingly apparent as a consequence of the influences of these non-state sites of constitutional power. Given the conclusions and analysis in this book, therefore, any constitutional pluralist discourse that provides a meaningful platform for new legal responses must recognise the continued salience of state structures, whilst also carving out areas where non-state and non-state-like sites of constitutional power can be considered and perhaps, where appropriate, recognised, and this is the nature of the discourses proposed here.

Temporal Criteria

Walker's temporal criteria are historical and discursive continuity. The former refers to the need for new forms of constitutionalism to maintain a 'plausible and recoverable causal connection with its historical origins' (2002: 334). Without this ability to trace the progression and evolution of constitutionalism it loses its context, and it then becomes difficult to make sense of and reconcile its differing uses in any coherent fashion. The second temporal criterion is related to the idea of historical continuity, but differs to the extent that it requires a consistent core of ideas that 'however radically transformed, are meaningfully connected between different times and places' (2002: 334). Walker explains discursive continuity thus (2002: 334–5):

> [W]hereas the requirement of historical continuity imposes a discipline of connection from the socio-political 'outside', the requirement of discursive continuity imposes a discipline of connection from the ideational 'inside'. These two disciplines, it is submitted, combine to provide the only plausible basis upon which the deep indeterminacy and disagreement which would debase constitutionalism's conceptual currency may be contested and averted.

The cumulative effect of historical and discursive continuity is a coherent progression forward that is inclusive of those allied to past discourses and those previously excluded by past discourses. In nation-states that have not been subjected to identity-based conflicts there is no evidence of a situation which requires the creation of a constitutional moment in time that provides a radical disjuncture from past events. The need for constitutional disjuncture occurs, I believe, as part of the birth of a new nation; the events in post-conflict societies such as South Africa and Sri Lanka come immediately to mind as examples of such scenarios.[30] But even still, post-conflict societies such as these need to maintain some level

30 More recently Kenya has signed a new constitution, which moves it away from the constitution it inherited as a part of decolonisation. The main thrust behind the new

of historical and discursive continuity, although not to the same degree as nation-states where no case can be made for a radical departure from the past.

Menski's model of law provides visual representation of both historical and discursive continuity in the context of this fresh perspective. The model shows, inter alia, historical continuity in its acceptance of the validity of a spectrum of jurisprudential accounts of law, and in its emphasis upon their role as influential factors to be negotiated by our many kites of law. Moreover, this model shows discursive continuity in its reliance on the core ideas of these previous jurisprudential accounts of law to inform its legally pluralistic perspective on law. In fact, this legally pluralistic account combines and reconciles dominant jurisprudence with other schools of thought.

In addition to the conceptualisation of law that informs these constitutional pluralist discourses, evidence of the temporal criteria can be seen in the supplementary and complementary character of these discourses. Whilst justice requires new legal responses to diversity, this does not obviate the need for current legal responses in the form of anti-discrimination legislation, current constitutional provisions, and human rights provisions which continue to provide significant legal responses to the challenges of justice in societies with diverse identities.

Further evidence of these criteria can be found in the relation between the triad of norms and these new discourses. The three norms of heterogeneity, expansive justice and post-colonial and post-9/11 peoples are vital to begin these discourses, although they are open to debate as part of the discourses. Recall, however, that these norms were presented as a modification of the norms that are promised by current legal responses to diversity, in order to take our evolving understanding of diverse identities into account. In this way the triad of norms support both the external and internal continuity that Walker articulates, precisely because they respect the successes and utility of historical discourses. Thus, they facilitate the maintenance of a connection with the core ideas of past discourses, and thereby promote discursive continuity. The norms of expansive justice, and post-coloniality and our post-9/11 worlds, in particular, also promote the temporal criteria in their specific content. The expansive nature of justice is premised upon the idea of justice as a concept that must be able to grow – not start anew – in pace with the evolution of our understandings and conceptualisations of justice in diverse worlds. In this sense, then, it is a norm that is firmly rooted within historical discourses, yet its expansive nature permits a forward-focused continuous ideological flow within these discourses.

The idea of citizens as post-colonial and post-9/11 peoples also embodies the temporal criterion of historical continuity. The need to understand living in diverse societies as, to some degree, a negotiation of its past legacies forces a very real connection with history that I argue has been missing in the past. Whilst our

constitution is to address the political corruption that seems to have blighted this nation. It is too early to assess or analyse this new constitutional moment in any meaninful manner.

past has never been denied, it has, on the whole, been viewed through rose tinted glasses; empire has been painted as embodying everything that is good, if not great, about a country, and the realities of colonisation have been glossed over. The final norm in my triad calls for a more realistic engagement with a nation-state's colonial history and its post-9/11 future, and is premised, therefore, upon the importance of continuity with our historical origins. The historical continuity of this fresh perspective on diversity is, in part, contingent upon taking this realistic approach to our colonial legacies and post-9/11 futures, with the further hope that this clear and unwavering gaze permits an understanding of contemporary citizenries as ones engaged in negotiating and navigating post-colonial and post-9/11 spaces; this, I submit, is the value of historical continuity.

The conceptual and analytical tool of identity markers evidences discursive continuity in the discourses I propose. One of the purposes of identity markers is to act as an analytical tool that facilitates an understanding of the constitutional dimensions to a diversity-focused form of justice. They are able to do this because they are a conceptual tool conceived to provide a better match between this diversity-focused justice, with its emphasis upon the value of our self-actualisation of identity, and the ways that diversity is understood. In one sense identity markers open a locked door to these constitutional dimensions that concepts such as culture, religion, race, ethnicity, nationality, gender, sexual orientation, beliefs, and so on, fail to access. Yet, this is not because identity markers have some elusive quality that these other concepts do not possess; rather, it is because identity markers are part of new discourses which move away from the narratives and concepts which underpin and limit current responses to diversity. These historical discourses have failed to appreciate that diversity might produce constitutional sites of power, and therefore the concepts that underpin them are too closely associated with these non-constitutional discourses to permit a proper focus upon the constitutional dimensions of diversity. Recall, however, that identity markers do not abandon these other concepts entirely, precisely because they continue to have salience in diversity discourses; this connection reflects the importance of discursive continuity. Identity markers would lose their value and meaning if they were presented as a concept that is entirely distinct from historical concepts within diversity discourses. The core ideologies of these historical discourses continue to have import and significance for this new vista on constitutionalism. To put this point another way, to proceed with this vista in terms entirely outside of these historical concepts would create a type of disconnect that would stall any potential legal responses. First, the connection between concepts such as religion and race and historical discourses that do not operate with constitutional dimensions, impedes the progress of our legal imaginings. Discourses that treat the Human Rights Act 1998 as a constitutional text,[31] for example, have had less of an impact than such a suggestion ought to

31 See, for example, O'Cinniede (2004), who clearly treats the Human Rights Act 1998 as a constitutional text. Further evidence of the constitutional nature of some Acts of

have received in the field of diversity. This, I believe, is because of the difficulty of changing the flow of an established discourse. In using a new conceptual tool that departs from the old paradigm, without completely abandoning these historical discourses, this particular obstacle is overcome. Secondly, the idea of justice that underpins these historical concepts is not in complete alignment with the notion of diversity as constitutionally significant. This mismatch, which again presents itself as an obstacle to new legal responses, is avoided when using a concept such as identity markers that sits more comfortably within a framework created by a diversity-focused understanding of justice.

The value of historical and discursive continuity can also be seen in my proposal for a new vista on constitutional pluralism in the form of discourses, as opposed to a new set of legal claims or a modified constitution. New legal grounds for claims or proposals for new constitutional frameworks are unfeasible without discourses that lead towards their substantive content. The benefit of discourses is that they promote dialogue and debate within a particular framework, and it is this dialogue that is better placed to lead to concrete proposals for new legal responses, precisely because it is through debate that a more comprehensive consideration of the questions raised by such a paradigm shift is possible. My proposal for constitutional pluralist discourses is based, therefore, upon achieving a paradigm shift whilst maintaining an historical and discursive connection that would not be feasible in proposals for new legislative or constitutional frameworks.

Normative Criteria

Walker's normative criteria are perhaps the most difficult of the three sets of criteria for renewal to summarise and illustrate compliance. The first criterion is inclusive normative coherence, by which he means to encapsulate a (2002: 336):

> [C]ommitment within constitutional theory and practice to a highly reflexive conception of democracy, one which is constantly vigilant; first, of its capacity to provide an adequate representation and reconciliation of the diversity of democracy-respecting interests and aspirations within and beyond the *demos* that may be affected by and thus have a legitimate claim to a voice in the political practice of that *demos*; and, secondly, and at a deeper level of reflection, of the appropriateness of the current (and always contingent) boundaries of its political self-characterisation as a *demos* as a framework to optimise that representative and reconciliatory capacity.

Parliament can be found in the *Metric Martyrs* case law. However, this line of normative reasoning has not had any significant impact upon the direction of diversity discourses.

To explain inclusive normative coherence Walker references Tully's concept of a constitutional arrangement which allows all parties with vested interests 'to enter into processes of contestation and negotiation of the rules of recognition' (Tully 1995: 477, quoted in Walker 2002: 336). In essence, inclusive normative coherence demands an open-ness that makes space for and accepts the reality of normative pluralism; that is, the reality that there are many different logics in the world that lead to a great variety of normative conclusions.[32] Constitutionalism must make enough space so that advocates of radically different normative arguments have access to and are able to participate in constitutional processes upon an equal footing; constitutionalism must be inclusive in its boundaries.[33]

The final criterion of constitutional renewal is external coherence and it seeks to fill any gaps left by internal normative coherence (2002: 336):

> [I]t is clearly not enough for constitutionalism merely to convince the constitutionalists. If constitutionalism is intended as a form of practical reasoning, it must have something relevant to say to those who are skeptical about the claims it makes … or, indeed, to those who make no such explicit critique of constitutional discourse but who simply choose to concentrate on other forms of practical reasoning but within areas which constitutionalist [*sic*] would also consider to be within *their* legitimate contemplation.

The normative arguments of constitutionalism must, therefore, be able to engage with and be relevant to other discourses, particularly those that criticise constitutionalism as having a tendency to claim to be a panacea to all.[34]

These are, perhaps, the most controversial of Walker's criteria for constitutional renewal. Nevertheless, the proposals made here fulfil these normative criteria in two separate ways. First, I propose constitutional pluralist *discourses*, rather than a new constitutional framework or set of legal claims, in order to promote dialogue and debate, and therefore pursue a reflexive approach to carving out legal responses to diversity. I use the term reflexive here in the sense that Pierre Bourdieu theorised it: the biases created by one's own position in social and legal structures must be recognised, and one way of achieving such cognisance is

32 I am again drawing upon Isaiah Berlin's (1997: 9) definition of pluralism.

33 An interesting point can be made here in reference to same-sex marriages. Osterlund (2009) argues that a side-effect of allowing homosexual couples to marry in Canada has been an underlying normalisation of processes of love. Love, she argues, must entail marriage and families, if the state message is to be believed. Presumably an inclusive normative coherence would require that couples are permitted to define love in a myriad of ways beyond marriage and having children.

34 This particular critique of constitutionalism, namely that it stretches its remedial capacities and potential too far, is termed 'constitutional fetishism' by Walker (2002: 324–7).

through collective participation in dialogue and debate.[35] In this regard, the claim I make that there are constitutional implications to diverse identities, as well as the parameters of the normative framework, remain open to debate as part of the constitutional pluralist discourses I propose. Furthermore, this clarifies why it would be inappropriate to go as far as constructing a new constitutional framework, or a set of legal claims, as this would bypass, and therefore forgo the benefits of, these reflexive processes.

Although the reflexive character of this discourse also goes a considerable way to realising the criterion of external normative coherence, it is further realised by an acceptance of the limits of such discourses. Whilst law has a burden to shoulder in realising the challenges of a diversity-focused form of justice, and constitutional pluralist discourses form *one* legal response to those challenges, it does not represent the whole story. The realisation of social justice, so that societies are at ease with their plurality, is not a goal that can be achieved fully through constitutions, or even law. The challenge of justice in such circumstances pervades into far more domains than merely legal arenas. Indeed, I believe that the challenges of justice in situations of diversity are unremittingly pervasive, and make demands across the whole spectrum of civil society. However, exploring the reach of the challenges of justice in diverse societies is not vital to the claim made here. Instead, the claim that the challenges of justice in diverse societies fall wider than the stretch of legal arenas can be sustained by cursory consideration of the limits of law.[36]

My concern here is not precisely where these limits lie, but rather that there are limits to the social transformation capacities of law, such that it cannot be considered to provide a comprehensive response to the challenges of justice. In accepting that law has limits, other, external, normative lines of reasoning which seek to respond to such challenges are validated. Moreover, the explicit recognition of the validity of a wide variety of forms of normative reasoning and the significance of a great number of social domains to the challenges of my conception of justice, allows discourses, such as the ones proposed here, to find allies amongst the sceptics and the uninterested, as Walker categorises them (2002: 336).

The precise boundaries of the limits of law are, I believe, open to debate and disagreement, and this debate must at least be informed by, if not to some degree occupied with, the definition of law. However, the claim that there must be limits to law's ability to transform or control societies or, to put it another way, engage in social engineering, is perhaps far less controversial and less contestable. Moreover, although the position of these limits may vary according to the definition of law upon which such claims are premised, differences in definitions of law do not negate the claim that law has limits, so long as we can

35 See, for example, Bourdieu (1990), Bourdieu and Wacquant (1992) and Bourdieu (2004); and for a synopsis of Bourdieu's approach to reflexivity see Deer (2008).

36 I borrow the idea and phrase, 'the 'limits of law', from Allott (1980).

agree that every rule, norm, principle, moral, and so on is *not* law and, therefore, that law is not to be found everywhere.[37] If we can agree upon these premises, then the idea that law cannot completely control societies is uncontroversial, perhaps even trite. Arguments in support of this assertion range from evidence of illegal activities, both criminal and civil, despite laws prohibiting such acts, to examples of laws that have responded to, rather than precipitated, changes in society. One stark example of the latter can be found in *R v R (Rape: Marital Exemption)* where the House of Lords in the UK overturned the common law rule that a husband could not be criminally liable for committing rape upon his wife (irrespective of whether the wife could reasonably be said to be consenting to intercourse) in 1991.[38]

Examples such as the Civil Partnership Act 2004 in the UK are perhaps more illuminating as to the existence of boundaries to law's capacity to effect social change. The explanatory notes to this Act states that its purpose 'is to enable same-sex couples to obtain legal recognition of their relationship by forming a civil partnership'. Whilst significant sections of Britain's societies believed, and campaigned for this legislation, upon the basis that same-sex couples must be entitled to avail themselves of the same legal rights as heterosexual couples, equally significant sections of Britain's societies opposed the Act on a variety of grounds; some believed that same-sex couples should not be permitted to enter into a marriage-like union, for both religious and non-religious reasons, and that this legislation would therefore dilute the institution of marriage; others opposed the Act on the basis that heterosexual couples did not have options to commit to each other outside of marriage and therefore the Act failed fully to go down the road of equality; and some sections of society felt that committed partners who chose not to go through any ceremony, whether partnership or marriage, should also be entitled to legal recognition.[39] The wide spectrum of opinions on this subject, in contrast to near universal acceptance of the principles underpinning the House of Lords' decision in *R v R*, evidence that this Act did not merely reflect a change in attitude across Britain to same-sex relationships, and instead was an attempt to encourage Britain's societies to accept the importance and value of equality for same-sex couples. Yet, this capacity for change has limits: Jacqui Smith, who was the Minister of State for Industry and the Regions and Deputy Minister for Women and Equality at that time, introduced the consultation papers for this Act acknowledging that it was an attempt to mould social attitudes towards same-sex couples, but that '[c]ulture change occurs not only by legal recognition but also by building on the significant and welcome change in attitudes towards lesbian, gay and bisexual people' (Smith 2003: 9). It is, of course, too early to

37 This is a complaint sometimes directed at theories of legal pluralism, particularly earlier ones.

38 [1991] 4 All ER 481.

39 See BBC News Online (2004), for an example of the broad range of public opinion on the Civil Partnership Act 2004.

assess the success of this Act in contributing towards a change in social attitudes, but alone it is highly unlikely to lead to comprehensive acceptance of same-sex relationships.

Another particularly salient example of legislation that seeks to transform societies, that is more amenable to assessment, is Britain's Race Relations Acts 1965–1976. Singh (2006: 135) describes the RRA 1976 as a 'speaking act', this being 'a law which seeks to do more than just lay down legal rules, which speaks to society and tries to influence behaviour by laying down a fundamental principle and setting out a vision of what we could become'.[40] Literature assessing the impact of this legislation provides evidence that laws can engage in social control, but that there are limits to this role. Hepple and Szyszczak's collection of papers, for example, examine the globally common theme that Britain's 'anti-discrimination laws have failed to fulfill the promise of equality which they hold out to disadvantaged groups' (1992: ix), and argue that, as the collection's title suggests, there are limits to discrimination laws. This is not to say that they are wholly ineffective. Indeed, upon the 30th anniversary of the RRA 1976, its successes were acknowledged with the conclusion that Britain is a country with far less explicit racism today than 30 years earlier (Bickerstaffe 2006: 140). It is possible that the limits of anti-discrimination legislation lie in law's inability to change the way that people think and make covert racism unacceptable. Martin Luther King famously said (1967):

> [A]lthough it may be true that morality cannot be legislated, behaviour can be regulated. Even though it may be true that the law cannot change the heart, it can restrain the heartless. Even though it may be true that the law cannot make a man love me, it can restrain him from lynching me.

My point in referencing these examples is that there are undoubtedly limits to law, although we may argue about where these limits lie, and this means there are limits to my proposal for constitutional pluralist discourses. Furthermore, this conclusion reinforces that it is vital to the external normative coherence of these discourses that they are recognised as partial, but nevertheless crucial, responses to the challenges of justice in diverse societies. In recognising the parameters of these discourses it becomes meaningful to those who sit outside of constitutionalism's lure, because it empowers and validates their voices as responses to the challenges of a diversity-focused justice.

Walker's criteria for constitutional renewal have made possible an exploration of the nature of the constitutional pluralist discourses that I propose. Moreover, they have allowed an illustration of the relations between these constitutional pluralist discourses and the normative framework that I have argued for. The aim

40 I have argued that a full and frank view of Britain's anti-discrimination legislation cannot view it solely as a legislative expression of equality discourses, as its inception is too closely linked to racially targeted immigration controls.

is that these constitutional pluralist discourses will further a debate that clarifies the nature of the questions and issues posed by diversity. In becoming clearer as to the questions raised by diversity, we are provided with a better opportunity to craft sound legal responses to the challenges of justice in diverse societies.

Chapter 11
Conclusions

Since the aim of my proposal for constitutional discourses is to provide a platform from which it is possible to have a clearer view of the challenges of my diversity-sensitive conception of justice, it seems premature to reach conclusions at this stage. Instead, I tie my normative framework to my proposal for constitutional pluralist discourses by using it as a lens to revisit *Ali v Ali*,[1] 'the case of the missing one pound' (Menski 2002: 47) and the question of wearing religious garments in the public sphere. This return visit allows me to demonstrate how constitutional pluralist discourses have the potential to illuminate alternative and much needed legal responses to diversity. Furthermore, this analysis illustrates how constitutional pluralist discourses can contribute both to current and new legal responses to diversity.

The Case of the Missing One Pound

I introduced the subtleties of the challenges of justice in diverse communities by considering the unreported case of *Ali v Ali*. I want to revisit that case and consider how viewing this case through a constitutional pluralist lens might offer an alternative perspective. In essence, Mr and Mrs Ali were unable to agree whether the £30,001 that had been agreed upon as *mahr* in their *kabhinama* had now become due to Mrs Ali, and so they found themselves arguing over this matter before an English court. Mr Ali put forth two arguments to justify denying Mrs Ali this *mahr* (Menski 2002: 49–50):

1. He denied that he had given his wife a *talaq*, without which Mrs Ali's claim to *mahr* would have to be forfeited, although he had initiated the divorce proceedings before the English courts.
2. He argued that he had been forced into agreeing such a high amount of *mahr*, an admission that Menski explains is inconsistent with the idea of maintaining one's social status, or *izzat*. Further, Mr Ali suggested that large amounts of *mahr* are promised in order to maintain one's *izzat*, whilst there is no intention that this money will ever be paid.

Through a constitutional pluralist lens *mahr* is understood as an identity marker that is a site of constitutional authority. The bargaining process that takes place

1 Unreported, Menski (2002: 47–52).

when agreeing the level of *mahr* 'reflects a contest over the relative status and financial standing in society of all participants to this negotiation' (Menski 2002: 48). Thus, the constitutional dimension of *mahr* as an identity marker is easily identifiable. By understanding *mahr* in this manner it is possible to see this dispute beyond an argument over a significant sum of money; clearly there were issues of *izzat*, or honour connected to identity processes, at stake here. Furthermore, through this lens, Mr Ali's arguments cast him as an unscrupulous husband who is engaged in manipulating English law, with the knowledge that it operates with monistic blinkers and is unable to understand the meaning of this dispute. Through a constitutional pluralist lens the characterisation of the dispute between Mr and Mrs Ali changes and offers a different, clearer view of the challenges of justice in their case. This is precisely because the concept of identity markers, together with their background of constitutional pluralism, allow us to see the significance of *mahr* and gain a clearer picture of what the dispute between this husband and wife is really about.

This constitutional pluralist lens also allows us to analyse the English court's response to this claim in more robust and clarified ways. Whilst inquiring into the reason for the English court awarding Mrs Ali £30,000, and not £30,001, Menski explains that '[b]y giving her £1 less, [the English judge] applied not Muslim law, but asserted the application of English law' and 'protected [it] from the unrelenting pressure to accept personal laws' (2002: 51). Menski's model of legal pluralism, together with the idea of identity markers, permit further clarification of this analysis of the decision in *Ali*. A constitutional pluralist perspective allows us to see a conflict between Islamic law and English law, a clash of laws that the judge in *Ali* was attempting to resolve. Moreover, the post-colonial and post-9/11 perspective that is part of this constitutional pluralist lens illuminates the power struggle taking place as part of this clash of laws. In this conceptualisation of *Ali*, the judge was concerned to ensure the dominant position of English law, as it came under fire from the colonial Other and terrorist potential of Islamic law. Furthermore, the path chosen by the judge in *Ali* fails to recognise the importance of encouraging heterogeneity, and the divisive impact that this subtle pursuit of homogeneity can have. *Ali* is a good example of the tacit nature of homogenous nation-building techniques and the role of official law in nation-building projects. The fact that the *mahr* was enforced by an English court appears progressive; however, the message of leaving out one pound is clear, namely that English law is the only applicable law of the land. This has implications for the ways that members of diverse communities participate in and access civil society. Thus, the injustice of this seemingly equitable decision is exposed. A constitutional pluralist perspective sheds light upon these layers of *Ali*, and permits their more coherent expression. Through this lens, the significance of the missing one pound becomes apparent.

Constitutional Pluralism and Religious Dress

I intend here to consider a topic that has received much attention, both judicial and otherwise, in order to demonstrate how a constitutional pluralist framework might alter the nature of the questions raised in difficult cases, and how we approach such cases.[2] I have chosen to focus upon the subject of religious dress in public places, because it represents an area where there is a great variety of non-judicial opinions, and also because it is proving to be a site of conflict across the globe. As such it presents a rich context against which a fresh perspective can be more clearly explained.

The debates surrounding religious dress can be understood along many different axes, some of which include gender equality, multiculturalism, pluralism, secularism, integration, internal religious plurality, liberalism and national identity.[3] However, these debates raise a broader question (McGoldrick 2006: 33, emphasis in original): '*how do people who disagree over profoundly different matters live together?*' It is this broad agenda that makes the issues encountered by Muslim women who veil themselves and Sikh men and women who choose to wear turbans an exemplar through which a constitutional pluralist discourse can be demonstrably explained.[4]

The issue of religious dress in public places is considerable in quantity and approaches, and therefore has a great variety of potential entry-points. My approach here is to consider two strands of jurisprudence in this field. The first strand of cases focuses upon prohibition of the Islamic practice of veiling in public spaces such as schools and universities.[5] The range of opinions within the

---

2 Claims for legal pluralism, or legally pluralistic perspectives, sometimes suffer on account of their inability to go further than theoretical and conceptual arguments and provide tangible examples of legal pluralism in action. My inclusion of examples of the application of a constitutional pluralist perspective is intended to address this criticism.

3 For a comparative approach to the Islamic veiling that looks at this subject across Europe see McGoldrick (2006). For an overview of some of the dimensions of debates that surround veiling see, in particular, McGoldrick (2006: 8–21, 208–310). The question of veiling is dealt with as one of religious obligation, an instrument of oppression of women, as a form of religious extremism, as a political statement, as evidence of the failure of integration by immigrants and as an aspect of terrorism. A wider perspective is also taken where veiling debates are used to explore national identity, multiculturalism, secularism and liberalism in the context of intense, often conflicting, normative pluralism.

4 Recent controversies in Europe over veiling have focused upon banning full veils in *all* public spaces, including, for example, public transport. See, for example, Davies (2010) on veiling in France. It appears to be important to send a clear message that this element of Islam is not welcome in these nation-states, and I believe this type of debate is another dimension of our post-9/11 condition that we are negotiating under the rubric of secularism.

5 I use the term veiling in a broad sense so that a spectrum of interpretations of the Islamic requirement of modesty are included, ranging from the *hijab* and *jilbab* to the

practice of veiling is intense in its plurality (not only are there wide ranges of opinion external to Islam on the practice, the interpretations internal to the faith are hugely varied), and the question of its place in public, secular, institutions has arisen within a human rights context, making it an excellent platform to consider how a constitutional pluralist discourse might provide a clearer picture of the challenges of justice in diverse societies. The second strand of cases also considers prohibitions of religious forms of dress in public spaces, but within the context of the RRA 1976. The House of Lords' decision in *Mandla*, which considers the Sikh turban and its place in the public sphere, best exemplifies this strand of cases. I propose to begin with a brief summary of the facts and judgments in these cases to inform my discussion of how a constitutional pluralist approach to religious dress might change the nature of this debate. I organise this discussion by showing how the three guiding norms in my local normative framework work to change the way these cases are considered.[6]

I argued for three norms (heterogeneity, expansive justice and post-colonial and post-9/11 peoples) that were designed to aid my fresh perspectives on law in overcoming the difficulties I identified in current official legal responses to diversity. The idea of a commitment to valuing difference (heterogeneity), an understanding of justice that allows it to evolve over time (expansive justice) and a structure that allows negotiation of colonial and 9/11 legacies (post-colonial and post-9/11 peoples) were, therefore, aimed at providing a sound normative foundation and making space for the expression of the local specificities of diversity.

Summary of Jurisprudence

In the last 15 years a significant line of veiling jurisprudence has built up, framed within the terms of the ECHR. Many of these cases did not pass the admissibility stage of proceedings and were declared to be manifestly ill-founded before they could be considered on their merits, although there are at least two cases which the ECtHR and the House of Lords have decided on their merits.

In *Karaduman v Turkey*,[7] a university graduate was refused a certificate confirming her qualifications because she would not submit a photograph with her head uncovered, as required by the university regulations. She alleged violation of her freedom to manifest her religion (Article 9 ECHR), but this case did not get past the admissibility stage. The ECtHR held that 'Article 9 of the Convention does not always guarantee the right to behave in the public sphere in a way which is dictated by such a belief' (para 108). The Court felt that the applicant's choice to

---

burqa and *niqab*. See Esposito (2003: 52, 112, 160) and Glassé (2008: 114, 204, 544) for consideration of this Islamic practice.

6 This method of organising a discussion of a constitutional pluralist discourse does not reflect the relative importance of this triad of norms in my normative framework. It is merely an expedient way of organising this discussion.

7 (1993) 74 DR 93.

study at a secular university implied her acceptance of these rules, which the Court went on to describe as securing 'respect for the rights and freedoms of others', and in particular those that were felt to be necessary in order to 'ensure that certain fundamentalist religious movements do not disturb public order' (para 108).

In *Dahlab v Switzerland* a public school teacher was asked to remove her *hijab* having worn it to work for five years.[8] She made an application alleging that her Article 9 ECHR rights had been violated. The ECtHR found Dahlab's application to be manifestly ill-founded, and employed a line of reasoning that has been followed in later Islamic dress cases. The ECtHR agreed with Switzerland's arguments that the banning of religious dress was justified by the principle of denominational neutrality and gender equality, as protected by the Swiss Constitution.

This reasoning was elaborated upon in *Leyla Şahin v Turkey*,[9] which was declared admissible and was considered on its merits. Leyla was a medical student at Istanbul University and was refused entry to lectures, access to examinations and enrolment upon courses, because she was wearing a *hijab*. At the time of her exclusion Istanbul University had issued a circular prohibiting headscarves and beards on the university campus.[10] Before the circular was issued Leyla had worn her *hijab* at the university, as well as completing four years of tertiary medical education at Bursa University whilst wearing her *hijab*. Leyla unsuccessfully challenged the circular in the Istanbul Administrative Court, and felt forced to abandon her medical training in Turkey upon the basis of her continued exclusion, choosing to complete her training in Austria at Vienna University instead.[11] She then challenged the ban in the ECtHR, alleging, inter alia, that her freedom of religion (Article 9 ECHR) and right to non-discrimination on the grounds of freedom of religion (Articles 9 and 14 ECHR) had been violated.[12] The Turkish Government argued that whilst there had been interference with the applicant's ECHR rights, these were justified by the Turkish constitutional principles of secularism and gender equality, and therefore they came within the acceptable limitations of ECHR rights since they were necessary in a democratic society for the protection of the rights of others and of public order.[13] The Grand Chamber

8 Dec no 42393/98, ECHR 2001-V.

9 GC no 44774/98, ECHR 2005 XI.

10 The circular was issued on 23 February 1998, and Leyla had enrolled at the Cerraphasa Faculty of Medicine, Istanbul University, on 26 August 1997. Prior to joining Istanbul University, which was her fifth year of medical school, Leyla studied at the Faculty of Medicine at Bursa University, where she was free to wear her *hijab*.

11 Leyla lodged her complaint in the Istanbul Administrative Court on 29 July 1998, just five months after the circular was issued. The Istanbul Administrative Court dismissed her complaint on 19 March 1999, and this decision was then affirmed by the Supreme Administrative Court on 19 April 2001.

12 Leyla also alleged that her right to respect for private life (Article 8), freedom of expression (Article 10) and right to education (Protocol 1, Article 2) had been violated.

13 The ECtHR has established jurisprudence which interprets the phrase 'necessary in a democratic society' (found in many of the limitation paragraphs of rights enshrined

found that there had been interference with Leyla's right to freedom of religion, as enshrined by Article 9(1) ECHR, but that the justificatory arguments put forward by the Turkish Government brought Leyla's exclusion within the permissible limits set out in Article 9(2) ECHR.[14] The Grand Chamber therefore pursued the same line of reasoning employed in *Dahlab*, namely that the principles of secularism and gender equality justified a ban on religious clothing in public places.

The *Begum* case, the facts of which have already been recited, need not be reiterated here. However, it is worth noting that the House of Lords employed analogous lines of reasoning to those used by the ECtHR, since their Lordships justified the school's decision not to allow Shabina to wear her *jilbab* on the grounds that it would secure the liberty of conscience of the other students and that it could not be squared with gender equality. *Azmi v Kirklees Metropolitan Borough Council* is the final veiling case that merits mention.[15] The facts were somewhat similar to *Dahlab*, as Aishah Azmi was a teaching assistant who was not permitted to wear a veil covering her head and her face whilst teaching in the presence of males. Along similar lines to *Dahlab*, Azmi argued that this constituted religious discrimination that was prohibited by regulation 3 of the Employment Equality (Religion or Belief) Regulations 2003.[16] The Employment Appeal Tribunal (EAT) dismissed her appeal and approved the decision of the Employment Tribunal (ET) that there was no religious discrimination in this case. The framework under the Employment Regulations is slightly different to Article 9 of the ECHR and the courts are required, inter alia, to use a comparator to assess whether a claimant has been treated less favourably on the grounds of religion. In its judgment the EAT approved the ET's choice of comparator as a woman, whether Muslim or non-Muslim, who covered her face for non-religious reasons.

The formula of testing for discrimination under the Employment Regulations is a slightly modified version of the one found in the RRA 1976. It is worth revisiting, briefly, the leading case under this legislation, *Mandla*, as it also concerns religious dress, in this case a Sikh's turban, in a state school. Here a Sikh student claimed discrimination under the RRA 1976 because of his school's failure

---

by the ECHR) as requiring analysis of whether the justifications put forward pursued a legitimate aim and were proportionate to that end. *Leyla Şahin* involved more legal considerations than I mention here, in particular, considerable time was spent on analysing whether the circular could come within the phrase 'prescribed by law', as set out in Article 9(2) ECHR. However, I have endeavoured to keep the strictly legal analysis to a minimum, preferring instead to take a socio-legal approach where the issues considered in this case form the focal point of my consideration, with the legal arguments providing context to their consideration.

14 The Grand Chamber went on to find that no separate issues arose under the other Articles pleaded by Leyla, and that the same considerations made under Article 9 ECHR were applicable to the claims made under Article 2 of Protocol No 1.

15 [2007] ICR 1154; [2007] All ER (D) 528 (Mar).

16 These regulations implement the Employment Directive that was discussed in Chapter 4.

to allow him to wear a Sikh turban at school. The House of Lords overturned the Court of Appeal's judgment and found in favour of the complainant. The judgment is particularly important as it clarifies the definition of 'ethnic group' under the RRA 1976. However, the British courts have used this definition to conclude that Rastafarians are not an ethnic group and therefore can be required to remove their *tams* and cut their dreadlocks, without any prohibited discrimination taking place.[17] Furthermore, Muslims, because they come from a great variety of different countries, cannot be considered as an ethnic group, and are therefore not entitled to protection from discrimination under the RRA 1976.[18]

These cases, both on their facts and the reasoning employed by the litigants and courts, provide a natural laboratory in which the dimensions of a constitutional pluralist discourse can be considered. They allow me to demonstrate how my normative framework informs the constitutional pluralist discourses I argue for. Moreover, these cases allow me to illustrate how a constitutional pluralist lens leads to asking new questions about the challenges of justice.[19]

Heterogeneity

The question of religious dress in public places indirectly poses questions about whether we value a diversity of religions, and how we ought to express the value that we attach to diversity. It probes deeply into this question by presenting us with a great internal diversity of religious interpretation, as well as a diversity of different religions, and asks us how this diversity ought to be organised. In the cases précised here, governments and courts frame this question in at least two ways:[20]

1. the threat of religious extremism and the consequent need to protect the liberties of others;
2. the gender inequality of female religious forms of dress, and the paternalistic oppression this clothing involves.

---

17 *Crown Suppliers (Property Service Agency) v Dawkins* [1993] ICR 517.

18 *Tariq v Young* Case 247738/88 EOR Discrimination Case Law Digest No 2.

19 I have not considered *R (on the application of Sarika Angel Watkins-Singh) v The Governing Body of Aberdare Girls' High School* [2008] EWHC 1865 (Admin), on the grounds that it is does not add anything further to the cases considered.

20 These two ways of framing the questions raised in these cases are not comprehensive. In particular, the courts also consider freedom of expression in terms of the public expression of religious beliefs. However, nothing turns on including this point, since the threat to freedom of expression correlates to the acceptability of the form of religious dress. Thus, prohibiting a *hijab* is a greater incursion on freedom of expression than prohibiting a *jilbab*. For the sake of brevity and clarity, I have, therefore, omitted this particular point.

Under the rubric of heterogeneity I want to consider this first line of reasoning. A constitutional pluralist approach would, I believe, have four related dimensions. First, it would introduce the importance of the nation-building messages carried by cases such as these. Secondly, it would consider the divisive nature of the injustice of prohibiting identity markers. Thirdly, it would reframe the way we discuss the nature of a school or university's duties to its students. Finally, it would force us to probe more deeply for solutions that avoid the injustice of prohibiting identity markers.

By framing the issue of religious dress as one concerning the threat of religious extremism, when we think about the acceptability of veiling, we are asked to consider whether we want to live in a nation-state where religious fundamentalism is allowed room to grow and spread. This leads to circular reasoning where we are promised that eliminating the threat of religious extremism will secure liberty of conscience. However, a commitment to heterogeneity requires an emphasis upon encouraging and welcoming difference. It means understanding that nation-building is an ongoing project in which our attitudes towards diversity are key, and that a failure to value diversity is divisive and fractures societies. Indeed, there is evidence that curtailing diversity, on the grounds that to do otherwise encourages fundamentalism, can actually construct the politicised Islamic subject: Islamic girls and women whose mothers and grandmothers have not veiled themselves are now beginning to adopt the veil themselves and it is believed that this a response to the current political climate; there is also evidence that some women are refusing to unveil themselves in any circumstances, including in female company, as a sign of Islamic feminism, rather than merely veiling themselves to preserve their modesty around men (Lyon and Spini 2004: 344). The construction of this political subject feeds, in part, from a failure to appreciate the changed nature of nation-building projects, the value of heterogeneity and the diminution of self involved in prohibiting (law-like) identity markers. Through a constitutional pluralist lens, diverse forms of religious dress would be approached upon the basis that a cohesive nation-state needs to embrace the ideology of heterogeneity if it is to have the twin pillars of justice in its sights. The fact that there are extremist Islamic groups ought to be no more relevant to veiling than extremist Sikh and Jewish groups are to turbans and *yamoulkas*.[21]

This does not, however, exclude the importance of considering a school or university's duties towards all of its students. These duties are based upon the idea of schools as 'miniature "communities of citizens", where pupils learn the

21 It is interesting that Baroness Hale's judgment in *Begum*, which stands out amongst the judgments of the other (male) Lords in its empathy towards (some) feminist perspectives of veiling, so easily divests male forms of religious dress of any political dimension and blithely concludes that when 'a Sikh man wears a turban or a Jewish man a *yamoulka*, we can readily assume that it was his free choice to adopt the dress dictated by the teachings of his religion' (para 94, HL).

principles of public citizenship' (Laborde 2005: 327).[22] A constitutional pluralist approach would not try to deny the significance of this issue, but would instead aim to realign the association between excluding veils and securing the religious freedom of the remaining students away from the logic employed in *Begum* and *Şahin*. The question of how to educate children and young adults appropriately on the principles of civic responsibility remains a burning issue, and one that has and will always have to consider how to protect children of a vulnerable age from extremist forms of thought, whether these are moral and/or political in nature. However, this particular approach questions whether limiting religious forms of dress has any legitimate contribution to a school's duty to protect vulnerable children against extremist forms of thought. Furthermore, it suggests that excluding a pupil based on an identity marker provides a poor and damaging lesson in the principles of citizenship to the excluded pupil and the broader student body, since it teaches them that conforming to a standard decided by others creates a harmonious school, as opposed to teaching them that diversity can also foster social cohesion. Students take this association of homogeneity and harmony into the wider world, and it perpetuates the faulty ideology that informs current nation-building techniques.

A similar approach can be taken to veiling cases that involve teachers, rather than students, as the complainant. In *Azmi* the veil was cast as an impediment to the complainant's ability to teach. However, because this constitutional pluralist perspective recognises the injustice of forcing Aishah Azmi to remove her veil, precisely because it is an identity marker that makes sovereign claims upon her, it leads to the question of the nature of the evidence that concludes that it impedes her ability to teach. In this case the courts deferred to evidence adduced by one of the parties to the litigation without any further probity, either by the court itself or through the introduction of evidence by other parties to the litigation. In fact, all the cases on veiling mentioned here reveal a judicial trend of deferring to local knowledge introduced by *one* of the parties to the litigation.[23] However, a framework in which requiring a teacher to unveil herself would be considered a

---

22 Laborde (2005: 327–8) identifies five interconnected ways in which *hijabs* can be seen as an incursion on the neutrality of state schools as part of the principle of secularism, or *laïcité* : (i) they bring private markers of difference and 'religious divisiveness' into the public sphere; (ii) their inclusion in public places permits the prioritising of religious belief over citizenship and national belonging; (iii) they infringe upon the school's obligation to treat all of the pupils equally and encourage divisive distinctions between groups; (iv) they make inroads upon the civic mission of state schools because they encourage parents to undertake a pick and mix approach, where exemptions from classes such as biology are sought, when there should be a universal form of education; and (v) they undermine religious freedoms because headscarves limit the liberty of conscience of others, especially at an age when children are vulnerable to the ostensible religious behaviour of others.

23 The idea of the margin of appreciation is not novel in ECHR jurisprudence, but it is interesting that the British courts are using an analogous technique of deferring to regional knowledge in cases such as *Begum* and *Azmi*. This trend has been picked up by commentators: Vakulenko (2007) argues that both are judicial techniques that enable

grave injustice forces a greater level of probity. It leads us to seriously ask ourselves whether there is any way of combining the veil with teaching, and to pursue any such possibility sincerely, given the injustice of failing to allow free participation in civil society on the basis of one of their identity markers.

Expansive Justice

Although the norm of expansive justice is broad enough to inform matters considered under the headings of the other two norms in this triad, it provides an opportunity to consider the second line of reasoning employed in this jurisprudence. An expansive form of justice encapsulates the idea that justice must be able to respond to the ebb and flow of societies and the evolutions in the way that we understand ourselves. Within the context of religious dress, and in particular veiling, this engages with the issues of intersectionality and religious dress as law. I use the term intersectionality to refer to the broad idea that we express our identities along many intersecting lines, and tend to draw inspiration from many of our affiliations, whether they be religion, gender, race, ethnicity, culture, sexual orientation, and so on, rather than in a singular manner. As a consequence, our identity markers reflect these intersections.

The idea of intersectionality is not novel in of itself, and this is evidenced in the approach of the ECtHR to veiling as one that includes gender equality, and also Baroness Hale's judgment in *Begum*, which stands out from those of the other Lords because of its consideration of Islamic veils as the manifestation of patriarchal cultural oppression. However, in the earlier exploration of identity processes and in the justification of identity markers, I argued that our intersecting affiliations cannot be satisfactorily separated from each other and that the boundaries between them are blurred and overlapping. It is this characteristic that needs to be taken into account when considering justice in the case of veils, and religious dress more generally.[24] Veiling jurisprudence frames the issue of intersectional affiliations by pitting religious freedom against gender equality, and thereby positioning

contentious questions to be avoided, and are part of a broader scheme of rights fetishism that is counterproductive in considering the question of Islamic dress.

24 Islamic veils provide an especially useful prism through which to understand the idea of intersectionality because they are widely accepted as raising issues of both religious freedom and gender equality. However, other forms of religious dress can equally be subjected to this model. Consider, for example, the Sikh turban which is widely assumed to be a religious requirement. In fact, there is no mention of this particular form of dress in the Sikh's central religious document, the *Guru Granth Sahib*. Instead, it derives its legitimacy from an oral account of a significant historical event for Sikhs, the foundation of the Khalsa by Guru Gobind Singh Ji. Is the continuance of this form of dress religious and/or cultural? Furthermore, the actions of Sikh women who wear turbans illustrate well how identity markers that are exclusively available to men raise questions that relate to gender equality. It is evident, therefore, that most, if not all, identity markers must be considered in terms of intersectionality.

them as conflicting priorities. In *Şahin* the ECtHR derived the general principles applicable from the conclusions in *Dahlab*, and argued that the *hijab* 'appeared to be imposed on women by a religious precept that was hard to reconcile with the principle of gender equality', and that 'wearing the Islamic headscarf could not easily be reconciled with the message of tolerance, respect for others and, above all, equality and non-discrimination' (para 111). Baroness Hale in *Begum* similarly conceptualised the *jilbab* as a question of balancing religious freedom against gender equality. She referenced the following passage from Raday (2003, quoted at para 98, HL):

> [A] mandatory policy that rejects veiling in state educational institutions may provide a crucial opportunity for girls to choose the feminist freedom of state education over the patriarchal dominance of their families. ... On the other hand, a prohibition of veiling risks violating the liberal principle of respect for individual autonomy and cultural diversity ... implementation of the right to equality is a complex matter, and the determination of the way it should be achieved depends upon the balance between these two conflicting policy priorities in a specific social environment.

However, the notion of intersectionality that grounds the concept of identity markers does not fit a conceptualisation of gender and religion as separate and conflicting priorities that we can choose between. A constitutional pluralist discourse must therefore discuss how we can achieve alternative conceptualisations of veiling, and more generally religious dress, which recognise the interconnected nature of the affiliations of our identity, and which reflect their intersections.

The premise that religious dress is a type of law is best explained by Menski's model of law. If, as an integral part of a constitutional pluralist discourse, we accept that wearing an Islamic veil, a Sikh turban, or a Jewish *yamoulka* involves following a law, this impacts the view taken of these practices. In particular, using the language of choice and decision-making does not capture the law-like quality of religious dress, and more generally of (some) identity markers. Consider the contradiction in Baroness Hale's statement in *Begum* (para 94, HL, emphasis added): 'If a Sikh man wears a turban or a Jewish man a *yamoulka*, we can readily assume that it was his *free choice* to adopt the dress *dictated* by the teachings of his religion'. How does one freely choose something that is dictated to them? The language of choice, as a way of exploring religion, fails to comprehend its nature and, more generally, the nature of identity markers which, I claim, can be law-like.[25] Furthermore, the language of choice is used to make the political dimensions of veiling incompatible with the rational free-thinker who is the embodiment of Enlightenment.

25 Mahmood's (2005, 2006) work on secularism, hermeneutics and empire eloquently explores how the language of choice is used to construct a rational free-thinking agent, and how this fails adequately to understand religiosity.

The House of Lords in *Begum* describe how Shabina was 'escorted' to school by her 'quite unnecessarily confrontational' activist brother on the day that she first wore a *jilbab*; he then went on to make the assistant head teacher feel 'threatened' with his talk of 'human rights and legal proceedings' when Shabina was told to go home and comply with the school uniform policy. Lord Scott concluded that 'the confrontational nature of the peremptory manner in which the jilbab issue was raised' meant it was 'very unlikely to have been chosen by Shabina, not yet 14 years of age' (para 80, HL). Whilst the question relating to Shabina's agency may be legitimately raised, its conflation with religious fundamentalism only serves to muddy the waters. Why was the young boy in *Mandla* not treated like a vulnerable child whose agency was in question? At the very least, he was as impressionable as the students whose liberty of conscience took priority over Shabina's right to manifest her religious beliefs. The difference was, of course, the context of religious fundamentalism that is portrayed as intrinsically linked to Islamic veiling. My point is that if religious dress is considered as a law, and we are led to remove the language of choice, it is not so easy to package religious dress with the question of whether and how vulnerable members of society are protected from extreme religious and moral beliefs. A constitutional pluralist approach must, then, include discourse on alternative ways of framing these issues and, I believe, leads to work on a more coherent account of religion, morals, ethics, society and modernity as sources of law. Moreover, this constitutional pluralist lens makes the challenges of justice in religious dress cases clearer, although I concede that it does not immediately present us with an answer to such cases. This, however, is not the short-term aim of the constitutional pluralist discourses I propose. Instead, the immediate aim is to construct dialogues that allow us to become clearer about what the questions are, and what the challenges of justice in diverse societies are.

Post-coloniality and Post-9/11 Peoples

Unlike heterogeneity and expansive justice, post-coloniality and considering a post-9/11 landscape reveals a hidden dimension to the jurisprudence on religious dress. This norm seeks to orient our approach to the challenges of justice by raising awareness that diverse citizens are navigating their way through post-colonial and post-9/11 spaces, with knowledge that our perceptions of the world are heavily associated with racial and religious hierarchies. This guiding norm, therefore, orients discourses towards consideration of the ways that religious dress is approached in a manner that reflects and sustains power relationships of superiority and inferiority. The dichotomy of religious dress and gender equality is one example of how this relationship is constructed. I have illustrated how Islamic veils are viewed as incompatible with gender equality, but the unspoken presupposition behind this approach is that non-Islamic, Western forms of dress are already compatible with gender equality. The very dichotomy of religious freedom and gender equality masks a form of chauvinism that presupposes that the West's own civilised house is already in order, and should more backward ways of life wish to be admitted into this (liberal) magic circle, they ought to get their houses in order too.

The language of choice is another cloak for this power relationship of superiority and inferiority evident in current approaches to religious dress. Brown asks (2006: 189): 'What makes choices "freer" when they are constrained by secular and market organizations of femininity and fashion rather than by state or religious law?' Furthermore, Vakulenko reminds us that 'it is telling that Western dress codes are routinely constructed as almost unlimited freedom of choice, while Islamic ones are cast as the complete lack thereof' (2007: 728). Other 14 year old girls are subjected to marketing trends that, in effect, tell them what they should be wearing. However, the idea that these constraints upon free choice cannot easily be squared with gender equality is not articulated in religious dress jurisprudence, because the unspoken framework within which Islamic veils are considered is one where liberal Western behaviour has reached a point that is beyond such scrutiny.[26]

The construction of opposing superior and inferior ways of life is a mechanism that aims to legitimate dominant behaviour as free, liberal and beyond scrutiny. However, the important point to note is that tacit chauvinism does not go unnoticed and unfelt. Those constructed as inferior subjects feel excluded from civil society. Moreover, this hierarchy fails to respect the value of diversity inherent in the first pillar of justice. A constitutional pluralist perspective reveals the damaging dimensions in this religious dress jurisprudence. In making the challenges of justice clearer, we are prompted to ask whether equality requires the acceptance of normative pluralism. We are led to seek ways of ensuring that certain groups are not required to present themselves as completed and coherent, whilst others evade scrutiny. This is not to say that questions relating to freedom of choice and gender equality could not be legitimately raised. Rather, a constitutional pluralist lens inspires us to find more just ways of framing these issues. Whilst the answers to these religious dress cases are not presented in this application of a constitutional pluralist discourse, this does not diminish the potency of this new vista on constitutional pluralism. Its potency lies in its capacity to reframe the ways that diversity is considered, and to allow the challenges of a diversity-conscious justice to become clearer.

---

26 This is reminiscent of one strand of Derrida's (1994) criticism's of Fukuyama's (1989, 1992) end of history thesis. In this particular strand of criticism Derrida argues that the idea that Western democracy represents some kind of end point reflects a Western hegemony where the East is imagined as following in the footsteps of the West. The West has already learnt its lessons and experienced the trajectory that the East is following, and in positioning itself at the end of history it paints itself as the wiser older mentor, ready to teach the East lessons it has already learnt.

Is Constitutional Pluralism a Form of Relativism?

Whilst the religious dress cases provide an opportunity to showcase the way the normative framework I argue for can ground constitutional pluralist discourses, going beyond cases found within the sphere of official law provides a twofold opportunity. First, it emphasises my proposal for discourses and demonstrates how this might be a beneficial initial step to take before moving on to consider new legal responses to diversity. Secondly, it provides the opportunity to address the possibility that constitutional pluralism and identity markers, as new conceptual tools, might merely act as a form of relativism where all forms of difference and normative pluralism are tolerated. In order to capitalise on these two opportunities, in the final section of this chapter I conclude by considering the framework in which the murder of a teenage girl in Canada by her father was discussed in one magazine article. I then go on to use fictional situations to argue further that constitutional pluralism and identity markers do not involve the acceptance of all non-dominant forms of behaviour.

In December 2007 Aqsa Parvez, a 16 year old girl who lived in a suburb of the Greater Toronto Area, was strangled to death by her Muslim father. Her story is a complex one that I argue we do not gain a clear picture of through the dominant lenses that are available to us. It was reported that Aqsa was murdered because she refused to wear a *hijab* and that her father was the one who reported her murder to the police. An account of her murder appeared in a magazine titled *Toronto Life* that was focusing on immigrant issues. I wish to use extracts from this article to show two things. First, I want to demonstrate how vital our normative frameworks are to how we approach diversity related injustices. Secondly, I want to illustrate that a constitutional pluralist discourse on the *Aqsa Parvez* case does not entail justifying, or even excusing, murder. Rather, with these discourses the emphasis is upon understanding the complexities of such cases so that we have a greater hope of preventing such injustices in the future.

Mary Rogan sets the tone to her article when she states (2008: 54):

> Canada prides itself on its multiculturalism and, to varying degrees of success, condemns institutionalized patriarchy. But there is growing concern that recent waves of Muslim immigrants aren't integrating, or embracing our liberal values. Aqsa's death – coming in the wake of debates about the acceptability of sharia law, disputes over young girls wearing hijabs at soccer games, and the arrest of the Toronto 18 – stoked fears about religious zealotry in our midst. Is it possible that Toronto has become too tolerant of cultural differences?

It is clear that Rogan writes from within a normative framework where immigrant values do not belong in liberal Canadian society, and the burden is upon these immigrants to integrate, or at the very least, embrace Canadian values. Although it is not absolutely clear what these Canadian values are, Rogan does respond to an imam's analysis that whilst the Koran does require the *hijab* to be worn, no-one can be forced to adhere to this, and murder is certainly not a response considered acceptable in Islam, with the following (2008: 57):

> His analysis wilfully ignores how Aqsa, like any teen, was just trying to emerge from her parents' shadow, to be herself in every way. The hijab was one falshpoint, but there were others: the friends she had, the hours she kept, the wishes she harboured. She wanted a boyfriend. She wanted to go to movies. She wanted to lose her virginity before she finished high school. 'She didn't turn her back on her culture,' Ashley says. 'She just wanted to have freedom; that's all she wanted'.

Earlier I considered the ways in which the language of choice is attributed to Western values, and so, in this instance, it is sufficient merely to landmark this issue here. Instead, I want to contrast the normative framework Rogan employs against a constitutional pluralist discourse on Aqsa Parvez's murder.

Through a constitutional pluralist lens we can begin to construct Aqsa as a teenager who was negotiating her identity processes. Wanting a boyfriend, wanting to go to the movies and wanting to lose her virginity were all identity markers for her; the same can be said of her desire not to wear a *hijab*. Whilst I do not claim that all or any of these identity markers were law-like for Aqsa, I do argue that the *hijab* was a law-like identity marker for Aqsa's father. This, I believe, is vital to understanding why he might get to the point of murdering his own daughter. If the *hijab* made no such sovereign claims on Muhammed, this murder becomes nothing short of senseless and, if that is the case, what hopes do we have of preventing any further loss of life? It cannot be overstressed that what I am arguing for here is not a legal defence for murder. Instead, I am proposing a discourse within a normative framework that will help us become clearer about why someone would commit such a heinous crime. Clearly Muhammed was aware that his actions were indefensible, and he, himself, was hugely conflicted: not only did he call the emergency services and tell them that he had killed his daughter, but both he and his son also pleaded guilty to the charges brought against them when the case came to trial.[27]

My intent is that by becoming clearer about the issues in such cases, we begin to open doors where we might discuss how to prevent such murders. If we accept that for Muhammed, the way his daughter dressed and behaved, constituted law-like identity markers and, moreover, that Aqsa was engaged in navigating her identity processes on her own terms, then the next step in our constitutional pluralist discourse might be to consider how these two conflicting scenarios can be resolved without the needless loss of life. We might discuss how important it is that pluralism and heterogeneity become bedrocks in our diverse societies so that those with non-dominant identities can have the space they need to negotiate who they are and who they want to be without undue pressures to conform. We might

27 See Mitchell and Javed (2010).

even talk about this by borrowing Ballard's concept of skilled cultural navigators (1994: 30–33) and ask how teenagers such as Aqsa can be supported to become skilled identity navigators. We might then go on to consider how official laws and civil society might rearrange its processes if it accepts that in diverse societies there are law-like identity markers that have sources beyond official laws, and that these identity markers make sovereign claims upon us. This might lead us to discuss processes that could help people such as Aqsa's father to negotiate the legal hybrids in his worlds, so that they can more adequately manage the conflicts of laws that appear to be irresolvable.

There are many other discussions that a constitutional pluralist discourse on the *Aqsa Parvez* case might engage in. However, my point is to illustrate two things. First, by changing the underlying normative framework, the views and panoramas we see dramatically alter. We could simply continue to censure criminals such as Muhammed Parvez using official laws and go no further than that, but can we be sure that we are doing our utmost to prevent any repeat cases? Secondly, the *Aqsa Parvez* case allows me to show that there are good and sound reasons for proposing discourses, as opposed to new legal responses or new constitutional frameworks. At the very least, these discourses do not stray into territory where murder can be excused. More importantly, whilst this approach might not provide us with immediate answers, I believe that we cannot afford to miss the initial steps of becoming clearer about questions and gaining a better understanding of what the challenges of justice in diverse societies are, before we try to find solutions; constitutional pluralist discourses have the potential to allow us to do just that.

There are a few final, and crucial, points that must be made, which are best addressed by posing some fictional scenarios. With these scenarios I intend to demonstrate further that my proposal for constitutional pluralist discourse is not a façade for a relativist approach. Consider the situation where instead of a piece of religious dress being prohibited, it is football shirts that cannot be worn to public schools, in place of school uniforms. A constitutional pluralist lens, which values diversity, would, I believe, mean sincere consideration of arguments as to the importance and value of one's association to a football team as an identity marker. However, it does not follow that by taking a sincere approach to these claims to identity markers that there is a blanket acceptance of all difference, not least because not all identity markers can be considered to make sovereign like claims upon us. Indeed, I do not argue that the prohibition on any of the identity markers I consider here should be lifted. I do, however, argue that the way that these questions are framed must change if a diversity-conscious conception of justice is to be duly respected. Moreover, I believe that the constitutional pluralist discourses that I propose in this project can achieve this change. Nevertheless, the decisions as to which identity markers merit prohibition, and which merit acceptance, must be the product of these discourses.

The football shirt example is useful but, to some degree, it trivialises the question of how constitutional pluralist discourses will respond to identity claims from dominant or powerful groups within majority communities. The answer to this question lies in the normative framework that grounds these discourses. A diversity-conscious conception of justice not only recognises the importance of the self-actualisation of authentic identities, it takes on the general meaning of free and fair participation in and access to civil society and it accepts the importance of nation-building techniques in achieving this goal. On this account, in order to do justice, consideration of the ways in which particular voices garner greater attention must be part of the discourses that discuss identity markers and claims for the law-like character of identity markers.

Finally, the question of whether this new vista on constitutional pluralism will fragment established (moral) prohibitions on certain practices must also be addressed. One such example can be found in the ban on corporal punishment in many schools around the world. Suppose a pupil, old enough to provide informed consent, signs a voluntary consent form agreeing that she is happy to receive corporal punishment, and that this reflects her religious identity. Arguably, this is an identity marker, but does it merit an exception to an established ban on corporal punishment? More significantly, this example raises the question of whether we ultimately need unitary constitutionalism as a necessary evil to impose a common framework within which pluralism can effectively flourish. I argue that this is not the case. Constitutional pluralism alters the way that the challenges of a diversity-conscious form of justice are perceived; it does not lead to a blanket acceptance of all difference, or all identity markers. Furthermore, if our reasons for banning corporal punishment were sound to begin with, I see no reason why they would be ineffective within a constitutional pluralist discourse. The potency of these discourses lies in their capacity to reframe the ways that diversity is considered and to allow the challenges of a diversity-conscious justice to become clearer. It does not signal a blanket acceptance of all forms of diversity.

Our current legal responses to diversity have undoubtedly had successes, and the world that we live in today is far more diversity-friendly than was previously the case. However, it is also clear that if we fail to move forward in this field, we will continue to ask the same questions and respond with the same answers, and those answers will not speak to developments that have taken place and continue to take place in diverse societies. I argue that we need to expand law's role and make this role one that has the capacity to continue to expand, if we wish to develop our legal responses to diversity. Furthermore, we must keep a clear focus upon justice as we continue to unravel the intense pluralities of the 21st century. My fresh perspectives on justice and law, which lead to a new vista of constitutional pluralism, aim to provide a clearer picture of the challenges of justice, with the hope that, as we become clearer about these challenges, we stand a better chance of meeting them.

Bibliography

Abraham, D. 2008. 'Constitutional Patriotism, Citizenship, and Belonging'. *International Journal of Constitutional Law*, 6(1), 137–52.

Adelman, S. 1998. 'Constitutionalism, Pluralism and Democracy in Africa'. *Journal of Legal Pluralism and Unofficial Law*, 42, 73–88.

Ahdar, R.J. (ed.) 2000. *Law and Religion*. Aldershot; Burlington USA: Ashgate.

Ahsan, M. 1995. 'The Muslim Family in Britain', in *God's Law Versus State Law: The Construction of an Islamic Identity in Western Europe*, edited by M. King. London: Grey Seal, 21–30.

Alexander, L. (ed.) 1998. *Constitutionalism: Philosophical Foundations*. Cambridge: Cambridge University Press.

Alexy, R. 1990. 'A Theory of Practical Discourse', in *The Communicative Ethics Controversy*, edited by S. Benhabib and F.R. Dallmayr. Cambridge, Mass.: MIT Press, 151–90.

Ali, N., V.S. Kalra and S. Sayyid (eds) 2006. *A Postcolonial People: South Asians in Britain*. London: Hurst and Co.

Allott, A.N. 1980. *The Limits of Law*. London: Butterworths.

Alston, P. (ed.) 2001. *People's Rights: The State of the Art*. Oxford: Oxford University Press.

Althusser, L. 1971. *Lenin and Philosophy, and Other Essays*. Trans. B. Brewster. London: New Left Books.

Anderson, B. 1991. *Imagined Communities: Reflections on the Origin and Spread of Nationalism*. London; New York: Verso.

Anderson, G.W. 2005. *Constitutional Rights After Globalization*. Oxford; Portland, Or.: Hart Publishing.

Andrew, A. 2004. 'Multiculturalism is Dead. Hurrah?' *The Guardian* [Online, 8 April] Available at http://www.guardian.co.uk/world/2004/apr/08/religion.race (last accessed 16 September 2010).

Angus, I. 2008. *Identity and Justice*. Toronto: University of Toronto.

Annett, K.D. 2001. *Hidden From History: The Canadian Holocaust: The Untold Story of the Genocide of Aboriginal Peoples by Church and State in Canada: A Summary of an Ongoing, Independent Inquiry into Canadian Native "Residential Schools" and their Legacy*. Vancouver, B.C.: Truth Commission into Genocide in Canada.

Appadurai, A. 1996. *Modernity at Large: Cultural Dimensions of Globalization*. Minneapolis; London: University of Minnesota Press.

Appiah, A. 1994. Identity, authenticity, survival: multicultural societies and social reproduction, in *Multiculturalism: Examining the Politics of Recognition*, edited by A. Gutmann. Princeton; Chichester: Princeton University Press, 149–63.

Appiah, A. 2005. *The Ethics of Identity*. Princeton; Woodstock: Princeton University Press.

Asad, T. 2003. *Formations of the Secular: Christianity, Islam, Modernity*. Stanford, Calif.: Stanford University Press.

Ashcroft, B., G. Griffiths and H. Tiffin (eds) 2006. *The Post-colonial Studies Reader*. London; New York: Routledge.

Athar Ali, M. 1997. 'The Perception of India in Akbar and Abu'l Fazl', in *Akbar and his India*, edited by I. Habib. Delhi: Oxford University Press, 215–24.

Baker, J.H. 1990. *An Introduction to English Legal History*. London; Boston: Butterworths.

Ballard, R. 1994. 'Introduction: The Emergence of *Desh Pardesh*', in *Desh Pardesh: The South Asian Presence in Britain*, edited by R. Ballard. London: Hurst, 1–34.

Banting, K. and W. Kymlicka 2003. 'Multiculturalism and Welfare'. *Dissent*, 50(4), 59–66.

Banton, M. 1967. *Race relations*. London: Tavistock.

Banton, M. 1983. *Racial and Ethnic Competition*. Cambridge: Cambridge University Press.

Banton, M. 1998. *Racial Theories*. Cambridge: Cambridge University Press.

Barendt, E. 1997. 'Is There a United Kingdom Constitution?' *Oxford Journal of Legal Studies*, 17(1), 137–46.

Barry, B.M. 2002. *Culture and Equality: An Egalitarian Critique of Multiculturalism*. Cambridge: Polity Press in association with Blackwell Publishers Ltd.

Barth, F. (ed.) 1969. *Ethnic Groups and Boundaries: The Social Organization of Culture Difference*. Bergen; London: Allen and Unwin.

Bauböck, R., A. Heller and A.R. Zolberg (eds) 1996. *The Challenge of Diversity: Integration and Pluralism in Societies of Immigration*. Aldershot: Avebury.

Bauman, Z. 2004. *Identity*. Oxford: Polity.

Baumann, G. 1996. *Contesting Culture: Discourses of Identity in Multi-ethnic London*. Cambridge; New York: Cambridge University Press.

BBC News Online. 1968. 'OnThis Day: 1968: Race Discrimination Law Tightened'. [Online, 26 November] Available at http://news.bbc.co.uk/onthisday/hi/dates/stories/november/26/newsid_3220000/3220635.stm (last accessed 16 September 2010).

BBC News Online. 1994. 'On This Day: 1994: Sunday Trading Legalised'. [Online, 28 August] Available at http://news.bbc.co.uk/onthisday/hi/dates/stories/august/28/newsid_2536000/2536115.stm (last accessed 17 September 2010).

BBC News Online. 2004. 'Gay couples to get joint rights'. [Online, 31 March] Available at http://news.bbc.co.uk/1/hi/uk_politics/3584285.stm (last accessed 17 September 2010).

BBC News Online. 2008. 'Australia Apology to Aborigines'. [Online, 13 February] Available at http://news.bbc.co.uk/1/hi/world/asia-pacific/7241965.stm (last accessed 17 September 2010).

Becker, L. and W. Kymlicka 1995. 'Symposium on Citizenship, Democracy, and Education – Introduction. *Ethics*, 105(3), 465–7.

Benhabib, S. 2002. *The Claims of Culture: Equality and Diversity in the Global Era*. Princeton; Oxford: Princeton University Press.

Berger, P.L. (ed.) 1999. *The Desecularization of the World: Resurgent Religion and World Politics*. Washington, D.C.: Ethics and Public Policy Center.

Berlin, I. 1997. 'The Pursuit of the Ideal', in *The Proper Study of Mankind: An Anthology of Essays*, edited by H. Hardy and R. Hausheer. London: Chatto and Windus, 1–16.

Bevan, V. 1986. *The Development of British Immigration Law*. London: Croom Helm.

Bhachu, P. 1986. *The Twice Migrants*. London: Tavistock.

Bhamra, M.K. 2007. 'On Cultural Diversity: The Importance of Normative Foundations for Legal Responses', in *Law and Ethnic Plurality: Socio-legal Perspectives*, edited by P. Shah. Leiden; Boston: Martinus Nijhoff Publishers, 9–30.

Bhargava, R. (ed.) 1998. *Secularism and its Critics*. Delhi; Oxford: Oxford University Press.

Bickerstaffe, R. 2006. 'Leadership and Legacy', in *30: At the Turning of the Tide*, edited by Commission for Racial Equality. London: Belmont, 140–42.

Bindman, G. 1976. 'The Law and Racial Discrimination'. *British Journal of Law and Society*, 3(1), 110–14.

Bindman, G. 1992. 'Proof and Evidence of Discrimination', in *Discrimination: The Limits of Law*, edited by B.A. Hepple and E.M. Szyszczak. London: Mansell, 50–66.

Blair, T. 2006. 'The Duty to Integrate: Shared British Values'. Speech at Downing Street, London.

Bogdanor, V. 1987. 'Constitutional Law and Politics'. *Oxford Journal of Legal Studies*, 7(3), 454–64.

Bogdanor, V. 1996. *Politics and the Constitution: Essays on British Government*. Aldershot: Dartmouth.

Bogdanor, V. 1999. *Devolution in the United Kingdom*. Oxford: Oxford University Press.

Bogdanor, V. 2004. *The British Constitution in the Twentieth Century*. Oxford: Oxford University Press.

Bogdanor, V. 2007. 'Publication Review: The Evolution of a Constitution: Eight Key Moments in British Constitutional History by Elizabeth Wicks'. *Law Quarterly Review*, 123, 480–84.

Bohman, J. 1994. 'Complexity, Pluralism, and the Constitutional State: on Habermas's *Faktizität und Geltung*'. *Law and Society Review*, 28, 897–930.

Borrows, J. 2002. *Recovering Canada: The Resurgence of Indigenous Law*. Toronto: University of Toronto.

Bourdieu, P. 1990. *In Other Words: Essays Towards a Reflexive Sociology*. Trans. M. Adamson. Stanford, Calif.: Stanford University Press.

Bourdieu, P. 2004. *Science of Science and Reflexivity*. Trans. R. Nice. Cambridge: Polity.

Bourdieu, P., and L. Wacquant 1992. *An Invitation to Reflexive Sociology*. Cambridge: Polity.

Boyd, S.B. (ed.) 1997. *Challenging the Public/Private Divide: Feminism, Law, and Public Policy*. Toronto; Buffalo: University of Toronto Press.

Bradney, A. 1993. *Religions, Rights and Laws*. Leicester: Leicester University Press.

Bradney, A. 2000. 'Faced by Faith', in *Faith in Law: Essays in Legal Theory*, edited by P. Oliver, S.D. Scott and V. Tadros. London: Hart, 89–105.

Bradney, A. 2009. *Law and Faith in a Sceptical Age*. Milton Park, Abingdon: Routledge-Cavendish.

Branigan, T. and J. Carvel 2007. 'Single Equality Act Under Threat, Warn Campaigners'. *The Guardian* [Online, 18 May] Available at http://www.guardian.co.uk/society/2007/may/18/politics.socialexclusion (last accessed 17 September 2010).

Brock, G. 2009. *Global Justice: A Cosmopolitan Account*. Oxford: Oxford University Press.

Brown, W. 2006. *Regulating Aversion: Tolerance in the Age of Identity and Empire*. Princeton: Princeton University Press.

Brubaker, R. 1996. *Nationalism Reframed: Nationhood and the National Question in the New Europe*. Cambridge: Cambridge University Press.

Brubaker, R. 2006. *Ethnicity Without Groups*. Cambridge, Mass.; London: Harvard University Press.

Calhoun, C.J. (ed.) 1992. *Habermas and the Public Sphere*. Cambridge, Mass.: MIT Press.

Calhoun, C.J. (ed.) 1994. *Social Theory and the Politics of Identity*. Oxford: Blackwell.

Carens, J. 1997. 'Liberalism and Culture'. *Constellations*, 4(1), 35–47.

Cathcart, B. 1997. 'The Long, Hard Fight for Justice'. *The Runnymede Bulletin*, 307, 8–9.

CBC News Online. 2008. 'Prime Minister Stephen Harper's Statement of Apology'. [Online, 11 July] Available at http://www.cbc.ca/canada/story/2008/06/11/pm-statement.html (last accessed 17 September 2010).

Chiba, M. (ed.) 1986. *Asian Indigenous Law: In Interaction with Received Law*. London; New York: KPI: Distributed by Routledge and Kegan Paul.

Chiba, M. 1989. *Legal Pluralism: Toward a General Theory Through Japanese Legal Culture*. Tokyo: Tokai University Press.

Chiba, M. 1998. 'Other Phases of Legal Pluralism in the Contemporary World'. *Ratio Juris*, 11(3), 228–45.

Choudhry, S. 2007a. 'Does the World Need More Canada? The Politics of the Canadian Model in Constitutional Politics and Political Theory'. *International Journal of Constitutional Law*, 5(4), 606–38.

Choudhry, S. 2007b. 'Editor's Note: Constitutionalism in Divided Societies'. *International Journal of Constitutional Law*, 5(4), 573–5.

Choudhry, S. (ed.) 2008. *Constitutional Design for Divided Societies: Integration or Accommodation?* Oxford: Oxford University Press.

Cohen, A. 1969. *Custom and Politics in Urban Africa: A Study of Hausa Migrants in Yoruba Towns*. London: Routledge and Kegan Paul.

Cohen, A. 1974a. 'Introduction: The Lesson of Ethnicity', in *Urban Ethnicity*, edited by A. Cohen. London: Tavistock, ix–xxii.

Cohen, A. 1974b. *Two-dimensional Man: An Essay on the Anthropology of Power and Symbolism in Complex Society*. London: Routledge and Kegan Paul.

Coleman, J.L. (ed.) 2001. *Hart's Postscript: Essays on the Postscript to The Concept of Law*. Oxford: Oxford University Press.

Collins, H. 2003. 'Discrimination, Equality and Social Inclusion'. *Modern Law Review*, 66(1), 16–43.

Commission for Racial Equality 1990. *Race Discrimination Law Report*. London: Commission for Racial Equality.

Commission for Racial Equality 2004. *40 Years of Law Against Racial Discrimination*. Northampton: Belmont Press.

Craig, P.P. 2001. 'Constitutions, Constitutionalism, and the European Union'. *European Law Journal*, 7(2), 125–50.

Craig, P.P. and G. de Búrca 1998. *EU Law: Text, Cases, and Materials*. Oxford: Oxford University Press.

Crawford, J. (ed.) 1988. *The Rights of Peoples*. Oxford: Clarendon.

Cretney, S.M., J. Masson and R. Bailey-Harris 2003. *Principles of Family Law*. London: Sweet and Maxwell.

Danielsen, D. and K. Engle (eds) 1995. *After Identity: A Reader in Law and Culture*. New York; London: Routledge.

Davie, E. 2005. 'Tebbit: "Cricket test" Could Have Stopped Bombings'. [Online, 18 August] Available at http://www.epolitix.com/latestnews/article-detail/newsarticle/tebbit-cricket-test-could-have-stopped-bombings/ (last accessed 17 September 2010).

Davies, L. 2010. 'France: Senate Votes for Mulsim Face Veil Ban'. *The Guardian* [Online, 14 September] Available at http://www.guardian.co.uk/world/2010/sep/14/france-senate-muslim-veil-ban (last accessed 21 September 2010).

Deer, C. 2008. 'Reflexivity', in *Pierre Bourdieu: Key Concepts*, edited by M. Grenfell. London: Acumen Publishing Ltd, 199–212.

Dean, M. (ed.) 2002. *Japanese Law: Text, Cases and Materials*. London: Cavendish.

Derrida, J. 1994. *Spectres of Marx: The State of the Debt, the Work of Mourning, and the New International*. Trans. P. Kamuf. New York: Routledge.

Derrida, J. 2001. *Writing and Différence*. Trans. A. Bass. London: Routledge.

De Smith, S.A. and R. Brazier 1998. *Constitutional and Administrative Law*. London: Penguin.
Dicey, A.V. and E.C.S. Wade 1959. *Introduction to the Study of the Law of the Constitution*. London: Macmillan.
Diduck, A. 2001. 'A Family By Any Other Name - or Starbucks™ Comes to England'. *Journal of Law and Society*, 28(2), 290–310.
Doshi, S.L. 2003. *Modernity, Postmodernity and Neo-sociological Theories*. Jaipur; New Delhi: Rawat.
Douzinas, C. and A. Gearey 2005. *Critical Jurisprudence: The Political Philosophy of Justice*. Oxford: Hart.
Du Gay, P., J. Evans and P. Redman (eds) 2000. *Identity: A Reader*. London; Thousand Oaks, Calif.: SAGE Publications in association with The Open University.
Dugard, J. 1978. *Human Rights and the South African Legal Order*. Princeton: Princeton University Press.
Dworkin, R. 1977. *Taking Rights Seriously*. London: Duckworth.
Dworkin, R. 1985. *A Matter of Principle*. London: Harvard University Press.
Edge, P.W. 2006. *Religion and Law: An Introduction*. Aldershot; Burlington, VT.: Ashgate.
Eisgruber, C.L. and Z. Mariah 2006. 'Religious Freedom in Canada and the United States'. *International Journal of Constitutional Law*, 4(2), 244–68.
Elster, J. and R. Slagstad (eds) 1988. *Constitutionalism and Democracy*. Cambridge: Cambridge University Press in collaboration with Maison des Sciences de l'Homme, Paris.
Engineer, A.A. 1998. 'Religion and Secularism', in *State Secularism and Religion: Western and Indian Experience*, edited by A.A. Engineer and U. Mehta. Delhi: Ajanta Publications, 1–20.
Engineer, A.A. and U. Mehta (eds) 1998. *State Secularism and Religion: Western and Indian Experience*. Delhi: Ajanta Publications.
Eriksen, T.H. 1988. *Communicating Cultural Difference and Identity: Ethnicity and Nationalism in Mauritius*. Oslo: Department of Social Anthropology, Occasional Papers, No 16.
Eriksen, T.H. 2002. *Ethnicity and Nationalism: Anthropological Perspectives*. London: Pluto.
Erikson, E.H. 1968. *Identity, Youth, and Crisis*. London: Faber and Faber Ltd.
Esposito, J.L. (ed.) 2003. *The Oxford Dictionary of Islam*. Oxford: Oxford University Press.
Evans, J.M. 1972. 'Immigration Act 1971'. *Modern Law Review*, 35(5), 508–24.
Ewing, K.D. 2004. 'The Law and the Constitution: Manifesto of the Progressive Party'. *Modern Law Review*, 67(5), 734–52.
Fabian, J. and M. Bunzl 1983. *Time and the Other: How Anthropology Makes its Object*. New York: Columbia University Press.
Feldman, D. 2005. 'None, One or Several? Perspectives on the UK's Constitution(s)'. *Cambridge Law Journal*, 64(2), 329–51.

Forst, R. 1997. 'Foundations of a Theory of Multicultural Justice'. *Constellations*, 4(1), 63–71.

Foucault, M. 1982. 'The Subject and Power'. *Critical Inquiry*, 8(4), 777–95.

Fournier, P. 2001–2002. 'The Erasure of Islamic Difference in Canadian and American Family Law Adjudication'. *Journal of Law and Policy*, 10, 51–95.

Fournier, P. 2006. 'In the (Canadian) Shadow of Islamic Law: Translating *Mahr* as a Bargaining Endowment'. *Osgoode Hall Law Journal*, 44, 649–77.

Fournier, P. 2010. *Muslim Marriage in Western Courts, Lost in Transplantation*. Aldershot: Ashgate.

Franck, T.M. 1999. *The Empowered Self: Law and Society in the Age of Individualism*. New York: Oxford University Press.

Fraser, N. 1997. *Justice Interruptus: Critical Reflections on the 'Postsocialist' Condition*. New York; London: Routledge.

Fraser, N. 2003a. 'Distorted Beyond All Recognition: A Rejoinder to Axel Honneth', in *Redistribution or Recognition? A Political-philosophical Exchange*, edited by N. Fraser and A. Honneth. London; New York: Verso, 198–236.

Fraser, N. 2003b. 'Social Justice in the Age of Identity Politics: Redistribution, Recognition and Participation', in *Redistribution or Recognition? A Political-Philosophical Exchange*, edited by N. Fraser and A. Honneth. London; New York: Verso, 7–109.

Fraser, N. 2005. 'Reframing Justice in a Globalizing World'. *New Left Review*, 36, 69–88.

Fraser, N. 2006. 'Dimensions of Justice'. Paper to the Social Justice and Public Policy Conference: Social Justice and Public Policy, Westminster, London, 6 December 2006.

Fraser, N. and A. Honneth (eds) 2003. *Redistribution or Recognition? A Political-Philosophical Exchange*. London; New York: Verso.

Fredman, S. 1997. 'Reversing Discrimination'. *Law Quarterly Review*, 113(Oct), 575–600.

Freeman, M.D.A. 2001. *Lloyd's Introduction to Jurisprudence*. London: Sweet and Maxwell.

Friedman, T.L. 2007. *The World is Flat: The Globalized World in the Twenty-first Century*. London: Penguin.

Füredi, F. 1998. *The Silent War: Imperialism and the Changing Perception of Race*. London: Pluto Press.

Fukuyama, F. 1989. 'The End of History?' *The National Interest*, 16, 3–18.

Fukuyama, F. 1992. *The End of History and the Last Man*. New York: Free Press.

Gardner, K. 1993. 'Desh-Bidesh: Sylheti Images of Home and Away'. *Man*, 28(9), 1–15.

Garet, R. 1983. 'Community and Existence: The Rights of Groups'. *Southern California Law Review*, 56, 1001–75.

Gates, H.L. 2008. *African American Lives 2*, DVD. Directed by G. Judd, L.A. Gladsjø, J. Sweet and J. Youngelson. Arlington, VA: PBS Home Video.

Gellner, E. 1983. *Nations and Nationalism*. Oxford: Basil Blackwell.

Gellner, E. 1987. *Culture, Identity, and Politics*. Cambridge: Cambridge University Press.

Ghai, Y. and J. Cottrell 2007. 'A Tale of Three Constitutions: Ethnicity and Politics in Fiji'. *International Journal of Constitutional Law*, 5(4), 639–69.

Glassé, C. 2008. *The Concise Encyclopaedia of Islam*. London: Stacey International.

Greenhouse, C. 1982. 'Nature is to Culture as Praying is to Suing: Legal Pluralism in an American Suburb'. *Journal of Legal Pluralism and Unofficial Law*, 20, 17–35.

Gregory, J. 1987. *Sex, Race and the Law: Legislating for Equality*. London; Newbury Park, Calif: Sage Publications.

Grenfell, M. (ed.) 2008. *Pierre Bourdieu: Key Concepts*. London: Acumen Publishing Ltd.

Griffin, S. 1990. 'Constitutionalism in the United States: From Theory to Politics'. *Oxford Journal of Legal Studies*, 10, 200–20.

Griffith, J.A.G. 1979. 'The political constitution'. *Modern Law Review*, 42, 1–21.

Griffiths, A. 2002. 'Legal Pluralism', in *An Introduction to Law and Social Theory*, edited by R. Bankar and M. Travers. Oxford: Hart, 289–301.

Griffiths, J. 1986. 'What is Legal Pluralism?' *Journal of Legal Pluralism and Unofficial Law*, 24, 1–56.

Grimm, D. 2005. 'Integration by Constitution'. *International Journal of Constitutional Law*, 3(2 and 3), 193–208.

Guild, E. 2000. 'The EC Directive on Race Discrimination: Surprises, Possibilities and Limitations'. *Industrial Law Journal*, 29(4), 416–23.

Gutmann, A. (ed.) 1994. *Multiculturalism: Examining the Politics of Recognition*. Princeton; Chichester: Princeton University Press.

Habermas, J. 1978. *Knowledge and Human Interests*. London: Heinemann.

Habermas, J. 1986. *The Theory of Communicative Action. Volume 1: Reason and the Rationalization of Society*. Trans. T. McCarthy. Cambridge: Polity Press.

Habermas, J. 1987. *The Theory of Communicative Action Vol 2: Lifeworld and System: A Critique of Functionalist Reason*. Cambridge: Polity Press.

Habermas, J. 1989. *The Structural Transformation of the Public Sphere: An Inquiry into a Category of Bourgeois Society*. Trans. T. Burger and F. Lawrence. Cambridge: Polity Press.

Habermas, J. 1990. *Moral Consciousness and Communicative Action*. Cambridge: Polity.

Habermas, J. 1992. 'Further Reflections on the Public Sphere', in *Habermas and the Public Sphere*, edited by C.J. Calhoun. Cambridge, Mass.: MIT Press.

Habermas, J. 1993. *Justification and Application: Remarks on Discourse Ethics*. Trans. C. Cronin. Cambridge, Mass.: MIT Press.

Habermas, J. 1994. 'Struggles for Recognition in the Democratic Constitutional State', in *Multiculturalism: Examining the Politics of Recognition*, edited by A. Gutmann. Princeton; Chichester: Princeton University Press, 107–48.

Habermas, J. 1996. *Between Facts and Norms: Contributions to a Discourse Theory of Law and Democracy*. Cambridge, Mass.: MIT Press.

Habermas, J. 1998. *The Inclusion of the Other: Studies in Political Theory*, edited by P. De Greiff and C. Cronin. Cambridge, Mass.: MIT Press.

Habermas, J. 2003. 'Intolerance and Discrimination'. *International Journal of Constitutional Law*, 1(1), 2–12.

Habermas, J. and P. Dews 1986. *Autonomy and Solidarity: Interviews with Jürgen Habermas*. London: Verso.

Hall, S. 1999. 'Introduction: Who Needs Identity?', in *Questions of Cultural Identity*, edited by S. Hall and P. Du Gay. London; Thousand Oaks, Calif.: Sage Publications, 1–17.

Hall, S. and P. Du Gay (eds) 1996. *Questions of Cultural Identity*. London; Thousand Oaks, Calif.: Sage Publications.

Hamilton, C. 1995. *Family, Law and Religion*. London: Sweet and Maxwell.

Handelmann, D. 1977. 'The Organization of Ethnicity'. *Ethnic Groups*, 1, 58–74.

Hart, H.L.A. 1963. *Law, Liberty and Morality*. Oxford; New York: Oxford University Press.

Hart, H.L.A. 1994. *The Concept of Law*. Oxford: Clarendon.

Hartley, T.C. 1998. *The Foundations of European Community Law: An Introduction to the Constitutional and Administrative Law of the European Community*. Oxford: Oxford University Press.

Held, D., A. McGrew, D. Goldblatt and J. Perraton 1999. *Global Transformations*. Cambridge: Polity Press.

Hepple, B.A. 1966. 'Race Relations Act 1965'. *Modern Law Review*, 29(3), 306–14.

Hepple, B.A. 1968a. 'Commonwealth Immigrants Act 1968'. *Modern Law Review*, 31(4), 424–28.

Hepple, B.A. 1968b. 'The Street Report on Anti-discrimination Legislation. Report of the Committee on Immigration and Appeals'. *Modern Law Review*, 31(3), 310–21.

Hepple, B.A. 1969. 'Race Relations Act 1968'. *Modern Law Review*, 32(2), 181–6.

Hepple, B.A. 1992. 'Have Twenty-five Years of the Race Relations Acts in Britain been a Failure?', in *Discrimination: The Limits of the Law*, edited by B.A. Hepple and E.M. Szyszczak. London: Mansell, 19–34.

Hepple, B.A. and T. Choudhury. 2001. *Tackling Religious Discrimination: Practical Implications for Policy-makers and Legislators*. Home Office Research Study 221. London: Home Office, Research, Development and Statistics Directorate.

Hepple, B.A., M. Coussey and T. Choudhury 2000. *Equality: A New Framework; Report of the Independent Review of the Enforcement of UK Anti-discrimination Legislation*. Oxford: Hart Publishing.

Hepple, B.A. and Runnymede Trust 1997. *Improving Equality Law: The Options*. London: JUSTICE.

Hepple, B.A. and E.M. Szyszczak (eds) 1992. *Discrimination: The Limits of Law*. London: Mansell.

Hindell, K. 1965. 'The Genesis of the Race Relations Bill'. *The Political Quarterly*, 36(4), 390–405.

Hirschl, R. 2004. *Towards Juristocracy: The Origins and Consequences of the New Constitutionalism*. Cambridge, Mass.; London: Harvard University Press.

Hoggett, B.M. and D. Pearl 1996. *The Family, Law and Society: Cases and Materials*. London: Butterworths.

Holmes, E. 2005. 'Anti-discrimination Rights Without Equality'. *Modern Law Review*, 68(2), 175–94.

Honneth, A. 1995. *The Struggle for Recognition: The Moral Grammar of Social Conflicts*. Trans. J. Anderson. Cambridge: Polity.

Honneth, A. 2003a. 'The Point of Recognition: A Rejoinder to the Rejoinder', in *Redistribution or Recognition? A Political-philosophical Exchange*, edited by N. Fraser and A. Honneth. London; New York: Verso, 237–67.

Honneth, A. 2003b. 'Redistribution as Recognition: A Response to Nancy Fraser', in *Redistribution or Recognition? A Political-philosophical Exchange*, edited by N. Fraser and A. Honneth. London; New York: Verso, 110–97.

Hooker, M.B. 1975. *Legal Pluralism: An Introduction to Colonial and Neo-colonial Laws*. Oxford: Clarendon Press.

Hughes, R.A. 1995. *Identity, Law, and Politics*. Armidale, NSW: University of New England Press.

Igarashi, K. 1990. *Einführung in das Japanische Recht*. Darmstadt: Wissenschaftliche Buchgesellschaft.

Ignatieff, M. 2003. *Empire Lite: Nation Building in Bosnia, Kosovo and Afghanistan*. London: Vintage.

Inden, R.B. 1990. *Imagining India*. Oxford: Blackwell.

Janardhan, M.S. 2006. 'Economy: UAE Recasts Weekend to World's Beat'. Inter Press Service [Online 3 June] Available at http://ipsnews.net/news.asp?idnews=33481 (last accessed 18 September 2010).

Jones, R. and G. Welhengama 2000. *Ethnic Minorities in English Law*. Stoke-on-Trent: Trentham and School of Oriental and African Studies.

JSB. 2008. 'Equal Treatment Bench Book. [Online: Judicial Studies Board] Available at http://www.jsboard.co.uk/etac/etbb/index.htm (last accessed 18 September 2010).

Juss, S.S. 1995. 'The Constitution and Sikhs in Britain'. *Brigham Young University Law Review*, 2, 481–533.

Kairys, D. (ed.) 1998. *The Politics of Law: A Progressive Critique*. New York: Basic Books.

Kallen, E. 2010. *Ethnicity and Human Rights in Canada*. 3rd Edition. Don Mills, Ontario: Oxford University Press.

Kalra, V.S. and R. Ballard 1994. *The Ethnic Dimensions of the 1991 Census: A Preliminary Report*. Manchester Census Group.

Kalra, V.S., R.K. Kahlon and J. Hutnyk 2005. *Diaspora and Hybridity*. London: SAGE.

King, M. (ed.) 1995. *God's Law Versus State Law: The Construction of an Islamic Identity in Western Europe*. London: Grey Seal.

King, M.L. Jr. 1967. 'The Other America'. A speech presented on 14 April at Stanford University, California.

Klug, H. 2000. *Constituting Democracy: Law, Globalism, and South Africa's Political Reconstruction*. Cambridge; New York: Cambridge University Press.

Knights, S. 2007. *Freedom of Religion, Minorities, and the Law*. Oxford; New York: Oxford University Press.

Koh, H.H. 2000. *1999 Country Reports on Human Rights Practices, U.S. Department of State*.

Krausz, E. 1971. *Ethnic Minorities in Britain*. London: MacGibbon and Kee.

Kroeber, A.L. and C. Kluckhohn 1952. *Culture: A Critical Review of Concepts and Definitions*. Cambridge, Mass.: Peabody Museum of American Archaeology and Ethnology, Harvard University.

Kuper, A. 1999. *Culture: The Anthropologists' Account*. Cambridge, Mass.; London: Harvard University Press.

Kymlicka, W. 1988. 'Liberalism and Communitarianism'. *Canadian Journal of Philosophy*, 18(2), 181–204.

Kymlicka, W. 1989. *Liberalism, Community and Culture*. Oxford: Clarendon Press.

Kymlicka, W. 1992. 'The Rights of Minority Cultures – Reply to Kukathas'. *Political Theory*, 20(1), 140–46.

Kymlicka, W. 1995. *Multicultural Citizenship: A Liberal Theory of Minority Rights*. Oxford; New York: Clarendon Press.

Kymlicka, W. 2001. *Politics in the Vernacular: Nationalism, Multiculturalism, and Citizenship*. Oxford; New York: Oxford University Press.

Kymlicka, W. 2002a. *Contemporary Political Philosophy: An Introduction*. Oxford: Oxford University Press.

Kymlicka, W. 2002b. 'Immigration, Citizenship, Multiculturalism: Exploring the Links'. *Political Quarterly*, 195–208.

Kymlicka, W. 2003. 'Being Canadian'. *Government and Opposition*, 38(3), 357–85.

Kymlicka, W. 2004. 'Marketing Canadian Pluralism in the International Arena. *International Journal*, 59(4), 829–52.

Kymlicka, W. 2007. *Multicultural Odysseys: Navigating the New International Politics of Diversity*. Oxford: Oxford University Press.

Kymlicka, W. and M. Opalski (eds) 2001. *Can Liberal Pluralism be Exported? Western Political Theory and Ethnic Relations in Eastern Europe*. Oxford: Oxford University Press.

Laborde, C. 2005. 'Secular Philosophy and Muslim Headscarves in Schools'. *Journal of Political Philosophy*, 13(3), 305–29.

Lacan, J. 2006. *Écrits: A Selection*. New York: Norton.

Laden, A.S. and D. Owen (eds) 2007. *Multiculturalism and Political Theory*. Cambridge, UK; New York: Cambridge University Press.

Larson, G. J. (ed.) 2001. *Religion and Personal Law in Secular India: A Call to Judgment*. Bloomington: Indiana University Press.

Le Sueur, A.P. and J.W. Herberg 1999. *Principles of Public Law*. London: Cavendish.

Legrand, P., I. Schoordijk and W.E.J. Tjeenk Willink BV 1999. *Fragments on Law-as-Culture*. Deventer: W.E.J. Tjeenk Willink.

Lester, A. 2006. 'Thirty Years On', in *30: At the Turning of the Tide*, edited by Commission for Racial Equality. London: Belmont, 21–6.

Lester, A. and G. Bindman 1972. *Race and Law*. Harmondsworth: Penguin.

Leuprecht, P. 2001. 'Minority Rights Revisited: New Glimpses at an Old Issue', in *People's Rights: The State of the Art*, edited by P. Alston. Oxford: Oxford University Press, 111–26.

Levy, G.B. and T. Modood (eds) 2008. *Secularism, Religion and Multicultural Citizenship*. Cambridge: Cambridge University Press.

Lijphart, A. 2004. 'Constitutional Design for Divided Societies'. *Journal of Democracy*, 15(2), 96–109.

Lowe, N.V. and G. Douglas 1998. *Family Law*. London: Butterworths.

Lustgarten, L. 2008. 'The Evolution of a Constitution by Elizabeth Wicks'. *Modern Law Review*, 71(1), 153–6.

Lyon, D. and D. Spini 2004. 'Unveiling the Headscarf Debate'. *Feminist Legal Studies*, 12, 333–45.

Macaulay, S. 1963. 'Non-contractual Relations in Business: A Preliminary Study'. *American Sociological Review*, 28(1), 55–67.

MacCormick, N. 1993. 'Constitutionalism and Democracy', in *Theories and Concepts of Politics: An Introduction*, edited by R. Bellamy. Manchester: Manchester University Press, 124–48.

Macklem, P. 2006. 'Militant Democracy, Legal Pluralism, and the Paradox of Self-determination'. *International Journal of Constitutional Law*, 4(3), 488–516.

Macklem, T. 2000. 'Reason and Religion', in *Faith in Law: Essays in Legal Theory*, edited by P. Oliver, S.D. Scott and V. Tadros. Oxford; Portland, Or.: Hart, 69–87.

Macklem, T. 2003. *Beyond Comparison: Sex and Discrimination*. Cambridge; New York: Cambridge University Press.

Mahmood, S. 2006. 'Secularism, Hemeneutics and Empire: The Politics of Islamic Reformation'. *Public Culture*, 18(2), 323–47.

Mahmood, S. 2005. *Politics of Piety: The Islamic Revival and the Feminist Subject*. Princeton; London: Princeton University Press.

Maitland, F.W. 1926. *The Constitutional History of England: A Course of Lectures*. Cambridge: The University Press.

Maitland, F.W. and F. Pollock 1952. *The History of English Law Before the Time of Edward I*. 2nd edition. London: Cambridge University Press.

Mallat, C. and J.F. Connors (eds) 1990. *Islamic Family Law*. London; Boston: Graham and Trotman.

Manji, A. 1999. 'Imagining Women's "Legal World": Towards a Feminist Theory of Legal Pluralism in Africa'. *Social and Legal Studies*, 8(4), 435–55.

Margalit, A. and J. Raz 1990. 'National Self-determination'. *Journal of Philosophy*, 87(9), 439–61.

Margolis, E. 2010. 'It's Not Easy Being Gay'. *The Guardian*, 3 September, G2 21.

Mason, D. 1995. *Race and Ethnicity in Modern Britain*. Oxford; New York: Oxford University Press.

McColgan, A. 2007. 'Reconfiguring Discrimination Law'. *Public Law*: 74–94.

McCrudden, C., D.J. Smith and C. Brown 1991. *Racial Justice at Work: Enforcement of the Race Relations Act 1976 in Employment*. London: Policy Studies Institute.

McDonald, M. 1991. 'Should Communities Have Rights? Reflections on Liberal Individualism'. *Canadian Journal of Law and Jurisprudence*, 4(2), 217–37.

McGoldrick, D. 2006. *Human Rights and Religion: The Islamic Headscarf Debate in Europe*. Oxford; Portland, Or.: Hart Publishing.

McGregor, R. 1997. *Imagined Destinies: Aboriginal Australians and the Doomed Race Theory, 1880–1939*. Carlton South, Vic.: Melbourne University Press.

McIlwain, C.H. 1947. *Constitutionalism: Ancient and Modern*. Ithaca, N.Y.: Cornell University Press.

McKinnon, C. and D. Castiglione (eds) 2003. *The Culture of Toleration in Diverse Societies: Reasonable Toleration*. Manchester; New York: Manchester University Press.

Melissaris, E. 2004. 'The More the Merrier? A New Take on Legal Pluralism'. *Social and Legal Studies*, 13(1), 57–79.

Menski, W.F. 1988a. 'Review of *Asian Indigenous Law in Interaction with Received Law* by M. Chiba'. *International and Comparative Law Quarterly*, 37, 750–51.

Menski, W.F. 1988b. 'English Family Law and Ethnic Laws in Britain'. *Kerala Law Times*, 1988(1), 56–66.

Menski, W.F. 1988c. 'Review of *English Law and Ethnic Minority Customs* by S. Poulter'. *International and Comparative Law Quarterly*, 37, 218–21.

Menski, W.F. 1991. 'Change and Continuity in Hindu Marriage Rituals', in *Hindu Ritual and Society*, edited by S.Y. Killingley. Newcastle: Grevatt and Grevatt, 32–51.

Menski, W.F. 1992. 'The Indian Experience and Its Lessons for Britain', in *Discrimination: The Limits of Law*, edited by B.A. Hepple and E.M. Szyszczak. London: Mansell, 300–43.

Menski, W.F. 1993. 'Asians in Britain and the Question of Adaptation to a New Legal Order: Asian Laws in Britain?', in *Ethnicity, Identity, Migration: The South Asian Context*, edited by M. Israel and N. Wagle. Toronto: University of Toronto, 238–68.

Menski, W.F. (ed.) 1995. *Coping with 1997: The Reaction of the Hong Kong People to the Transfer of Power*. Stoke-on-Trent: Trentham Books and School of Oriental and African Studies.

Menski, W.F. 1999. 'Publication Review: Ethnicity, Law and Human Rights: The English Experience by Sebastian M. Poulter'. *Law Quarterly Review*, 115, 139–43.

Menski, W.F. 2000. *Comparative Law in a Global Context: The Legal Systems of Asia and Africa*. London: Platinium.

Menski, W.F. 2002. 'Immigration and Multiculturalism in Britain: New Issues in Research and Policy'. *KIAPS: Bulletin of Asia-Pacific Studies*, XII, 43–66.

Menski, W.F. 2006. *Comparative Law in a Global Context: The Legal Systems of Asia and Africa*. Cambridge: Cambridge University Press.

Menski, W.F. 2009. 'Flying Kites: *Banglar Ghuri – Iccher Ghuri*. Managing Family Laws and Gender Issues in Bangladesh'. *Stamford Journal of Law*, 2(1).

Menski, W.F. 2010. 'Slumdog Law, Colonial Tummy Aches and the Redefinition of Family Law in India. Review Article'. *South Asia Research*, 30(1), 67–80.

Merry, S.E. 1988. 'Legal Pluralism'. *Law and Society Review*, 22(5), 869–96.

Miller, D. 1995. *On Nationality*. Oxford: Clarendon Press.

Miller, D. and M. Walzer (eds) 1995. *Pluralism, Justice, and Equality*. Oxford: Oxford University Press.

Milsom, S.F.C. 1981. *Historical Foundations of the Common Law*. London: Butterworths.

Mitchell, B.G. 1967. *Law, Morality, and Religion in a Secular Society*. London: Oxford University Press.

Mitchell, B. and N. Javed 2010. 'I Killed My Daughter … With My Hands'. *The Toronto Star* [Online, 16 June] Available at http://www.thestar.com/news/gta/article/824133 (last accessed 21 September 2010).

Modood, T. 1990. 'British Asian Muslims and the Rushdie Affair'. *Political Quarterly*, 61(2), 143–60.

Modood, T. (ed.) 1997. *Church, State and Religious Minorities*. London: Policy Studies Institute.

Modood, T. 2007. *Multiculturalism: A Civic Idea*. Cambridge: Polity Press.

Modood, T. and R. Berthoud 1997. *Ethnic Minorities in Britain: Diversity and Disadvantage*. Policy Studies Institute.

Modood, T. and Runnymede Trust 1992. *Not Easy Being British: Colour, Culture and Citizenship*. Stoke-on-Trent: Runnymede Trust and Trentham.

Moerman, M. 1965. 'Who Are The Lue: Ethnic Identification in a Complex Civilization'. *American Anthropologist*, 67, 1215–29.

Monahan, P.J. 2006. *Constitutional Law*. 3rd Edition. Toronto: Irwin Law Inc.

Moore, S.F. 1978. *Law as Process: An Anthropological Approach*. London; Boston: Routledge and Kegan Paul.

Morrill, J.S. (ed.) 1992. *Revolution and Restoration: England in the 1650s*. London: Collins and Brown.

Mouritsen, P. and K.E. Jorgensen (eds) 2008. *Constituting Communities: Political Solutions to Cultural Differences*. Basingstoke: Palgrave Macmillan.

Mudimbe, V.Y. 1988. *The Invention of Africa: Gnosis, Philosophy and the Order of Knowledge*. Bloomington: Indiana University Press.

Murray, C. and R. Simeon. 2007. 'Recognition Without Empowerment: Minorities in a Democratic South Africa'. *International Journal of Constitutional Law*, 5(4), 699–729.

Norris, P. and R. Inglehart 2004. *Sacred and Secular: Religion and Politics Worldwide*. Cambridge: Cambridge University Press.

O'Cinneide, C. 2002. *A Single Equality Body: Lessons From Abroad*. Manchester: Equal Opportunities Commission.

O'Cinneide, C. 2004. 'Democracy, Rights and the Constitution – New Directions in the Human Rights Era', in *Current Legal Problems, vol. 57*, edited by J. Holder, C. O'Cinneide and M. Freeman. Oxford: Oxford University Press, 172–211.

O'Dair, R. and A.D.E. Lewis (eds) 2001. *Law and Religion: Current Legal Issues 2001*. Oxford; New York: Oxford University Press.

Oda, H. 1992. *Japanese Law*. London: Butterworths.

Offe, C. 1998. '"Homogeneity" and Constitutional Democracy: Coping With Identity Conflicts Through Group Rights'. *Journal of Political Philosophy*, 6(2), 113–41.

Oliver, P.S., S. Douglas-Scott and V. Tadros (eds) 2000. *Faith in Law: Essays in Legal Theory*. Oxford: Hart.

Osterlund, K. 2009. 'Love, Freedom and Governance: Same-sex Marriage in Canada'. *Social and Legal Studies*, 18(1), 93–109.

Outhwaite, W. (ed.) 1996. *The Habermas Reader*. Oxford: Polity Press.

Parekh, B. 1990a. 'Britain and the Social Logic of Pluralism', in *Britain, a Plural Society: Report of a Seminar Organised by the Commission for Racial Equality and the Runnymede Trust, October 1988*, edited by Commission for Racial Equality and Runnymede Trust. London: Commission for Racial Equality, 58–76.

Parekh, B. 1990b. 'The Rushdie Affair: Research Agenda for Political Philosophy'. *Political Studies*, 38, 695–709.

Parekh, B. 1997. 'Dilemmas of a Multicultural Theory of Citizenship'. *Constellations*, 4(1), 54–62.

Parekh, B. 2000. *Rethinking Multiculturalism: Cultural Diversity and Political Theory*. Basingstoke: Palgrave.

Parekh, B. 2008. *A New Politics of Identity: Political Principles for an Interdependent World*. Basingstoke; New York: Palgrave Macmillan.

Parekh, B. and Runnymede Trust 2000. *The Future of Multi-ethnic Britain: Report of the Commission on the Future of Multi-ethnic Britain*. London: Profile Books.

Paxman, J. 2007. *Who Do You Think You Are?* Series 2, DVD. Directed by A. Baron, R. Oord and S. Chu. London: BBC.

Pearl, D. 1983. 'Legal Decisions Affecting Ethnic Minorities and Discrimination No. 19'. *New Community*, X, 496.

Pearl, D. and W.F. Menski 1998. *Muslim Family Law*. London: Sweet and Maxwell.

Pennock, J.R. and J.W. Chapman 1979. *Constitutionalism*. New York: New York University Press.

Perry, M.J. 2007. *Toward a Theory of Human Rights: Religion, Law, Courts*. Cambridge; New York: Cambridge University Press.

Petersen, H. and H. Zahle (eds) 1995. *Legal Polycentricity: Consequences of Pluralism in Law*. Aldershot: Dartmouth.

Phillips, M. and T. Phillips 1998. *Windrush: The Irresistible Rise of Multi-racial Britain*. London: HarperCollins.

Pierik, R. 2004. 'Conceptualizing Cultural Groups and Cultural Difference: The Social Mechanism Approach'. *Ethnicities*, 4(4), 523–44.

Pinxten, R., G. Verstraete and C. Longman (eds) 2004. *Culture and Politics: Identity and Conflict in a Multicultural World*. New York; Oxford: Berghahn Books.

Poole, T. 2007. 'Tilting at Windmills? Truth and Illusion in "the Political Constitution"'. *Modern Law Review*, 70(2), 250–77.

Pospišil, L. 1975. *Anthropology of Law: A Comparative Theory*. New York: Harper and Row.

Poulter, S. 1986. *English Law and Ethnic Minority Customs*. London: Butterworth.

Poulter, S. 1990. *Asian Traditions and English Law: A Handbook*. Stoke on Trent: Runnymede Trust with Trentham.

Poulter, S. 1992. 'The Limits of Legal, Cultural and Religious Pluralism', in *Discrimination: The Limits of Law*, edited by B.A. Hepple and E.M. Szyszczak. London: Mansell, 172–92.

Poulter, S. 1998. *Ethnicity, Law and Human Rights: The English Experience*. Oxford: Oxford University Press.

Radan, P., D. Meyerson and R.F. Croucher 2005. *Law and Religion: God, the State and the Common Law*. New York, London: Routledge.

Raday, F. 2003. 'Culture, Religion, and Gender'. *International Journal of Constitutional Law*, 1(4), 663–15.

Rawls, J. 1993. *Political Liberalism*. New York: Columbia University Press.

Raz, J. 1986. *The Morality of Freedom*. Oxford: Oxford University Press.

Raz, J. 1998a. 'Multiculturalism'. *Ratio Juris*, 11(3), 193–205.

Raz, J. 1998b. 'On the Authority and Interpretations of Constitutions. Some Preliminaries', in *Constitutionalism: Philosophical Foundations*, edited by L. Alexander. Cambridge: Cambridge University Press, 152–93.

Rex, R. 1993. *Henry VIII and the English Reformation*. Basingstoke: Macmillan.

Roberts, S. 1979. *Order and Dispute: An Introduction to Legal Anthropology*. Oxford: Martin Robertson.

Robertson, G. and H. Street. 1991. *Freedom, the Individual and the Law*. Harmondsworth: Penguin Books.

Robertson, R.T. 2003. *The Three Waves of Globalization: A History of a Developing Global Consciousness*. New York: Zed Books.

Robilliard, St. John A. 1984. *Religion and the Law: Religious Liberty in Modern English Law*. Manchester: Manchester University Press.

Rogan, M. 2008. 'Girl, Interrupted'. *Toronto Life*, December, 53–8.

Rosen, L. 1989. *The Anthropology of Justice: Law as Culture in Islamic Society*. Cambridge: Cambridge University Press.

Rosen, L. 2006. *Law as Culture: An Invitation*. Princeton; Oxford: Princeton University Press.

Russell, C. 1990. *The Causes of the English Civil War*. Oxford: Clarendon.

Sachdeva, S. 1993. *The Primary Purpose Rule in British Immigration Law*. Stoke-on-Trent: Trentham Books and School of Oriental and African Studies.

Said, E.W. 1995. *Orientalism*. London: Penguin.

Sandel, M.J. 1982. *Liberalism and the Limits of Justice*. Cambridge: Cambridge University Press.

Santos, B. de S. 2002. *Toward a New Legal Common Sense: Law, Globalization, and Emancipation*. London: Butterworths.

Scheuerman, W.E. 1997. 'Review Article: Constitutionalism and Difference'. *University of Toronto Law Journal*, 47(2), 263–80.

Scheuerman, W.E. 1999. 'Between Radicalism and Resignation: Democratic Theory in Habermas's *Between Facts and Norms*', in *Habermas: A Critical Reader*, edited by P. Dews. Oxford: Blackwell, 153–77.

Sen, A.K. 2001a. *Identity and Justice*. Paper to the Fifteenth Dr Eric Williams Memorial Lecture: Bank of Trinidad, 21 March 2001.

Sen, A.K. 2001b. 'Other People', in *Proceedings of the British Academy, Vol. 111*, 319–35.

Sen, A.K. 2006. *Identity and Violence: The Illusion of Destiny*. New York: W.W. Norton and Co.

Shachar, A. 2001. *Multicultural Jurisdictions: Cultural Differences and Women's Rights*. Cambridge: Cambridge University Press.

Shachar, A. 2009. *The Birthright Lottery: Citizenship and Global Inequality*. Cambridge, Mass.: Harvard University Press.

Shah, P. 2000. *Refugees, Race and the Legal Concept of Asylum in Britain*. London: Cavendish.

Shah, P. (ed.) 2005. *The Challenge of Asylum to Legal Systems*. London: Cavendish.

Shah, P. (ed.) 2007. *Law and Ethnic Plurality: Socio-legal Perspectives*. Leiden; Boston: Martinus Nijhoff Publishers.

Shah, P. 2009. 'Transnational Hindu Law Adoptions: Recognition and Treatment in Britain'. *International Journal of Law in Context*, 5(2), 107–30.

Shah, P. 2009. 'Activism in the European Court of Justice and Changing Options for Turkish Citizen Migrants in the United Kingdom', in *Vatandaşlık, Göç,*

Mülteci ve Yabancılar Hukukundaki Güncel Gelişmeler (Current Developments in Citizenship, Immigration, Refugee Law and Law of Foreigners), edited by K. Hailbronner et al. Ankara: Union of Turkish Bar Associations, 299–326.

Shah, P. 2010. 'The Indian Dimension of An-Na'im's *Islam and the Secular State*', in *Islam and Europe: Crises are Challenges*, edited by M. Foblets and J. Carlier. Leuven: Leuven University Press, 153–66.

Shah P. and C.F. Doebbler (eds) 1999. *United Kingdom Asylum Law in its European Context*. London: Platinium and GEMS.

Singh, G., M. O'Beirne, S. Choudhry, P. Smith and B. Webb 2003. 'Perceptions of Racial Prejudice and Discrimination in England and Wales', in *2001 Home Office Citizenship Survey: People, Families and Communities*, edited by C. Attwood, G. Singh, D. Prime and R. Creasey. London: Home Office Research and Statistics Directorate, 27–53.

Singh, G. and D.S. Tatla 2006. *Sikhs in Britain: The Making of a Community*. London; New York: Zed Books.

Singh, R. 2006. 'The Right Direction', in *30: At the Turning of the Tide*, edited by Commission for Racial Equality. London: Belmont, 135–37.

Smith, J. 2003. 'Foreword', in *Civil Partnership: A Framework for the Legal Recognition of Same Sex Couples*, DTI and Women and Equality Unit, 9. London: DTI and Women and Equality Unit.

Soysal, Y.N. 2000. 'Citizenship and Identity: Living in Diasporas in Post-war Europe?' *Ethnic and Racial Studies*, 23(1), 1–15.

Sparrow, A. 2010. 'Eliza Manningham-Buller at the Iraq Inquiry'. *The Guardian* [Online, 20 July] Available at http://www.guardian.co.uk/global/blog/2010/jul/20/iraq-war-inquiry-iraq (last accessed 21 September 2010).

Spencer, I.R.G. 1997. *British Immigration Policy Since 1939: The Making of Multi-racial Britain*. London; New York: Routledge.

Starkey, D. (ed.) 1991. *Henry VIII: A European Court in England*. London: Collins and Brown in association with the National Maritime Museum.

Steiner, H.J. and P. Alston 2000. *International Human Rights in Context: Law, Politics, Morals: Texts and Materials*. Oxford: Oxford University Press.

Tamir, Y. 1993. *Liberal Nationalism*. Princeton; Chichester: Princeton University Press.

Taylor, C. 1989. *Sources of the Self: The Making of the Modern Identity*. Cambridge: Harvard University Press.

Taylor, C. 1994. 'The Politics of Recognition', in *Multiculturalism: Examining the Politics of Recognition*, edited by A. Gutmann. Princeton; Chichester: Princeton University Press, 25–73.

Taylor, C. 1998. 'Modes of Secularism', in *Secularism and its Critics*, edited by R. Bhargava. Delhi; Oxford: Oxford University Press, 31–53.

Taylor, C. 2004. *Modern Social Imaginaries*. Durham; London: Duke University Press.

Taylor, C. 2007. *A Secular Age*. Cambridge, Mass.; London: Belknap Press of Harvard University Press.

Teubner, G., ed. 1997. *Global Law Without a State*. Aldershot: Dartmouth.

Thomas, S. 2005. *The Global Resurgence of Religion and the Transformation of International Relations: The Struggle for the Soul of the Twenty-first Century*. New York; Basingstoke, Hampshire: Palgrave Macmillan.

Thompson, L. 1960. *The Unification of South Africa, 1902–1910*. Oxford: Clarendon Press.

Thornberry, C. 1965. 'Commitment or Withdrawal? The Place of Law in Race Relations in Britain'. *Race and Class*, 7(1), 73–85.

Tie, W. 1999. *Legal Pluralism: Toward a Multicultural Conception of Law*. Aldershot: Ashgate.

Tierney, S. 2006. *Constitutional Law and National Pluralism*. Oxford: Oxford University Press.

Tierney, S. 2007. 'Giving With One Hand: Scottish Devolution Within a Unitary State'. *International Journal of Constitutional Law*, 5(4), 730–53.

Tomkins, A. 2005. *Our Republican Constitution*. Oxford: Hart.

Tonkin, E., M. McDonald and M. Chapman (eds) 1989. *History and Ethnicity*. London: Routledge.

Townshend-Smith, R. 1998. *Discrimination Law: Text, Cases and Materials*. London: Cavendish Publishing.

Tully, J. 1995. *Strange Multiplicity: Constitutionalism in an Age of Diversity*. Cambridge; New York: Cambridge University Press.

Tully, J. 2005. 'The Unfreedom of the Moderns in Comparison to Their Ideals of Constitutional Democracy'. *Modern Law Review*, 65, 204.

Tully, J. 2008. 'Academic profile'. [Online: University of Victoria, Department of Political Science] Available at http://web.uvic.ca/~polisci/tully/profile.htm (last accessed 30 April 2009).

Tully, J. and A. Gagnon (eds) 2001. *Multinational Democracies*. Cambridge; New York: Cambridge University Press.

United Kingdom. Parliament. 1999. *Report of an Inquiry by Sir William Macpherson of Cluny*. (Cmnd 4262-I), London: HMSO, Home Office.

United Kingdom. *Final Report of the Commission on Integration and Cohesion: Our Shared Future*, 2007. Yorkshire: Commission on Integration and Cohesion.

United Kingdom. Parliament. 2008. *Framework for a Fairer Future – The Equality Bill*. (Cmnd 7431) London: HMSO. Government Equalities Office.

Vakulenko, A. 2007. 'Islamic Dress in Human Rights Jurisprudence: A Critique of Current Trends'. *Human Rights Law Review*, 7(4), 717–39.

Van Dyke, V. 1977. 'The Individual, the State, and Ethnic Communities in Political Theory'. *World Politics*, 29(3), 343–69.

Van Dyke, V. 1982. 'Collective Entities and Moral Rights: Problems in Liberal-Democratic Thought'. *Journal of Politics*, 44(1), 21–40.

Vertovec, S. 2008. *Transnationalism*. London: Routledge.

Vertovec, S. 2007. 'Super-diversity and its Implications'. *Ethnic and Racial Studies*, 30(6), 1024–54.

Vertovec, S. and R. Cohen (eds) 1999. *Migration, Diasporas and Transnationalism*. Cheltenham: Edward Elgar.
Vile, M.J.C. 1967. *Constitutionalism and the Separation of Powers*. Oxford: Clarendon Press.
Visram, R. 2002. *Asians in Britain: 400 Years of History*. London: Pluto Press.
Wade, H.W.R. 1996. 'Sovereignty: Revolution or Evolution?' *Law Quarterly Review*, 112, 568–75.
Waldron, J. 1992. 'Minority Cultures and the Cosmopolitan Alternative'. *University of Michigan Journal of Law Reform*, 25(3), 751–93.
Walker, N. 1996. 'European Constitutionalism and European Integration'. *Public Law*, 266–90.
Walker, N. 2000. 'Beyond the Unitary Conception of the British Constitution?' *Public Law*, 383–404.
Walker, N. 2002. 'The Idea of Constitutional Pluralism'. *Modern Law Review*, 65(3), 317–59.
Walsh, D. 2005. 'The Rescuers'. *The Guardian*, 9 December.
Walzer, M. 1983. *Spheres of Justice: A Defense of Pluralism and Equality*. New York: Basic Books.
Walzer, M. 1992. 'Comment', in *Multiculturalism: Examining the Politics of Recognition*, edited by A. Gutmann. Princeton: Princeton University Press, 99–103.
Weedon, C. 2004. *Identity and Culture: Narratives of Difference and Belonging*. Maidenhead: Open University Press.
Weller, P., A. Feldman and K. Purdham 2001. *Religious Discrimination in England and Wales*. Great Britain, Home Office, Research, Development and Statistics Directorate.
Wheatley, S. 2005. *Democracy, Minorities and International Law*. Cambridge: Cambridge University Press.
Wicks, E. 2006. *The Evolution of a Constitution: Eight Key Moments in British Constitutional History*. Oxford: Hart.
Williams, B. 1976. *Morality: An Introduction to Ethics*. Cambridge: Cambridge University Press.
Williamson, J.A. 1944. *Great Britain and the Empire: A Discursive History*. London: A. and C. Black.
Wilson, A. 2006. *Dreams, Questions, Struggles: South Asian Women in Britain*. London; Ann Arbor, MI: Pluto.
Woodman, G.R. 1998. 'Ideological Combat and Social Observation. Recent Debate about Legal Pluralism'. *Journal of Legal Pluralism and Unofficial Law*, 42, 21–59.
Young, I.M. 1990. *Justice and the Politics of Difference*. Princeton: Princeton University Press.
Young, I.M. 1997. 'A Multicultural Continuum: A Critique of Will Kymlicka's Ethnic-nation Dichotomy'. *Constellations*, 4(1), 48–53.
Young, I.M. 2000. *Inclusion and Democracy*. Oxford: Oxford University Press.

Young, I.M. 2001. 'Equality of Whom? Social Groups and Judgements of Injustice'. *Journal of Political Philosophy*, 9(1), 1–18.

Young, I.M. 2006. 'Responsibility and Global Justice: A Social Connection Model'. *Social Philosophy and Policy*, 23(1), 102–30.

Zaman, S. 2008. 'Amrikan Shari'a: The Reconstruction of Islamic Family Law in the United States'. *South Asia Research*, 28(2), 185–202.

Index

For Product Safety Concerns and Information please contact our EU representative GPSR@taylorandfrancis.com
Taylor & Francis Verlag GmbH, Kaufingerstraße 24, 80331 München, Germany

www.ingramcontent.com/pod-product-compliance
Ingram Content Group UK Ltd.
Pitfield, Milton Keynes, MK11 3LW, UK
UKHW020011200926
475702UK00014B/1831
* 9 7 8 1 1 3 8 2 5 4 5 2 7 *